D1063046

Black Feminist Anthropology

BLACK FEMINIST ANTHROPOLOGY

Theory, Politics, Praxis, and Poetics

Edited by
IRMA McCLAURIN

RUTGERS UNIVERSITY PRESS
New Brunswick, New Jersey, and London

*GN
33.8
.B53
2001*

PHOTO CREDITS

A. Lynn Bolles photo, p. 24: University of Maryland Photographic Services, University of Maryland, College Park
Irma McClaurin photo, p. 49: Ray Carson
Kimberly Eison Simmons photo, p. 77: Courtesy of the author
Carolyn Martin Shaw photo, p. 102: Gena Foucek-Sinopoli
Karla Slocum photo, p. 126: Courtesy of the author
Angela M. Gilliam photo, p. 150: Melissa Schoemaker
Cheryl Mwaria photo, p. 187: Courtesy of the author
Paulla A. Ebron photo, p. 211: Courtesy of the author
Cheryl Rodriguez photo, p. 233: Daphne Thomas

**JKM Library
1100 East 55th Street
Chicago, IL 60615**

Library of Congress Cataloging-in-Publication Data

Black feminist anthropology : theory, politics, praxis, and poetics /
    edited by Irma McClaurin
        p. cm
    Includes bibliographical references and index.
    ISBN 0-8135-2925-5 (cloth : alk. paper)—ISBN 0-8135-2926-3
    (pbk. : alk. paper)
    1. Feminist anthropology. 2. Afro-American anthroplogists.
    3. Ethnology—Philosophy. I. McClaurin, Irma.

GN33.8 .B53 2001
305.42—dc21

00-045686

British Cataloging-in-Publication data for this book is available from the British Library.

This collection copyright © 2001 by Rutgers, The State University
Individual chapters copyright © 2001 in the names of their authors

All rights reserved
No part of this book may be reproduced or utilized in any form or by any means, electronic or mechanical, or by any information storage and retrieval system, without written permission from the publisher. Please contact Rutgers University Press, 100 Joyce Kilmer Avenue, Piscataway, NJ 08854–8099. The only exception to this prohibition is "fair use" as defined by U.S. copyright law.

Manufactured in the United States of America

This book is dedicated to Black women in the African Diaspora who survived the brutality of slavery with dignity and continue to survive the threats of postcolonialism; to our mothers, whose lives are lessons we are still learning; to the memories of Audre Lorde and Barbara Christian—beacons of Black feminist light; to the memory of my dear student Jennifer Drayton; to ourselves, for continuing the rebellious legacy of Black women; and to our daughters and sons, who we pray will make a better day.

Contents

Foreword

The three words that launch the title of this book have not always kept company with each other—and in the minds of many both inside and outside of the academy, they should remain separate. In this sense, Irma McClaurin and her sister anthropologists have given us a work that is not only pioneering but also bold.

Why is there such discomfort in joining the terms Black feminist, Black anthropology, feminist anthropology, and all three, Black feminist anthropology? The answer, of course, is that such combinations challenge the very idea that there could be more than one way to do anthropology—ways other than "the way we've always done it." But anthropology is clearly better off precisely because in this book, nine Black feminist anthropologists do it differently.

Any review of the history of the discipline reveals that the overwhelming majority of those who practiced it (as opposed to those upon whom it was practiced) were white. And while there have always been larger numbers of women in anthropology than in many other disciplines in the academy, it is only since the 1970s that a substantial body of anthropological scholarship came into existence that focuses on gender issues.

Black studies in the 1960s and women's studies in the 1970s

challenged the field of anthropology with respect to who was traditionally studied, by whom, in what ways, and toward what end. Why were virtually all of the folks studied poor people of color from non-Western cultures and virtually all of those doing the studying white, middle-class men from the United States and Europe? Why did the results of these studies end up in publications that not only were inaccessible to the people who had been studied but made little or no contribution to improving the conditions of their lives? And why was so much emphasis put on the need for objectivity?

As anthropology reinvented itself in response to such criticisms, the number of women and people of color who engaged in fieldwork increased. In what has come to be called native anthropology, more people from marginalized communities began to do anthropology "on them," and the very notion of applied anthropology earned far greater acceptability. These substantial changes laid the foundation for feminist anthropology, Black anthropology, and the very focus of this book—Black feminist anthropology.

Each of the essays in this impressive anthology is in some way a response to mainstream anthropology and "the way we've always done it." While the goal of objectivity is not simply tossed to the side, the sister anthropologists are in tune with the view of the sociologist C. Wright Mills, who said that while he would strive for objectivity, he would never claim to be detached from the people and the problems he was studying.

Among each of these sister anthropologists is an openness to any discipline that can inform their work and bring insights into the lives of the folks they are studying. Of course most often the folks being studied are Black women, individuals with whom these anthropologists feel a close kinship. There is also among sister anthropologists a willingness, even an eagerness, to use the tools of literature, sociology, history, and the interdisciplinary arenas of Black studies and women's studies. And the issues addressed in these chapters are not foreign to these sister anthropologists; indeed they are issues that these scholar-activists know about experientially or through close relationships with people in their most immediate communities. So it is that in chapter after chapter, the authors are engaged at intersections where the personal is political and professional. These intersections are sometimes full of tension, but not one of these sister anthropologists wants to move to a different place.

In the final paragraph of the introduction to this edited volume, Irma McClaurin poses the question, "Who sez Black folk, and Black women especially, don't do theory?" A definitive answer can be found in this volume, the first collection of writings in Black feminist anthropology. Chapter after chapter goes to the heart of the stereotype that Black folks and women folks, particularly Black women folks, are not intellectuals. And chapter after chapter presents important results of fieldwork and theorizing by Black women anthropologists. We might add yet another question: Who sez only Black men are change agents? Indeed, virtually all written accounts and verbal discussions of the Civil Rights movement and any effort for improved human rights sound as if only African American men were involved. But the sister anthropologists in this volume move through the world with a commitment to the kind of praxis that addresses changing the condition of their people, their discipline of anthropology, and indeed, themselves.

Johnnetta B. Cole
President Emerita, Spelman College
Presidential Distinguished Professor of Anthropology, Women's
Studies, and African American Studies, Emory University
August 2000

Preface

The gestation for this collection began in 1996 when my colleague France Winddance Twine and I agreed to co-organize a panel for the next annual meeting of the American Anthropological Association. We felt that most of the presentations and sessions that we had encountered over the last few years had failed to address the urgent questions: What is the relationship between one's racial/ethnic identity and one's anthropological praxis? And, what has feminism got to do with our lives as Black women?

The 1997 Invited Session titled "The Politics and Poetics of Black Feminist Anthropology," jointly sponsored by the Association of Black Anthropologists and the Association for Feminist Anthropology, was successful beyond our wildest expectations. At one point, in observing the capacity-filled room, we realized that this was one place where cultural diversity was manifest. In attendance were Black women, white women, Latina women, lesbians, heterosexual women, old women, and young women. All responded enthusiastically to the papers presented, many of which are included in this volume. Further, the audience demanded that we "do something" with the ideas so eloquently presented.

Without the support of that audience, those of us whose words and thoughts grace the pages of this book might not have had the courage to publicly display our vulnerabilities as Black feminist an-thropologists. We are forever grateful for that support, and although we do not know each name to recount here, we can still feel their spirits strong.

This book owes a great deal to conversations with three women—true sistahfriends—whose judgment, ideas, and support I have come to rely on and value immensely: Kesho Yvonne Scott has been an ever-present beacon in my life and has supported me through a personal crisis that threatened to slow down this book; Beverlyn Lundy Allen offered me sanctuary in her home during a difficult period, and my own chapter was written at her kitchen table; and France Winddance Twine, who because of other obligations could not participate, held numerous critical and challenging conversa-tions with me by phone about why this book needed to exist, its content, and possible contributors. I thank each of you for your friendship, spiritual support, intellectual guidance, and true sistah-hood. My thanks also to Dawn Banks and Abby Jenkins for their research assistance.

The final debt of gratitude must go, of course, to my sistah con-tributors. Without each of your individual and collective visions of Black feminism, this work would not have been birthed. It has been a labor of love, a labor of intensity, but most importantly, a labor of conscious participation in the process of theory build-ing and knowledge production in the field of anthropology and feminism.

Irma McClaurin

Black Feminist
Anthropology

IRMA MCCLAURIN

INTRODUCTION
Forging a Theory, Politics, Praxis, and Poetics of Black Feminist Anthropology

The lack of a discernible tradition has been a silencing agent in the history of Blacks, of women, of Black women, of indeed marginalized groupings. Without a "tradition" into which to fit us, we have been misunderstood, misinterpreted, and finally, often quickly dismissed.

—P. Gabrielle Foreman, "Looking Back from Zora, or Talking out Both Sides of My Mouth for Those Who Have Two Ears," 1990

Yes, he certainly knows his higher mathematics, and he can read Latin better than many white men I know, but I cannot bring myself to believe that he understands a thing he is doing. It is all an aping of our culture. All on the outside. You are crazy if you think that it has changed him inside in the least. Turn him loose, and he will revert at once to the jungle. He is still a savage, and no amount of translating Virgil and Ovid is going to change him. In fact, all you have done is to turn a useful savage into a dangerous beast.

—Unknown author, quoted in Zora Neale Hurston, "What White Publishers Won't Print," 1979 [1950]

The words of these epigraphs conjure up a description of a social environment in which the intellectual acumen of Blacks in the United States, both men and women, is continuously called into question.[1] It is against this backdrop of historical social and scholarly malignment and academic racism that this book emerges. In positioning itself as an approach derived from but frequently in opposition to mainstream feminist anthropology, Black feminist anthropology becomes a conscious act of knowledge production and canon formation. Despite postmodern critiques of grand theory, master narratives, and canon formation, the reality is that graduate and undergraduate curricula still largely rely upon canonical

1

works in training students. At the same time that Black feminist anthropology constructs its own canon that is both theoretical and based in a politics of praxis and poetics, it seeks to deconstruct the institutionalized racism and sexism that has characterized the history of the discipline of anthropology in the United States and Europe. This analysis pertains directly to the history of North American anthropology.

This book, *Black Feminist Anthropology*, is formulated out of a set of ideologies, theories, ethnographic methodologies, and social commitments that owe much to ideas both inside and outside anthropology. It is self-consciously fashioned as an act of knowledge production and sees itself as a form of cultural mediation between the world of Black scholars and the entire Western intellectual tradition, between Black anthropologists and the rest of the discipline, and between Black and white feminists. But more importantly, it is an intervention—a Black feminist anthropological intervention.[2]

As a strategy, interventions serve to either halt or resolve conflict. Medical interventions are intended to aggressively stem the onset of disease or other illness. Political interventions interfere in domestic or international political and economic affairs. An anthropological intervention, as this works deems itself, is intended to interrupt/disrupt the elitist, sexist, and racist dynamics that have plagued anthropology historically and that continue to inform its training, research funding, scholarly recognition, professional networks, and publications—in a phrase, all anthropological knowledge production and reproduction.

Both Lee D. Baker, a new critical historian of anthropology, and Faye V. Harrison, Black feminist anthropological theorist and ethnographer, have documented the way in which this less than stellar history of anthropology, replete with its pervasive biases, has reduced, marginalized, and erased the contributions of Black anthropologists in general, and U.S. Black women anthropologists specifically.[3] In his assessment of a crucial moment in the discipline's history when Black anthropologists attempted to carve out an intellectual space for themselves, Baker notes that

> the editors of, and contributors to, the *JAFL* [*Journal of American Folklore*] fashioned Negro folklore into an important thrust within the anthropological discourse on race and culture. How-

ever, African American scholars who forayed into the anthropological field of folklore immediately met with marginalization. They
were limited in their access to funds and to publishers.[4]

Observing the contemporary scene in anthropology, Faye V. Harrison concludes that little has changed in these conditions of
marginalization. She argues in a persuasive commentary, "Auto-
Ethnographic Reflections on Hierarchies in Anthropology" (based
on her own positionality), that although studying anthropology
provided her with a level of intellectual confidence, the types of
limitations and constraints Baker identified as characterizing the
early history of anthropology continue today: Black anthropologists (and others with nonhegemonic positions and/or perspectives)
continue to be ignored and marginalized, and their scholarship
minimized. Harrison notes that

> when "academic Others" do successfully live up to . . . [anthro-
> pology's] productivity standards—and in some cases even surpass
> them—they rarely receive full recognition and reward for their
> hard-earned accomplishments. . . . Furthermore, the politics of
> canon formation results in the peripheralization and erasure of
> much of the scholarship which people of color and women
> produce.[5]

Harrison goes on to argue that the absence of citations of Black
American anthropologists in the academic literature gives the appearance that they have not contributed much to the discipline.
However, she warns that this is misleading because it has been "constructed within a disciplinary context of racialized power dispari-
ties wherein intellectual validation and authorization have been and
are conferred on a basis other than value-free, color- and gender-
blind merit."[6] It is out of these flames of racism, sexism, and Euro-
ethnocentricism (which has shaped much of Western intellectual
thought, and anthropology in particular) that this book rises like
a mythical phoenix. Black feminist anthropology is marked by its
acknowledgment of theoretical, ideological, and methodological
diversity among it practitioners. This is largely because those Black
women who dare proclaim themselves feminists draw on the
tenets of feminism alongside those of anthropology and embrace
an intellectual repertoire that includes women's studies, African
American studies, ethnic studies, and African, Caribbean, and Latin

American studies. They also embrace the critiques, ideas, metaphors, wisdom, and grounded theories of organic intellectuals in the form of preachers, community activists, street-corner philosophers, and beauty shop therapists alike, who are eloquent about the way in which scholarship has rendered them victims, symbols of poverty, or people without histories; and who would agree with Othman Sullivan in *Drylongso*: "I think this anthropology is just another way to call me a nigger."[7]

Most of the contributors to *Black Feminist Anthropology* are explicit about how their present-day thinking was forged out of a tradition of Black American resistance rooted in the politics, praxis, and poetics of runaway slaves, slave rebellions, Maroons, the underground railroad, slave narratives, Negro spirituals, anti-lynching campaigns, the Civil Rights movement, black organizations, the Black Nationalist movement, the Black Aesthetic, and most recently, reggae and consciousness hip-hop. These elements constitute significant cultural variables and moments in the collective memory of Black Americans (and they also have an importance beyond U.S. geographical boundaries). They stand as reminders (indicators) that social inequality, and especially Black America's resistance to it, is structural, symbolic, and ever present in the cultural fabric of the United States, where we remain (as the words of Foreman, Hurston, and Sullivan remind us) part of the fringe work.

It is at this site, an imagined theoretical space/place, where Black feminist anthropology locates itself. It uses the description, analysis, and interpretations of social inequality and the concomitant resistance as an entry point to construct its own theory, praxis, politics, and poetics. It derives its content/data from the ethnographic study of African-descended people in the United States, Africa, the Spanish-, Dutch-, French-, and English-speaking Caribbean, Central and Latin America, and in other geographical spaces where the African Diaspora is located. Within this theoretical/spatial context, the multifarious dimensions of women's lived experience in the Diaspora become a unifying and central element. What better entry point for a theory, politics, praxis, and poetics of Black feminist anthropology than the description, analysis, and interpretation of social inequality and the concomitant resistance? What better entry point for Black feminist anthropology than the ethnographic study of African-descended people? And what could be a worthier task than the study of Black women's lives in these multiple contexts?

CONSTRUCTING A GENEALOGY OF BLACK ACTIVIST FEMINISM

The excavation of Black women's lives and the theorization of lived experience and culture in the African Diaspora through the lens of feminism do not begin with this book; nor is the idea of a praxis that insists on research directed to reveal contradictions and affect social problems our novel idea. Few traditions—scholarly or otherwise—begin in a vacuum. Rather, they emerge from various historical moments, social movements, and the assemblage of intellectual consensus and unite to create the appearance of a seamless web of intellectual, political, and activist communities. As Black feminists, we cannot claim our genealogy exists *ab origine* (from day one).[8] What we can claim is our own desire and political right to fashion (fictive) kin ties and seek ancestors from the past and present, and derive from their work a tradition composed of Black intellectual thought, feminism, and the gendered experience of African-descended people. Not all of those we claim as kindred would necessarily embrace the label of feminist or Black feminist, but fictive kin are made, not born (see table 1).

A Black feminist anthropological theory, and indeed the chapters in the this book, draws its inspiration from two very distinctive traditions (Black intellectual thought and feminism) that at different moments in time have overlapped, and sometimes conflicted, but frequently have shared a common vision of social transformation, equity, and justice. As part of a Black intellectual tradition, we claim a consciousness that identifies race as a social construction bolstered by a structural reality that is harsh and striking in its economic, political, and social ramifications. To understand how the "race" concept has come to pervade the thinking and policies of U.S. society and resulted in some of the most dehumanizing institutions, practices, and behaviors that defy rationality, morality, and spirituality, we trace our genealogy through the writings and speeches of Sojourner Truth, Frederick Douglass, W.E.B. Du Bois, Ida B. Wells, Anna Cooper, Zora Neale Hurston,

Table 1.   Timeline of Selected Black Women/Feminist Anthropologists

1930s–1960s

Carolyn Bond Day	*A Study of Some Negro-White Families in the United States* (1932)
Ellen Irene Diggs	First MA in sociology from Atlanta University (1933)
	Co-founder of *Phylon* Magazine with W.E.B. DuBois (1940)
	Ph.D. from University of Habana (1944)
	Black Chronology (1983)
Zora Neale Hurston	"Dance Songs and Tales from the Bahamas" (1930)
	Mules and Men (1935)
	Tell My Horse (1938)
Katherine Dunham	First dance anthropology performance, "L'Ag'ya" (1938)
	Founded School of Arts and Research Institute for Dance (1943)
	"Form and Function in Primitive Dance" (1941)
	Island Possessed (1969)
Pearl Primus	Solo (dance) performance at Cafe Society (1945)
Manet Fowler	First African American woman to earn a Ph.D. in anthropology from a U.S. university (Cornell, 1952)
Vera Green	Collected data for Oscar Lewis's *La Vida* (1963)
	"The Confrontation of Diversity within the Black Community" (1970)
	Migrants in Aruba (1974)
	Founding member and first president of the Association of Black Anthropologists (1977)

1970s–1980s

Angela Gilliam	"From Roxbury to Rio—And Back in a Hurry" (1970)
	"Clase, raza y etnicidad en Brasil y México" (1976)
	"A Black Feminist Perspective on the Sexual Commodification of Women in the New Global Culture" (2001)
Sheila Walker	*Ceremonial Spirit Possession in African and Afro-America* (1972)
	Co-editor, *African Christianity* (1979)
	The Religious Revolution in the Ivory Coast (1983)
Diane K. Lewis	"Anthropology and Colonialism" (1973)
	"A Response to Inequality: Black Women, Racism, and Sexism" (1977)
	"Black Women Offenders and Criminal Justice" (1981)
Niara Sudarkasa	"Where Women Work" (1974)
(Gloria Marshall)	"African and Afro-American Family Structure (1980)
	President, Lincoln University (1987–1998)
Leith Mullings	"Women and Economic Change in Africa" (1976)
	Editor, *Cities of the United States* (1987)
	Race, Class, and Gender (1992)
	On Our Own Terms (1997)
Claudia Mitchell Kernan	Co-editor, *Language, Thought, and Culture* (1977)
	Co-editor, *Television and the Socialization of the Minority Child* (1982)
	Co-editor, *The Decline in Marriage among African Americans* (1995)
Theresa Singleton	*The Archaeology of a Pre-18th-Century House Site in St. Augustine* (1977)
	The Archaeology of the Diaspora in the Americas (1995)

Table 1. Continued

A. Lynn Bolles	"Going Abroad" (1979)
	"Kitchens Hit by Priorities" (1983)
	"Anthropological Research Methods for the Study of Black Women in the Caribbean" (1987)
	Sister Jamaica (1996)
	"Seeking the Ancestors" (2001)
Johnetta B. Cole	"Women in Cuba: The Revolution within the Revolution" (1980)
	Editor, *All American Women* (1986)
	Editor, *Anthropology for the Eighties* (1982)
	President, Spelman College (1987–1998)
Yolanda Moses	"Female Status, the Family, and Male Dominance in a West Indian Community" (1977)
	President, American Association for Anthropologists (1995)
	President, City University of New York (1995–1999)
Filomena Chioma-Steady	*The Black Woman Cross-Culturally* (1981)
	"African Feminism: A World-Wide Perspective" (1987)
Faye V. Harrison	"An African Diaspora Perspective for Urban Anthropology" (1988)
	Editor, *Decolonizing Anthropology* (1991)
	"Auto-Ethnographic Reflections on Anthropology" (1995)
	"The Persistent Power of 'Race' in the Cultural and Political Economy of Racism" (1995)
Helán Page	"Dialogic Principles of Interactive Learning in the Ethnographic Relationship" (1988)
	"No Black Public Sphere in White Public Space" (1999)
Brackette Williams	"A Class Act: Anthropology and the Race to Nation across Ethnicity" (1989)
	Stains on My Name, War in My Veins (1991)
	"The Impact of the Precepts of Nationalism on the Concept of Culture" (1993)
	Editor, *Women Out of Place* (1996)
Gwendolyn Mikell	*Cocoa and Chaos* (1989, 1992)
	"African Feminism" (1995)
	African Feminism (1998)
	"Feminism and Black Culture in the Ethnography of Zora Neale Hurston" (1999)

1990s

Irma McClaurin	"Incongruities: Dissonance and Contradiction in the Life of a Black Middle-Class Woman" (1990)
	Women of Belize (1996)
	"Salvaging Lives in the African Diaspora" (1999)
	"Theorizing a Black Feminist Self in Anthropology" (2001)
Karla Slocum	"Managing Markets and Households" (M.A. thesis, 1991)
	"Negotiating Identity and Black Feminist Politics in Caribbean Research" (2001)
France Winddance Twine	Co-producer, *Just Black?* (1992)
	"O hiato de genero nas percepçoes de racismo" (1996)
	Racism in a Racial Democracy (1997)
	"Bearing Blackness in Britain" (1999)
	Co-editor, *Racing Research/Researching Race* (2000)
Ruth Wilson	*Hairston and Wilson Family Papers, 1800–1895* (1992)
Evelyn L. Barbee	"Ethnicity and Women Abuse in the United States" (1992)
	Co-author, "Health, Social Class, and African-American Women" (1993)

Table 1.   Continued

Beverly Tatum	*Teaching for Change* (1993)
	Facing Racism in Education (1996)
Audrey Smedley	*Race in North America* (1993)
Kimberly Eison Simmons	"Dominican Women" (M.A. thesis, 1994)
	"Reconfiguring Dominicanness" (Ph.D. dissertation, 2000)
	"A Passion for Sameness" (2001)
Carolyn Martin Shaw	*Colonial Inscriptions* (1995)
	"Disciplining the Black Female Body" (2001)
Patricia Guthrie	"Mother Mary Ann Wright: African-American Women, Spirituality, and Social Activism" (1995)
	Co-author, "Catching Sense" (1997)
Cheryl Rodriguez	"African-American Anthropology and the Pedagogy of Activist Community Research (1996)
	"Recapturing Lost Images" (1998)
	"A Homegirl Goes Home" (2001)
Cheryl Mwaria	"Physician-Assisted Suicide" (1997)
	"The Immorality of Collective Punishment" (1999)
	Co-editor, *African Visions* (2001)
	"Biomedical Ethics, Gender, and Ethnicity" (2001)
Maria Franklin	"'Power to the People': Sociopolitics and the Archaeology of Black Americans" (1997)
Paulla A. Ebron	"Regional Differences in African American Culture" (1999)
	"Tourists as Pilgrims" (1999)
	Performing Africa (2001)
	"Contingent Stories of Anthropology, Race, and Feminism" (2001)
Kesha Fikes	"Domesticity in Black and White" (1999)

2000s

| Irma McClaurin | Editor, *Black Feminist Anthropology: Theory, Politics, Praxis, and Poetics* (2001) |

Note: This timeline is not intended to be exhaustive. It builds on the geneology first developed by St. Clair Drake in several key articles ("Reflections on Anthropology and the Black Experience," *Anthropology and Education Quarterly* 9, 2 (1978): 85–109; and "Further Reflections on Anthropology and the Black Experience," *Transforming Anthropology* 1, 2, (1990): 1–14 and continued by Ira E. Harrison and Faye V. Harrison, eds., in *African American Pioneers in Anthropology* (Urbana: University of Illinois Press, 1999). Still and yet, there are many worthy contemporary Black women and women-of-color anthropologists doing important research who are not included here. The contemporary selections are somewhat arbitrary in that I have included scholars with whose work I am familiar, those who were suggested by colleagues, and some who were cited by the contributors to this book. Placement on the timeline is determined by date of first published work or other significant activities. I view this timeline as the beginning of an effort to document the contribution of Black women/Black feminist anthropologists and welcome any information that will help me refine this information for future editions. As Lynn Bolles indicates in chapter 1, by 1967, only eight U.S. Black women held Ph.D.'s in anthropology. Thus, a crucial area for future reach is a study of the number of Black women teaching in anthropology departments and an analysis of whether our numbers are increasing or decreasing. My own anecdotal observations indicate that the number of U.S. Black women teaching in anthropology departments is low. Many Black anthropologists teach in fields other than anthropology, such as sociology, African American studies, and women's studies, where they feel more welcome.

Katherine Dunham, Irene Diggs, and St. Clair Drake, to name only a few.[9] To create our unique kinship links obligates us to step outside the disciplinary boundaries of anthropology and look to research and writing in history, literature, art, sociology, psychology, economics, and political science. The result is a richness in our research and writing that is historically grounded and interdisciplinary in its foci, anthropological holism notwithstanding.

In following the Black intellectual tradition, Black feminist anthropological theory follows the direction of Pan-Africanism and posits a comparative (global) perspective as central to its enterprise. In this respect, it builds on the concepts promulgated by scholars such as W.E.B. Du Bois, St. Clair Drake, and Ruth Simms Hamilton, best captured by the notion of an African Diaspora. According to St. Clair Drake, the African Diaspora "involves the concept of a 'homeland' and various situations outside of it into which individuals have migrated and where persisting 'diaspora communities' survive."[10] This diasporic perspective is evident in the way that Black feminist anthropologists' ethnography is designed to look outward (at Africa, the Caribbean, Latin America, and Europe), a direction consistent with the aims of the conventional anthropological gaze, and simultaneously to look inward (at the United States), in keeping with the aims of a Black intellectual tradition. Black feminist anthropology and ethnography are transgeographical.

On the other side of our genealogical chart is feminism. The contributions of the non-Black feminists we draw upon are too numerous to recount here, but works such as Sandra Morgen's *Gender and Anthropology*, Faye Ginsburg and Anna Tsing's *Uncertain Terms: Negotiating Gender in America Culture*, Henrietta Moore's *Feminism and Anthropology*, and Micaela di Leonardo's *Gender at the Crossroads* are standard-bearers that we gratefully acknowledge.[11] The theorization of race and gender profoundly affected by class can be found in Karen Brodkin Sacks's 1989 seminal essay, "Toward a Unified Theory of Race, Class and Gender."[12] And Carol Stack's compelling ethnography, *All Our Kin*, brought ethnographic dignity to understanding the plight of poor Black women struggling to survive in a hostile urban environment.[13] Unfortunately, true to the cultural history of the United States, words such as *feminism* that claim inclusiveness do not always rise to the challenge.

In all of these anthologies, Black women anthropologists and other women-of-color anthropologists are a minimal or absent presence.

Thus, those of us in this volume who pronounce ourselves Black feminist anthropologists follow the divergent line in our genealogy chart where the Black intellectual tradition and white feminism meet—Black feminism. It is through this branch, produced as much out of silence as out of the testimonials, autobiographies, novels, poetry, music, and songs of the Black women who are our foremothers, that we trace our lineage. The very fact that we must create a genealogy should bear witness to the way in which anthropology has institutionalized our silence and erasure through the development and maintenance of institutional racism, as evidenced by the canon that is currently taught.

Despite the vastness of anthropology's curricula, its implicit critique of ethnocentrism, and its allegiance to the idea of cultural relativity, the content of most anthropology courses remains remarkably Eurocentric. Rarely are the works of Blacks included in the curricula of graduate and undergraduate anthropology courses. The exceptions are the few folklore programs that, often grudgingly, admit that perhaps Blacks had something to say on the topic. Most significantly, we are not included in the courses taught on theory and methodology, despite the innovative research, writing, and practices of anthropologists such as Zora Neale Hurston, Katherine Dunham, St. Clair Drake, and John Gwaltney. White feminist anthropologists have been co-conspirators in this enterprise of silence and erasure. Core courses on feminist anthropology frequently fail to include the works of Black feminist anthropologists in their repertoire of feminist theorists—the excuse given is that our works are not readily accessible. This book is intended as a response.

As editor of this new anthology, my intention was to build upon the experiences of the many sistah scholars who have researched and written about their challenges to the inequities of race, class, and gender. *Black Feminist Anthropology* is intended to pay tribute to the historical efforts of Black feminist scholars in other disciplines. Thus, I chose not to reproduce the breadth, scope, and historical range of works such as Beverly Guy-Sheftall's *Words of Fire*.[14] Nor is this the herculean effort of a single author, such as Patricia Hill Collins's awe-inspiring *Black Feminist Thought: Knowledge,*

Consciousness and the Politics of Empowerment.[15] Rather, guided by the historical breadth of Guy-Sheftall's anthology and similar works as well as by the theoretical clarity and insightfulness of Hill Collins, the agenda of *Black Feminist Anthropology* is quite modest—it is intended to document and elucidate the theoretical perspectives of contemporary Black American feminist anthropologists. In this respect, it is the first archive to compile in one place original essays that speak specifically, and from an anthropological perspective, about the way in which race, gender, and sometimes class have produced an ethnographic praxis informed by identity, social race, discriminatory practices in the academy and society, and field encounters influenced by colonialism.

The inspiration for this book owes its conceptual genesis to the 1997 invited session "The Politics and Poetics of Black Feminist Anthropology," co-organized by myself and France Winddance Twine for the annual meeting of the American Anthropological Association in Washington, D.C. Beyond the original panelists, an invitation broadly cast but by no means exhaustive was sent to many who were not on the panel but who have made important contributions to studying the lives of Black women cross-culturally or theorizing around the issues of race, class, and gender. Unfortunately, a number of our sister anthropologists, including Twine and two panelists, could not participate for good reasons that included prior commitments, conflicting time schedules, their own scholarly enterprises, and professional demands.[16]

A unifying element for the book was the fact that as a group, Black Americans have the longest history of scholarly involvement in the discipline of North American anthropology. Perhaps the earliest anthropological work written by a Black American is Martin R. Delany's *Principia of Ethnology: The Origins of Race and Color, with an Archaeological Compendium of Ethiopian and Egyptian Civilization from Years of Careful Examination and Enquiry*, published in 1879 by Harper and Brothers. In fact, Black anthropologists have produced a wealth of anthropological research and ethnographies (vindicationist, applied, and critical). To anthropology's loss, most of this work is not read alongside the discipline's classics because it was published in non-anthropological journals. Despite such a dubious relationship, it is important to acknowledge that contrary to most other academic disciplines, Black women have been active (albeit unrecognized) agents in the field of North American anthropology throughout its history. From Caroline Bond Day who studied physical anthropology with Earnest A. Hooton at Harvard in the 1920s, to Zora Neale Hurston who studied folklore under the tutelage of "Papa" Franz Boas at Barnard and Columbia University, to Katherine Dunham who studied ethnology under the guidance of Robert Redfield at the University of Chicago in the 1930s and who first introduced dance performances influenced by anthropological research, Black American women have played pivotal roles (frequently introducing innovative and creative approaches) in challenging, redirecting, and transforming North American anthropology.

Zora Neale Hurston represents the apex of this legacy.[17] Scarcely acknowledged in most histories of anthropology, Hurston trained under Franz Boas, the "father" of North American anthropology, although she never completed her Ph.D.—the reason often cited to explain her exclusion. Yet many white men of the same period were allowed to contribute to the anthropological canon, as well as teach, without academic credentials. Moreover, the discipline has embraced them, while Hurston remains an outcast. We can only assume that the real reason for her exclusion is her race and gender.

Despite her erasure from the anthropological canon, Hurston's ethnographic research and methodology were brilliant, to say the least. Subjecting her research methodology to the rigors of Boas's intensive ethnographic field method and certainly influenced by his theory of historical particularism, Hurston forged her own unique reflexive ethnographic style. A woman out of step with her times, at the height of scientific objectivism, Hurston consciously adopted a native anthropological approach for the study of Black American folklore, music, and life in the United States, the Caribbean, and Latin America.[18] Moreover, while today anthropologists debate the blurring of boundaries between literature and ethnography, five decades earlier Hurston wrote and published novels that were ethnographically rich, and compiled essays and books about folklore that were literary and insightful.

Indeed, Hurston considered the problems of what James Clifford later called "ethnographic authority."[19] This is evident in the reasons she proffers for conducting research in her native Eatonville, Florida: it is safe; folk will put her in her place, if need be; and there was a wealth of folklore to collect. In *Mules and Men*, she explains:

> And now, I'm going to tell you why I decided to go to my native village first. I didn't go back there so that the home folks could make admiration over me because I had been up North to college and come back with a diploma and a Chevrolet. I knew they were not going to pay either one of these items too much mind. I was just Lucy Hurston's daughter, Zora. . . . I hurried back to Eatonville because I knew that the town was full of material and that I could get it without hurt, harm or danger.[20]

Through Hurston it is possible to see that the roots of the foundation upon which Black feminist anthropology is built are crosscultural, historical, interdisciplinary, literary, and deeply ethnographic.

A third important lineage for Black feminist anthropology is a more recent addition to the genealogy chart. In 1979, Filomena Chioma Steady's book, *The Black Woman Cross-Culturally*,[21] exposed us to the diversity of ethnographic research on Black women in Africa and the African Diaspora. Almost a decade later, Rosalyn Terborg-Penn, Sharon Harley, and Andrea Benton Rushing followed with *Women in Africa and the African Diaspora*.[22] In this interdisciplinary reader covering theoretical, methodological, and interpretive issues, Black feminist anthropologists were well represented. In the first edition, Filomena Chioma Steady surfaced again to advocate a theoretical model to guide research and analysis, in an article titled "African Feminism: A Worldwide Perspective"; A. Lynn Bolles discussed the methodological problematic of being a native anthropologist in the field in "Anthropological Research Methods for the Study of Black Women in the Caribbean"; and Niara Sudarkasa, in "The 'Status of Women' in Indigenous African Societies," engaged the debates about status and roles that have plagued the ethnographic literature on women in Africa. In the second edition, Sheila S. Walker's "The Feast of Good Death: An Afro-Catholic Emancipation Celebration in Brazil" was added;[23] it opened an important ethnographic window on gender, resistance, and religion in Brazil. There is no doubt that *African Feminism*, edited by

Gwendolyn Mikell, has also made a significant contribution to our thinking about global feminism, gender, and Africa.[24] Mikell's commitment to polyvocality has created an important space/place from which our African sisters can dialog with those of us from the north about critical topics on the state, family, economic policy, and feminism. *Black Feminist Anthropology* differs in that its contributors have conducted research not only in Africa but in the Caribbean, the Middle East, and the United States. We intend this work to compliment all of the important Black feminist precursors mentioned here.

Other Black women anthropologists whose works have served as guideposts for the development of this volume include Faye V. Harrison, editor of *Decolonizing Anthropology*, Leith Mullings, author of *On Our Own Terms*, and Brackette F. Williams, editor of *Women Out of Place*.[25] These authors and editors have engaged us theoretically, methodologically, and ethnographically as we traveled our own peculiar path toward a transformative Black feminist anthropology. No doubt there are many sister anthropologists whom we have failed to mention. Mea culpa in advance. Unfortunately, like real genealogies, fictive ones are also subject to memory lapses. We take this opportunity to acknowledge our debt to those we have named as well as to the unnamed Black women anthropologists both past and present whose works have inspired us. This volume stands as a bridge (and our promise) to future kinfolk.

FASHIONING A THEORY OF BLACK FEMINIST ANTHROPOLOGY

> A question that must be raised is this: when natives of the various cultures denied history and intellectual authority do indeed theorize, are those theories legitimated? Are they even acknowledged as higher order explanations?
>
> —Faye V. Harrison, "Anthropology as an Agent of Transformation: Introductory Comments and Query," 1997 [1991]

> It is a curious fate to write for a people other than one's own and it is even stranger to write to the conquerors of one's people.
>
> —Joseph Memmi, *The Colonizer and the Colonized*, 1991 [1965]

What is it that Black feminist anthropology proposes? First, as a theory it seeks to locate the experiences of Black women around the world at the apex of a feminist anthropology. Second, it has as its objective "the study of gender, of the interrelation between women and men, and of the role of gender in structuring human societies, their histories, ideologies, economic systems and political structures."[26] And, third, because histories, ideologies, institutions, and social relations do not operate in a vacuum, and because historically the place of Black people in the anthropological discourse on culture has been treated with indifference and our lives interpreted as deviant, a strong vindicationist thread runs through Afro-American (a k a Black) anthropology. It is where these two approaches intersect, with their common concern for elucidating the constitution of social inequality and people's varied responses to it, that Black feminist anthropology carves out a place.

Why advance a theory of Black feminist anthropology? Because if, as R. Jon McGee and Richard L. Warms assert, data without theory are meaningless precisely because our understanding of data "is derived from . . . [a] theoretical perspective,"[27] then knowledge of the specific strategies that Black women anthropologists deploy to make sense out of their ethnographic data is crucial to our understanding their research and analysis. That is, all ethnographic practice is theorized. And while both poststructuralism and postmodernism implicitly advance beliefs about how to deconstruct conventional explanatory paradigms, they are theories nonetheless.

Black feminist anthropological theory asserts that by making the complex intersection of gender, race, and class as the foundational component of its scholarship, followers gain a different and, we are convinced, fuller understanding of how Black women's lives (including our own) are constituted by structural forces. The multiplicity of coping strategies and forms of resistance that Black women adopt globally to contend with the structural and psychocultural dimensions of racism, sexism, and the other myriad forms that social inequality can assume in people's lives are an essential component of a Black feminist anthropological theorization. In taking on the role of producing meaning, we as Black feminist anthropologists align our commitment, skills, and resources with those of the existing coterie of "organic intellectuals" that can be found in every community and who "[represent] the interests of the oppressed, raising their consciousness of exploitation, and leading them in the direction of resistance and counter-hegemony."[28]

Taking on this role of scholar-activist (or public intellectual) mandates an ethos of praxis; thus, the research of Black feminist anthropologists is frequently directed toward action and achieving some outcome that will help ameliorate the oppressive/subordinate conditions to which Black women historically have been and continue to be subjected. While it is true that all Black women are not the same, Ruth Simms Hamilton has made a compelling argument that a persistent and pervasive condition of economic and political disenfranchisement as well social and cultural denigration characterizes the people of the African Diaspora: "the African diaspora represents a type of social grouping characterized by a historical patterning of particular social relationships and experiences. . . . Two structures of inequality, race and class, are particularly crucial in assessing the black diaspora."[29] The kind of ethnographic research described in the following chapters validates Hamilton's observations; it also demonstrates that oppression frequently is manifested in very gendered forms, by which I mean that men's and women's experiences cannot be conflated.

TOWARD AN ANTHROPOLOGY FOR LIBERATION

The politics of Black feminist anthropology can be found in our self-conscious positioning of ourselves as Black women (first) who do anthropology (second). There is no debate for the contributors to this book about which has more saliency—our lives as Black women or our lives as anthropologists. In making the lived experience of Black women the focal point of Black feminist anthropology, we reject rigid classifications that force us to choose between these dual aspects of our existence. Rather, we use our identity as a seminal point of departure for our theorization and simultaneously as a point of entry for our ethnographic research. It is within this context that we seek to fashion an engaged, scholarly, reflexive, and political anthropology—what Faye V. Harrison calls "an anthropology for liberation." As she reminds us, "knowledge production and praxis are inseparable."[30] All of this, however, means little without ethnography. If Afro-Scottish artist Maude Sulter is to be believed, without the textualization of our knowledge we remain invisible; in a world in which literacy and the written word are icons of power and privilege, writing down what we know and the very production of this book are political acts: "Transmitting our stories by word of mouth does not possess archival importance. Survival is visibility."[31]

The compilation of such a book as *Black Feminist Anthropology* moves in the direction of ensuring the type of cultural survival and visibility of which Sulter speaks through its deployment of a "cultural poetics." Such a poetics of culture grows out of our desire to interpret "the collective making of distinct cultural practices and inquiry into the relations among these practices."[32] This direction and commitment require several things. It dictates that we recognize that African Americans indeed have culture and indigenous forms of theorizing, out of which enduring cultural beliefs and practices have developed in unique and diverse ways in the United States and throughout the African Diaspora. It also demands that we position ourselves as vigilant scholars and cultural mediators ever ready to explicate such practices for ourselves and to the world.

The first chapter in this volume, "Seeking the Ancestors: Forging a Black Feminist Tradition in Anthropology," by A. Lynn Bolles, is a conscious attempt to create a tradition for Black feminist anthropology. Through a genealogical exploration of the careers of one elder, Katherine Dunham, and four ancestors, Caroline Bond Day, Zora Neale Hurston, Vera Green, and Irene Diggs, Bolles tries to answer a question that all of us who have contributed to this volume hope to answer for ourselves: What calls Black women to anthropology? For Bolles, whether or not these women proclaimed themselves feminists, they are our ancestors—because of their invisibility in the academy, because of the way in which the history of anthropology has rendered them mute, and because they were all impassioned by the research they conducted on Black people in the United States and in the African Diaspora. According to Bolles, we would be remiss not to claim such ancestors as kin.

In chapter 2, "Theorizing a Black Feminist Self in Anthropology: Toward an Autoethnographic Approach," Irma McClaurin advocates the use of autoethnography as a literary form ripe with possibilities for Black feminist anthropologists. Through autoethnography, which blends autobiography and ethnography, Black feminist anthropologists, she argues, encounter a form that enables them to use their personal experiences as a lens through which to describe and analyze ethnographic data. Holding up Zora Neale Hurston as the erudite autoethnographer, McClaurin argues that autoethnography, a form of cultural mediation, autobiographical reflexivity, and ethnographic representation, "is an innovative strategy of knowledge production" for Black feminist anthropologists and any other "speakers of subjugated discourses."

Kimberly Eison Simmons, in chapter 3, "A Passion for Sameness: Encountering a Black Feminist Self in Fieldwork in the Dominican Republic," grapples with identity and anthropology in a way very different from how these issues are treated in conventional anthropology and by mainstream feminists. She argues that sameness, as well as difference, can be used as a way to "(re)focus attention in anthropology on the critical importance of race and racial constructions of gender and class." Using her own (autoethnographic) fieldwork in the Dominican Republic as a point of departure, she shows how we, as outside researchers who, when we study people who may resemble us in historical, economic, and political circumstances, as well as phenotypically, can still be implicated as insiders. We can even become intimately entangled in racial constructions that vary significantly from those to which we are accustomed. Still, and yet, African Diaspora narratives of color, position, and gender emerge and intersect in ways that Simmons claims enable her to link her agenda as a Black feminist to that of a local Black women's organization in the Dominican Republic.

Visible markers of race and gender impact our lives in strange, constricting, and new ways, according to Carolyn Martin Shaw in chapter 4, "Disciplining the Black Female Body: Learning Feminism in Africa and the United States." Drawing on discourse analysis, Martin Shaw demonstrates, through a narrative of her own coming of age in a postsegregated United States, and later in Africa, that "the construction of subjectivity through powerful competing and complementary discourses . . . [may] structure identity but does not deny individual choice and agency." It is the contrasting, and contradictory, images of Marilyn Monroe, Mau Mau, and *Sputnik* that form iconographies of sexuality, colonialism, and progress. They allow Martin Shaw to see how her own em*bodied* identity is formed and reformed as she first desires, then investigates, and later challenges what these icons represent in her personal life and in her scholarship.

In chapter 5, "Negotiating Identity and Black Feminist Politics in Caribbean Research," Karla Slocum grapples with what it means to be a "native" anthropologist in the field. As a Black woman anthropologist studying Black women in St. Lucia, she, unlike Simmons, finds constant disjunctures between how she is viewed by her informants and how she would like to be viewed, despite commonalties in their experiences of race and gender. After being relegated to the status of child/daughter, because of her lack of knowledge about the culture, and after conceding that parity is not possible, because of educational and class differences, Slocum abandons her initial naiveté and adopts a Black feminist approach that asserts "it is more significant how we position ourselves in terms of the politics surrounding our social and professional identities as Black feminist anthropologists."

Angela Gilliam, in chapter 6, "A Black Feminist Perspective on the Sexual Commodification of Women in the New Global Culture," is also concerned with how Black feminist anthropologists position themselves in the field. Using narrative vignettes that crisscross in time and place, Gilliam takes us on a journey of her coming of age as a Black feminist anthropologist. From Papua New Guinea to Brazil, we travel with her down roads and in languages that seem diverse but that ultimately connect with each other and with her as she structures her research agendas around how the Black woman's body through time and space is "both an instrument of prurient fascination and an historical symbol of service-oriented labor." For Gilliam, the crossroads of slavery, capitalism, and gender and sexual oppression conjoin in the "carnivalization of poverty" and the "sexual commodification of Brazilian women."

Like Gilliam, Cheryl Mwaria in chapter 7 also takes up the subject of Black women's bodies—as medical research subjects. In "Biomedical Ethics, Gender, and Ethnicity: Implications for Black Feminist Anthropology," she uses a biocultural approach to analyze how bioethics have historically avoided discussions of race, class, and gender as significant factors. As a result, Blacks and women, and Black women especially, have been the victims of medical experimentation. Tracing a history of medical experimentation that begins in slavery, and "presaged those of Nazi doctors," Mwaria demonstrates how Black women's position as property made them dispensable to both their owners and the doctors to whom they were loaned. Unfortunately, according to Mwaria, the atrocities of medical experimentation are still visited upon the poor, Blacks, and others who live on the margins of society. She eschews being a "distant and dispassionate observer" and advocates, instead, a Black feminist anthropology that requires us to "raise a different, more critical set of questions than those currently being raised in bioethical debates." According to her, we must use the "lenses of race, class, and gender" so that we may, as organic intellectuals in general and Black feminist anthropologists specifically, inform public policy and global medical technology and research.

On a different track in chapter 8, "Contingent Stories of Anthropology, Race, and Feminism," Paulla A. Ebron explores the way memory and social history conjoin to produce personal and intellectual understanding. She unabashedly critiques African Americans for imagining Africa in ways that construct it as our "Other." On a provocative journey, fueled by memories, Ebron provides a vivid etiology of her identity in which nationalism and feminism frequently collide and in which she disciplines them to co-exist. Ebron concludes that identity, theory, and praxis are best viewed as performances.

Although most of the chapters grapple with issues of identity, power differentials of race, class, and gender, feminism, and nationalism in exotic places, far, far away, what better place to begin to engage in a tranformative praxis designed to impact policy and wider arenas of power than at home? Or so Cheryl Rodriguez asserts in chapter 9, "A Homegirl Goes Home: Black Feminism and the Lure of Native Anthropology." Using a short story by Alice Walker, "Everyday Use," as a way to forewarn of the potential alienation of Black intellectuals from the folk, Rodriguez traces how her own engagement with anthropology has been very much grounded in home and the folk. Moreover, she is explicit about using Black feminism and native anthropology as twin complementary approaches that enable her to effectively engage in ethnographic research at home. The fusion of these two methodologies is a challenging one. According to Rodriguez, "Native Black feminist anthropology involves negotiating the challenges of our lives as Black women who are also feminists and researchers. It involves reinventing ourselves not just as anthropologists but also as those who are capable of building bridges across contradictory realities."

Who sez Black folk, and Black women especially, don't do theory? This volume is our way of defying this belief that hangs over us like Damocles' sword, whether spoken out loud or not. Indeed, these chapters represent an "archaeology" of Self and Black feminist anthropology in the best Foucaldian sense of the word. We present it to anthropology as a signal that we are prepared to engage in critical cultural mediation, and to our readers as a theoretical and political intervention on identity, knowledge production, and power so that they too will understand "What draws Black women—and other marginalized people—to anthropology?" For all of us, as our chapters reveal, are attracted to the theory, the politics, the praxis, and the poetics. We are attracted to being part of the knowledge producers of the world. We are drawn to making Black women's lives both visible and audible. We are drawn indeed to the possibilities of anthropology in general and the promise of Black feminist anthropology especially.

NOTES

1. While I acknowledge the tremendous diversity of experiences in the African Diaspora, I use the terms "Black" and "Black American" interchangeably to refer to men and women of African descent born in the United States.
2. I extend my heartfelt thanks to my friend and colleague France Winddance Twine for suggesting this concept of intervention and for pressing me to "call the skillet black" by explicitly discussing the constraints we face in anthropology as a result of our race and gender.
3. Lee D. Baker, *From Savage to Negro: Anthropology and the Construction of Race, 1896–1954* (Berkeley: University of California Press, 1998); and Faye V. Harrison, "Auto-Ethnographic Reflections on Hierarchies in Anthropology," *Practicing Anthropology* 17, 1–2 (winter/spring 1995): 48–50.
4. Baker, *From Savage to Negro,* 144.
5. Harrison, "Auto-Ethnographic Reflections," 50.
6. Ibid. Harrison's critique highlights the need for more systematic research, and the compilation of data, on the number of Black scholars who receive Ph.D.'s, the number of Blacks with Ph.D.'s actually teaching in anthropology departments, and the representation of Black women among the ever-growing number of women anthropologists in the academy.
7. John L. Gwaltney, *Drylongso: A Self-Portrait of Black America* (New York: The New Press, 1993), xix.
8. J. I. Rodale, *The Synonym Finder* (Emmaus, Pa.: Rodale Press, 1978), 816. I thank Kamari Clarke for her suggestions in the development of this Black feminist "genealogy" and France Winddance Twine for encouraging me to construct a timeline (see table 1) for future generations to use and improve upon.

9. See Baker, *From Savage to Negro*, 165–168, for an enlightening description of the activist contributions of Katherine Dunham and Irene Diggs.

10. St. Clair Drake, as cited on the title page of *Transforming Anthropology* 6, 1–2 (1997).

11. Sandra Morgen, *Gender and Anthropology: Critical Reviews for Research and Teaching* (Washington, D.C.: American Anthropological Association, 1986); Faye Ginsburg and Anna Tsing, *Uncertain Terms: Negotiating Gender in American Culture* (Boston: Beacon Press, 1990); Henrietta Moore, *Feminism and Anthropology* (Minneapolis: University of Minnesota Press, 1988); and Micaela di Leonardo, *Gender at the Crossroads* (Berkeley: University of California Press, 1992).

12. Karen Brodkin Sacks, "Toward a Unified Theory of Race, Class, and Gender," *American Ethnologist* 16 (3): 534–550.

13. Carol Stack, *All Our Kin: Strategies for Survival in a Black Community* (New York: Harper and Row, 1974).

14. Beverly Guy-Sheftall, ed., *Words of Fire: An Anthology of African-American Feminist Thought* (New York: The New Press, 1995).

15. Patricia Hill Collins, *Black Feminist Thought: Knowledge, Consciousness and the Politics of Empowerment* (1990; reprint, New York and London: Routledge, Chapman and Hall, 1991).

16. We acknowledge the tremendous leadership contributions of Johnnetta B. Cole, president emerita of Spelman College; Niara Sudarkasa, former president of Lincoln University; Yolanda Moses, a former president of CUNY and the American Anthropological Association; and Claudia Mitchell-Kernan, vice-chancellor of academic affairs at UCLA. We also salute Brackette Williams for her achievement as a 1999 McArthur Genius Award recipient.

17. See Gwendolyn Mikell, "Feminism and Black Culture in the Ethnography of Zora Neale Hurston," in *African-American Pioneers in Anthropology*, ed. Ira E. Harrison and Faye V. Harrison (Urbana: University of Illinois Press, 1999); and Graciela Hernández, "Multiple Subjectivities and Strategic Positionality: Zora Neale Hurston's Experimental Ethnographies," in *Women Writing Culture*, ed. Ruth Behar and Deborah A. Gordon (Berkeley: University of California Press, 1995). I am currently working on a project with the goal of reclaiming Hurston for anthropology; I thank the Beinecke Rare Book and Manuscript Library at Yale University for awarding me a Donald C. Gallup Fellowship in American literature in May 2000 to conduct research on the Zora Neale Hurston papers located in their James Weldon Johnson Collection.

18. Cf. Zora Neale Hurston, *Mules and Men* (1935; reprint, Bloomington: Indiana University Press, 1963), 9; and idem, *Tell My Horse: Voodoo and Life in Haiti and Jamaica* (1938; reprint, New York: Perennial Library, 1990). Hurston conducted research on folklore in the Bahamas, Haiti, the Honduras, as well as the United States.

19. James Clifford, "On Ethnographic Authority," in *The Predicament of Culture: Twentieth Century Ethnography, Literature, and Art* (Cambridge: Harvard University Press, 1988).

20. Hurston, "Introduction," *Mules and Men*, 9.

21. Filomina Chioma Steady, ed., *The Black Woman Cross-Culturally* (Cambridge, Mass.: Schenkman Publishing Company, 1981).

22. Rosalyn Terborg-Penn, Sharon Harley, and Andrea Benton Rushing, eds., *Women in Africa and the African Diaspora: A Reader*, 1st ed. (Washington, D.C.: Howard University Press, 1987).

23. Sheila S.Walker, "The Feast of Good Death: An Afro-Catholic Emancipation Celebration in Brazil," in *Women in Africa and the African Diaspora: A Reader*, 2nd ed., ed. Rosalyn Terborg-Penn and Andrea Benton Rushing (Washington, D.C.: Howard University Press, 1996), 203–214.

24. Gwendolyn Mikell, *African Feminism: The Politics of Survival in Sub-Saharan Africa* (Philadelphia: University of Pennsylvania Press, 1997).

25. Faye V. Harrison, ed., *Decolonizing Anthropology: Moving Further toward an Anthropology for Liberation*, 2nd ed. (1991; reprint, Arlington, Va.: Association of Black Anthropologists and American Anthropological Association, 1997); Leith Mullings, *On Our Own Terms: Race, Class, and Gender in the Lives of African American Women* (New York: Routledge, 1997); and Brackette F. Williams, ed., *Women Out of Place: The Gender of Agency and the Race of Nationality* (New York and London: Routledge, 1996).

26. Henrietta Moore, *Feminism and Anthropology* (Minneapolis: University of Minnesota Press, 1988), 6.

27. R. Jon McGee and Richard L. Warms, *Anthropological Theory: An Introductory History*, 2nd ed. (Mountain View, Calif.: Mayfield Publishing Company), 1.

28. Christine G. T. Ho, "Popular Culture and the Aestheticization of Politics: Hegemonic Struggle and Postcolonial Nationalism in the Trinidad Carnival," *Transforming Anthropology* 9, 1 (2000): 3.

29. Ruth Simms Hamilton, *Creating a Paradigm and Research Agenda for Comparative Studies of the Worldwide Dispersion of African Peoples*, Monograph no. 1, African Diaspora Research Project (East Lansing: Michigan State University, 1990), 18–19.

30. Harrison, *Decolonizing Anthropology*, 10.

31. Maude Sulter, quoted in Polly T. Rewt, "Introduction: The African Diaspora and Its Origins," *Research in African Literatures* 29, 4 (winter 1998): 8. Maude Sulter is an artist of Afro-Scottish descent. She addresses issues of power and representation, the image, and the spoken word. Her photographs and exhibits are often accompanied by her own poetry. This line is taken from a photo caption (Telrprischore) in a series of nine portraits called Zabat (1989). For more on Sulter, see Jim Mahon, "Europe's African Heritage in the Creative Work of Maude Sulter," *Research in African Literatures* 29, 4 (winter 1998): 148–155.

32. Greenblatt cited in José Limon, *Dancing with the Devil: Society and Cultural Poetics in Mexican-American South Texas* (Madison: University of Wisconsin Press, 1994), 14.

1

A. LYNN BOLLES

SEEKING THE ANCESTORS
Forging a Black Feminist Tradition in Anthropology

What would Black women anthropologists who have passed on, such as Caroline Bond Day, Zora Neale Hurston, Vera Green, and Irene Diggs, or the elders who are still among us, such as Katherine Dunham, say about being included in a discussion of Black feminist anthropology? More likely than not, they would remind us that we cannot make the historical record say what it does not—nor can we make them say what they have not. Although each of these women clearly understood her situation as a woman, not all of them interpreted that experience as one of "domination"; rather, some saw being a woman as *difference* in its most mild form, or as a practice of social asymmetry, with each gender playing a traditional role.

In this day of women and gender studies programs, such a perspective is untenable. Yet, the historical record tells us that for some women, in particular Black women, gender oppression has not placed high in their list of priorities, neither has it always served as the focal point of their scholarship and their activism. Despite this historical gender-neutral stance, the experiences and plights of these Black women anthropologists have been the seeds from which the current Black feminist tradition in anthropology has germinated. Further, whether or not they acknowledge themselves to be our intellectual forebears, those of us who consider ourselves Black feminist anthropologists have found inspiration and solace in their scholarship, and in the compromises and contradictions with which they were confronted for daring to declare themselves "Black" or "Negro" women anthropologists.

A SEED IS PLANTED

For almost as long as there have been graduates of anthropology departments, there have been Black women who studied this field of inquiry. Most have yet to be acknowledged in the most recent canon-setting texts of the discipline,[1] and few are recognized by the field—notwithstanding the election of the Black woman anthropologist Yolanda Moses in 1995 as president of the American Anthropological Association. The existence of a cadre of Black women in American academic anthropology in the early part of the twentieth century is a "thrice-told tale" of social relations.[2]

So-called American anthropology developed in the antebellum period (1840s) and evolved into an academic discipline during the 1880s. From then until the 1980s, the number of Black women in the discipline has not moved beyond the low double digits. Despite being few in number, Black women have been an integral part of the intellectual and knowledge production traditions of American anthropology, contributing innovations in innumerable ways. This chapter illustrates how Black women anthropologists contributed to the discipline through service to the profession, while continuing a tradition of African American intellectual thought.

Before the 1980s, the presence of Black women in anthropology could be viewed as underscoring the liberal agenda of the field in general and the academy at large. This agenda contained enough symbolic land mines, however, to make most departments and institutions unhealthy places for these early pioneers.[3] Their very presence raised havoc in a number of ways throughout departments across the country. What makes their story most poignant, though, is their silencing in the ways that "count."

What counts in the academy includes having one's work and scholarship valued and cited by colleagues, receiving financial support, and generally being referred to as a scholar in a positive manner. In this system of academic accounting, Black women's intellectual work was often torn apart, devalued, or ignored, and rarely was it supported financially.[4] Given this history of often being unwelcomed and unwanted, the question of "What calls Black women to anthropology?" is truly a profound one. Further, with the emergence of feminist anthropology in the 1970s, how has this positionality as unwelcomed guest or "outsider within" become a useful tool for the development of a Black feminist anthropology?[5] Finally, what might our Black women anthropologist ancestors say about all of this?

A THRICE-TOLD TALE

This historical exploration of female intellectual ancestors and the emergence of a Black feminist anthropology is traced through three "tales." The first is an exploration of the intersection of anthropology and the African American intellectual tradition. Using a historical framework allows me to situate Black women in the field of anthropology and pose the question "Why anthropology?"

The second "tale" of this chapter traces the development of a Black feminist anthropology. I look at Black feminisms and the matrices of domination that are used by Black women anthropologists, both on a personal level and as a tool of analysis to conduct research on and write about particular populations or communities.[6] Finally, in the third "tale," I examine the lived experiences of the four women ancestors and one elder. My goal is to analyze and offer my own exegesis of what the ancestors might have thought and what the elders do think about the confluence of being Black, female, and anthropologist and where, if at all, being a feminist fits into their identity formulations.

ANTHROPOLOGY AND AFRICAN AMERICAN INTELLECTUAL TRADITIONS

In trying to answer the question "Why anthropology?" I turn to Francille Rusan Wilson, an African American feminist who studies the history of Black intellectuals. She observes that most Black women working on academic advanced degrees in the first half of the twentieth century were primarily centered in sociology programs.[7] Most, emulating the dictates of middle-class decorum, often married and, following the history of Black women as an integral part of the U.S. labor force, continued to work professionally. They usually became social workers or teachers but rarely completed their doctorates. It is Leith Mullings who asserts that the "esoteric nature of anthropology made it difficult for anyone to envision it as a viable vehicle through which one concerned with the racial progress, a major goal of the day for the Black middle-classes, intellectuals, and elites, in particular, could achieve specific goals."[8] As Mullings also reminds us, those goals were (and still are) (1) the charge of uplifting the race, (2) dealing with the social and material conditions of the race, and (3) finding "a cure for inequality."[9]

Because anthropology's origins lay in the developing world and served at that time as a true tool of the colonial world, the discipline did not lend itself to understanding social relations within the United States. Despite its inauspicious, and to some a seemingly recondite, legacy, anthropology was viewed by the handful of Black women who studied the discipline from about 1915 through the 1950s as a tool to locate the sources of inequality, and in some instances, as a place where one could participate in finding the "cure."

Although considered by many today to be "the child of imperialism," anthropology has the ability to serve as a positive social force for advancing equality among people.[10] This capacity is to be found in the way in which anthropology proceeds. Contrary to most academic disciplines concerned with disciplinary purity and boundary maintenance, anthropology luxuriates in its own eclecticism. Because anthropology derives much of its perspective from a fusion of the humanities, social sciences, and natural sciences, some dimension of it is usually attractive to all and of value to many. Its uniqueness is in its point of view, which is at once holistic, comparative, particularistic, and general. Individual anthropologists describe and analyze the world they encounter in a variety of forms emanating from the four classical areas of anthropological study: archaeology and biological/physical, linguistic, and social-cultural anthropology. At the core of each of these approaches lies some concept of culture, which provides the social arena in which all else occurs. While culture is the axis upon which the discipline rotates, the methods employed by anthropologists to illustrate culture as phenomena are diverse.[11] It is this eclecticism of anthropology and its overarching concern with the human condition that align it with the historic goals of the African American intellectual tradition, out of which comes the perspective called African American anthropology. The African American intellectual tradition can be seen as most often corrective, meaning that Black intellectuals are compelled to expend tremendous energies answering "stupid questions posed by others; striving often with no more success than Sisyphus, to push the paradigms steeped in racism, sexism, ethnocentrism, and cold contempt."[12] In the course of correcting these dominant paradigms, African American scholars focus on accurate descriptions and a reclamation of a history of cultures constructed under, at best, hostile circumstances. "Setting the story straight," Mullings notes,[13] requires not only lauding the accomplishments and victories over domination but also understanding and giving meaning to the structures of oppression that frame and underscore the creativity and history of an oppressed people. It is this synergy that eloquently responds to the question of "Why anthropology?" for Black intellectuals.

One of the most prominent Black anthropologists, president emerita of Spelman College, Johnnetta Betsch Cole, has described how she was captivated by anthropology during her first year at Oberlin College.[14] Cole recalls listening to a white man (George Eaton Simpson) not only give information about a part of Black culture but describe it so poetically that he inspired her realization that one could study culture—one's own or that of others—and represent it truly and eloquently rather than use the stance of an objective observer as a way to dominate others. Mullings aptly defines this as "the possibilities of anthropology."[15] This approach to anthropology enables nonmainstream anthropologists who are racially identifiable or of marked ethnicities (and a few unmarked ones as well) to follow intellectual guidelines for responsible research that provide an opportunity for exchange, increase accuracy, foster mutual respect, and create a sharing of civic responsibility between the researcher and those they study.[16]

Because racism and the omnipresence of oppression are significant factors in the lived experiences and identity formations of female and male African American anthropologists, the "fit" or synergism of the discipline and the African American intellectual tradition was, and still is, comfortable. Further, whatever the mandates of anthropology may be to study the "Other," almost to a person the research of African American anthropologists has had as its focus Africans or African-descended people at home and abroad.

FORGING A TRADITION

The first Black person to earn a graduate degree in anthropology was a woman, Caroline Bond Day. She graduated in the class of 1919 from Harvard/Radcliffe and received her Master of Science degree from there in 1932.[17] Beginning a tradition of working on topics germane to the Black intellectual tradition, she wrote her thesis on race crossing, and color and intelligence among mulatto Black Americans in Atlanta and Washington, D.C. Although Day's work used the prevailing theoretical and interpretive frameworks of physical and cultural anthropology of her time, she attempted to argue against eugenics.[18] However, her book, *A Study of Some Negro-White Families in the United States*, also included a foreword and notes by Earnest A. Hooton, an anthropometric who professed that physical inheritance explained mental and cultural differences between the races.[19] Although Day's research argued against such biologizing of racial differences, Hooton, her adviser, ironically considered her "a credit to her race" because, in his estimation, as a light-skinned colored woman, she physically and intellectually proved his thesis.

From this modest beginning to the present, African American anthropologists have produced works on race, ethnicity, inequality, expressive cultural ways, self-validating rituals, and the political, economic, and social practices of people in Africa and the African Diaspora. Moreover, they have written about how these accomplishments frequently have occurred in environments of adversity.[20] This scholarship not only reflected their use of esoteric anthropological traditions but was and is clearly involved in the traditional aims of the Black intellectual tradition—racial uplifting, analysis of the social and material conditions of the race, and locating sites of inequality.

Despite some long-standing and innovative contributions, particularly in the area of urban and American anthropology, which only in the late 1960s were brought into the fold of "real" anthropology, the African American anthropological tradition is neither valued nor lauded by the academy. This can be attributed primarily to its devotion to discerning and analyzing the nonwhite American domestic scene and/or to its devout antiracist agenda. As a result of the applied focus of their work and as a consequence of being ignored by mainstream anthropology, only a few Black anthropologists have worked in the academy, and mostly on the periphery, at historically Black colleges or universities (e.g., Irene Diggs). Others have found themselves devalued and invisible in mainstream academic settings (e.g., Vera Green). Suffice it to say, uncategorically, that despite significant intellectual contributions, the works of Black anthropologists are rarely recorded or acknowledged.[21]

Neither St. Clair Drake (1911–1990) nor Allison Davis (1902–1983) received in life the recognition or appreciation they deserved from their colleagues in the discipline; moreover, what praise they have been granted posthumously seems to have been conferred begrudgingly.[22] Both Zora Neale Hurston and Katherine Dunham must be counted among some of the true innovators in cultural anthropology—Hurston for her reflexive ethnographic method used decades before it was embraced by anthropologists or postmodernists, and Katherine Dunham for creating the field of dance anthropology. Although both women are now recognized by a wider audience, neither are included as contributors in the current borderless discourses of postmodern and postcolonial theories and practices.[23] And significantly, rarely are they discussed in conventional histories of the field of anthropology.[24]

Zora Neale Hurston in the literary world, like the resurrected Mexican artist Frida Kahlo, is now deified and has become the token representative of the misbegotten "before her time" temperamental, tormented artist. Unlike Kahlo, however, whose paintings, drawings, and other works are carefully and critically examined in the art world by feminist scholars such as Evelyn Beck,[25] Hurston has yet to be critically analyzed "as an anthropologist" in the same manner by someone in the discipline. Most works on Hurston seem preoccupied with her personality and literary production, giving little attention to a deep analysis of her ethnographic work and her alternative research methods.[26]

From my own count, by 1967 only eight Black women held a Ph.D. in anthropology. They are Irene Diggs (1944, Havana); Manet Fowler (1954, Cornell); Diane Lewis (1965, Cornell); Audrey Smedely (1965, Victoria University of Manchester, England); Vera Green (1967, Arizona); Johnnetta Betsch Cole (1967, Northwestern); Claudia Mitchell-Kernan (1967, University of California, Berkeley); and Niara Sudarkasa (née Gloria Marshall) (1967, Columbia).[27]

Surveying the institutions at which these women earned their degrees establishes that these Black women received outstanding graduate educations at predominately white institutions of higher learning. The racial and classist undertones embedded in the phrase "predominately white institutions" should not be lost on anyone. Predominantly white institutions maintained exclusionary admissions practices (particularly for graduate programs), based on notions of social incompatibility, and other academic criteria that were suspect at best, invalid at worst, and rooted in the presumed intellectual inferiority of Blacks. In practice, these institutions carefully guarded their gates and limited those who applied, were accepted, matriculated, and graduated. Anthropology itself, although a liberal discipline, was not ready for "the natives" to study themselves or anyone else. And while today the numbers of Black graduate students may be growing, "native anthropology" is still disdained, and the notion of Black anthropologists studying themselves is generally discouraged.[28]

For these women and their predecessors, being Black and female compounded their situation in the academy. If in the 1920s the discipline did not know what to do with a Margaret Mead going into the field, it could not even imagine a Black woman anthropologist embarking on fieldwork. For most of these women, isolation as the only person of color and an inattentive adviser were the rule rather the exception. Of course, a few lucky ones found caring advisers who supported them, made sure that the appropriate jobs were lined up, and wrote glowing letters of recommendation. In these instances, anthropological liberalism operated as a double-edged sword.

Such liberal advisers practiced the "pet Negro" syndrome, as Zora Neale Hurston called it. They relied on Black students to reaffirm their liberal tendencies, yet withheld the amount or type of resources that would ensure their students' transformation into professional anthropologists.[29] For example, before the late 1950s, Black anthropology graduate students were constrained from conducting research in Africa. Melville Herskovits, one of the leading figures in Africanist and Caribbeanist anthropology, believed that Black Americans could not be objective in their studies of African societies.[30] His gatekeeping policies affected the graduate careers of St. Clair Drake and later his own student, Johnnetta B. Cole.[31] Hurston's struggles to find funding for the fieldwork that gave birth to *Mules and Men* is one of the more famous examples of Black scholars having to subject themselves to alternate and sometimes demeaning—as in the case of Hurston's benefactress—circumstances to acquire funding for their intellectual work.[32]

THE AFRICAN AMERICAN ANTHROPOLOGICAL TRADITION AND FEMINISMS: AWKWARD COMPANIONS

By the early 1970s, feminist anthropology was in full swing. As an approach within anthropology, it moved beyond the mere inclusion of women as suitable subjects for anthropological inquiry toward the development of a goal of understanding social relations of power, women's individual and collective identities, and the fabric of meaning and value in society relative to sex roles.[33]

The impact and growing influence of women in anthropology are exemplified by the way in which standard textbooks and curricula have been modified to include gender, the incorporation of discussions of women's roles and gender-related issues in all areas of anthropology, the increased proportion of women in the profession, and the prominence of women in leadership positions in the discipline's main professional societies.[34] Some "old boys" argue that the "feminization" of anthropology is eroding the core of the discipline.

Despite the enormous advances of women in anthropology over the last two decades, Black women remain invisible and silenced where it counts, [35] although many have been active participants in the wide-ranging debates and discussions that helped shape feminist anthropology.[36] Ironically, mainstream feminist anthropology continues the practice of the discipline.[37] That is, it too follows the classic liberal agenda when it comes to including nonmainstream (i.e., racially identifiable, marked and unmarked ethnic) anthropologists. When we are called on to speak, it is usually in the context of a multicultural format: one Asian, one African American, one lesbian (usually Euro-American), one Latina, and so forth.[38] This exclusion of Black American feminist anthropologists (who comprise the largest minority) makes little sense, given that they have been making a way for themselves in anthropology since the 1960s. Moreover, their scholarly visibility is impressive; for example, in 1995–1997 alone, Black American feminist anthropologists published almost a dozen books (e.g., *Sister Jamaica* and *We Paid Our Dues* by A. Lynn Bolles; *Women of Belize* by Irma McClaurin; *African Feminisms* by Gwendolyn Mikell; *On Our Own Terms* by Leith Mullings; *Colonial Inscriptions* by Carolyn Martin Shaw; and *Racism in a Racial Democracy* by France Winddance Twine).[39] We have authored numerous refereed articles that have appeared in such mainstream journals as *Anthropology and Educational Quarterly* ("African American Anthropology and the Pedagogy of Activist Community Research" by Cheryl Rodriguez), *Annual Review of Anthropology* ("The Persistent Power of 'Race' in the Cultural and Political Economy of Racism" by Faye Harrison), and *Ameri-*

can Anthropologist ("Black Male Imagery and Media Containment of African American Men" by Helán Page).[40] Black feminist anthropologist Brackette Williams was awarded a MacArthur genius prize in 1999, and others have served as presidents of the American Anthropological Association (Yolanda Moses, 1995–1997), the African Studies Association (Gwendolyn Mikell, 1996–1997), and the Caribbean Studies Association (A. Lynn Bolles, 1997–1998). The achievements of Black women anthropologists also extend beyond the conventional domain of scholarship as they assume key leadership positions as presidents and top administrators of a wide range of institutions of higher learning: Johnnetta Betsch Cole (president emerita of Spelman College), Niara Sudarkasa (president of Lincoln University, Pennsylvania), Yolanda T. Moses (a former president of CUNY), and Claudia Mitchell-Kiernan (dean/vice chancellor of academic affairs at UCLA).

The intersection of the African American anthropological tradition and feminism has matured in the rather sophisticated way often fostered by oppression, and it is out of the ensuing tension that Black feminist anthropology has grown. In effect, Black women in anthropology came to feminism not because of what they found there, but because of what they felt they could contribute to the analysis of gender inequality. Most often this meant paying greater attention to the interactiveness and simultaneity of race, class, and gender.[41] As products of the 1960s, and often as political workers inside and outside of the academy, Black feminists constructed an approach to race, class, and gender that brought it all home—linking anthropologists in a more integral way to the communities in which they worked and inviting the communities to speak back to anthropology. Mullings asserts that it was her search for child care that brought class, race, and gender issues together in a very personal way, while for Johnnetta Cole it was conducting research in Cuba, where because institutional racism was outlawed, she was able to see sexism operating in more blatant, fundamental ways.[42]

The thread that connects Black feminist theorizing both inside and outside anthropology is the concept of "the simultaneity of oppression." That is, race, class, gender are conceptualized as combining in various ways that are always historical and contextual.[43] Following Rose Brewer's lead and the "simultaneity of oppression" model, I suggest that to theorize about the simultaneity of oppression and struggle leads to an understanding of the embeddedness and relationality of race, class, and gender in a synergistic way. Furthermore, the analysis and description of the lived experiences, historical positioning, cultural perceptions, and social construction of Black women (who are enmeshed in and whose ideas emerge out of that experience) result in a feminism whose organizing principle is one firmly rooted in class, culture, gender, and race interacting. Black feminism, then, is an anthropologist's theoretical dream come true.

Contributing to this synergistic approach—yet complicating it too—is the fact that the researcher and those under study often have much in common as a result of these matrices of domination. Conducting fieldwork, especially with other Black or nonwhite women, demands that the Black feminist anthropologist be simultaneously analytical, political, and reflexive. Patricia Hill Collins's work on Black women's standpoint theory provides the necessary context for understanding this type of interaction between the Black feminist anthropologist researcher and the women she encounters in the fieldwork situation.[44] It is in the synthesis of the Black feminist concept of the simultaneity of oppression with the African American anthropological tradition that the foundation for contemporary Black feminist anthropology becomes evident. However, the time prior to the articulation of this gendered theoretical perspective is the entry point for Black women ancestors and elders. Trying to derive some meaning out of and some understanding of why they failed to prioritize gender or study sexual inequality enables us to historicize how theoretical perspectives are sometimes born out of omissions and silences.

WOMEN ANCESTORS: RECLAIMING OUR PAST

In the 1994 edition of *Island Possessed*, while reflecting back on her entrance into the field of anthropology, Katherine Dunham recalls:

> Harold Courlander had been there and Melville Herskovits had just published the first serious and sympathetic study of the people and their social structure. They were white and male, these writers. Of my kind I was a first—a lone young woman easy to place in the clean-cut American dichotomy of color, harder to place in

the complexity of Caribbean color classifications; a mulatto when occasion called for, an in-between, or "griffon" actually, I suppose; of as "noir"—not exactly the color black, but the quality of belonging with or being at ease with black people.[45]

In this moment, Dunham positions herself in opposition to the anthropologist of the day—she is the "perspiring student" of "dance and anthropology" ready to begin her study of kinetic expressions among the "real Haitian people." She is cognizant that no one expects a visiting researcher to be female, a U.S. citizen, a student, *and* to be of African descent. In one human package, Dunham breaks all of the rules.

Looking at the careers of three deceased anthropologists, Zora Neale Hurston, Vera Green, and Irene Diggs, and one living elder, Katherine Dunham, we see the commonalties but also the differences among these women forebears. All of them chose anthropology because of the incredible power of the concept of culture, which enabled them to capture and embrace the contributions of Creole and Africa in the New World. Three of them—Hurston, Dunham, and Diggs—worked in the areas of expressive culture: oral literatures, music, and dance. At that time, great importance was placed on finding and demonstrating retentions encoded in the expressive culture that enabled a people to maintain its history through performance and artistry. Green analyzed the impact of race and ethnicity in family life and the ways variation in forms of social inequality influenced social mobility. The early work of all four of these anthropologists was located in the Caribbean—Haiti, Cuba, Aruba, and Jamaica.

Each had a personal understanding of the meaning of racism, how it affected their lives, and what the people at home, and the people with whom they worked, did to adapt to and negotiate this oppression. In terms of social class, Dunham was of middle-class origins, while Vera Green characterized her Chicago parents and family as being members of "the rented-room poor."[46] Irene Diggs was raised in a small town in southern Illinois with an even smaller working-class Black population. Her mother and father were considered "hard-working people." Like Diggs, Zora Neale Hurston came from a working-class background; she grew up in Eatonville, Florida, one of a very few Black townships in the state (not just

the Black side of a white town). All of these women won scholar-
ships to pursue their undergraduate degrees. All were dependent
on grants and prizes to make ends meet. Their economic situations
could at best be described as precarious during the height of the
Depression; at times, Hurston was compelled to assume jobs as a
manicurist and maid to finance her education.

Each of these women worked closely with people considered
important intellectual leaders in the African American community
or the field of anthropology. For example, Irene Diggs spent eleven
years as W.E.B. Du Bois's research assistant at Atlanta University.[47]
She earned the first master's degree in sociology from Atlanta University, and when she traveled to Cuba on holiday, she vowed to
return to the island and continue her exploration of another black
culture that was not her own. At the University of Havana, Diggs
became a student of Fernando Ortiz.[48] In the pre-Revolutionary racial climate of Cuba, Diggs, whose status as a student implied that
she was middle class, found her phenotype socially "lightened."
While in Cuba, she collected songs, poetry, and recorded the music and dance of Afro-Cubans in the western part of the country
for her dissertation. Later, after a year of study in Argentina and
Uruguay, Diggs returned to the United States and never again conducted fieldwork outside of the country; instead, she taught sociology and anthropology at Morgan State for almost thirty years.[49]

Vera Green's engagement with anthropology began as a child,
when she used to criticize Hollywood's portrayals of Native Americans in the movies she watched on Saturday afternoons in Chicago.
Her early undergraduate mentor at Roosevelt University in Chicago
was St. Clair Drake,[50] who encouraged her to pursue her education
at Columbia University in New York. Green worked for a number
of years as a social worker in the Cabrini-Green housing projects
in Chicago to save for her graduate school tuition. At Columbia,
she studied with Charles Wagley, Elena Padilla, and Gene Weltfish.[51] It was while working with Padilla in East Harlem that Green
found the topic for her own research.

Her master's thesis was on romantic love and familial responsibility among new Puerto Rican migrants in El Barrio (East Harlem).
At the midpoint of her master's work, Green was strongly discouraged
(politely denied advanced candidacy) from entering the doctorate

program at Columbia, and she terminated her studies with a master's degree in 1955. Turning back to social work, Green joined a UNESCO community development team in Mexico and lived there for a number of years. She also was a UNESCO community worker in India. After her return to the United States in 1963, Oscar Lewis persuaded Green to become his research assistant for his work in San Juan. Material collected in the project was the basis for Oscar Lewis's 1966 National Book Award volume and most controversial book, *La Vida: A Puerto Rican Family in the Culture of Poverty—San Juan and New York.*[52] Lewis recognized the value and sensitivity of Green's fieldwork in El Barrio with Padilla and her UNESCO training. After the Puerto Rico project was completed, Lewis gave Green the mentoring nudge to finish her doctorate at the University of Arizona. Continuing her work on migration and community, Green focused her dissertation on migrants to Aruba and the relationships between ethnicity, poverty, and family life. Demonstrating a great facility with languages (she spoke Spanish, French, Papiamento, Dutch, German, and Urdu), Vera Green developed a scholarly career researching and writing about the issues of ethnicity, poverty, and family life in the United States and the Caribbean. Green, a firm believer in social networks, served on the executive board of the American Anthropological Association, a position that represented the highest elected post held by a Black until the election of Yolanda Moses as president in 1995. Green was the first president of the Association of Black Anthropologists (1977–1978).

Zora Neale Hurston is perhaps the best known of the ancestors, although she is usually cited for her contributions to literature rather than anthropology. As a student of Franz Boas (or Papa Boas, as she called him),[53] she participated in his study of cranial capacity and national origins in the late 1920s. This research was Boas's critique and refutation of the anthropometric tendencies that still had some credence in the discipline.[54] Hurston quickly gained a reputation in Harlem for her "random selection techniques" of human subjects: walking up and down one of New York's major thoroughfares, Harlem's 125th Street, Hurston would simply stop people, measure their heads, foreheads, breadth of nose, and so forth, and then just keep on going.

Hurston also skillfully used her gift of storytelling to further her anthropological research. She trained her ear to listen well and took seriously the value of the insider's (emic) perspective well before it was popular in anthropology. Believing that the wisdom held by the common Black man and woman was valuable, Hurston recorded folktales in Florida, New Orleans, Jamaica, the Bahamas, Haiti, and Harlem. Her association with the Harlem Renaissance literary world and her benefactor are well documented.[55] It is likely that the tension between the pull of social science and the push of fiction writing was responsible for Hurston's reluctance to accept university teaching as a career option.[56] The academy required total allegiance—something Hurston was unable to give.

Although Hurston is often cited for her contributions to folklore (especially in terms of the quality of the data she collected and her fieldwork ethics and interactions), she should also be acknowledged for her development of alternative research methods. The best example of these can be found in her ethnography, *Tell My Horse.*[57] During a period in anthropology when positivist, scientific approaches were the order of the day, Hurston's ethnography provides a sharp contrast. It is self-reflexive, community-masking, and genre-bending—in fact, the reader is hard pressed to distinguish between what is fiction and what is social science analysis.[58]

It is this dimension of Hurston's contributions that has been appropriated, but without proper acknowledgment of its origin. Everyone speaks of the wonderful "content" of Hurston's work, but rarely is she acknowledged as an innovator of theory and method—yet she clearly was. An exception is Gwendolyn Mikell, who, in her chapter on Hurston in *African-American Pioneers in Anthropology*, focuses on Hurston's training as an anthropologist, her research style, and her methods that mirrored the Boasian tradition of meticulous detail. Hurston's work took its own direction, and her development of alternative methods of collecting materials and new forms of interpretation proved unsatisfactory to the scientific community. More than likely it is this uncomfortable fit that propelled Hurston into producing literary works (novels, short stories, and plays) rather than continuing to interpret the cultural production of the folk as a social scientist.

With the exception of Zora Neale Hurston, none of these

women ancestors was known to work explicitly on women's issues. Although they included women in their analyses, they did not engage in a feminist or gender-based approach. In contrast, Zora Neale Hurston's gendered approach to understanding culture and society can be found in "Women in the Caribbean," a chapter in *Tell My Horse*. In this chapter, Hurston describes how women are excluded from vast areas of culture and do not receive the advantage of education. Looking at poor Black women in Jamaica, Hurston writes, "women get no bonus just for being female down here. She can do the same labor as a man or a mule and nobody says anything about it."[59] Hurston also argues that while mulatto/middle-class Jamaican women are assured of marrying men from their own social class, they, like their working-class counterparts, are subjected to the male whims of a sexual double standard.

Hurston's avowedly "feminist" perspective was unique for the times, but all of these ancestors were concerned with issues that were the order of the day for African American intellectuals. They wanted to correct the story about African Americans, to describe accurately their lived experiences, and to create new paradigms with which to dismantle the existing racial hierarchy. In interviews, both Diggs and Green characterized feminism as another way for whites to claim what was commonly assigned to Black people—oppression.[60] They saw the women's liberation movement as a distraction from the Black liberation movement. When asked specifically about feminism, Irene Diggs remarked that "those were not my issues." As far as she was concerned, feminism and women's studies was by and for women of European descent. Vera Green's sentiments were clearly demonstrated by her lack of enthusiasm for the women's studies program at Rutgers. In the late 1970s, the push to fund women's studies at the university was perceived by Green as a call to decrease the funds available to African and Latin American studies. As director of Latin American studies, Vera Green provided space for feminist events on campus, but she did so in the name of scholarly exchange rather than as a supporter of feminism.[61]

In the lived experience of ancestors such as Green, racism was the primary enemy, not sexism. As Black women, they certainly felt the reality of both racism and sexism, and they must have experienced the connection between the two, but they failed to recognize the simultaneous nature of race, class, and gender oppression. Even Katherine Dunham, who has spoken about the varying nature of domination, sees race as paramount, followed by class status.[62] For our ancestors—those women who have passed on—and the elders who remain, the color line was and still is the issue for the twenty-first century.[63]

ONWARD AND UPWARD INTO THE TWENTY-FIRST CENTURY

The call to anthropology was heeded by the five ancestors and the elder, who were drawn by the discipline's framework and its grounding of culture, history, and social practice. As Black intellectuals, this group recognized the possibilities of anthropology to provide the cure, or the method, to discover some answers to why racism continued as a fundamental element in social inequality.[64] All of these women followed St. Clair Drake's idea of vindicationist praxis in their work.[65] Grounded in the African American intellectual pattern of the time, their scholarship also included the following elements: research was to be conceived and conducted as a form of activism; historical and comparative methods were emphasized; racism was viewed as a central problem in the contemporary world; race was believed to intersect with class on both national and international levels; and alternative methods and theories were to be employed or examined.[66] With this history in mind, the critical question is how can we today claim these women as foremothers of a Black feminist anthropological tradition when a gendered approach, save for Hurston, was not on their agenda?

One thing that can be said about history is that it does not always cooperate. Trying to extract a feminist past from these women may seem like an impossible task, for although they all might have agreed with the concept of simultaneous oppression, it is unlikely that they would have made use of this approach in their own scholarship. Yet, despite their unwillingness to position themselves within a feminist perspective, I argue that they can and should be claimed as predecessors to the existing Black feminist anthropology tradition that is alive and well in the discipline today. In claiming them, however, I realize that I risk accusations of revisionist history—but history is, after all, a matter of interpretations.

Nineteenth-century Black women public speakers and writers such as Ida B. Wells and Victoria Earle Matthews worked as individuals and leaders in the Black clubwomen movements, expressing their own personal sentiments about being Black and female.[67] The next generation of Black women anthropologists heard the call to feminism—a personal and political stance—because of the circumstances of their own lives or as a result of fieldwork experience.[68]

What is unique about the Black feminist perspective is its collective expression, which first surfaced in the early 1970s with Toni Cade Bambara's classic, *The Black Woman*. This anthology of writings by artists, social scientists, and activists examined how the Civil Rights movement was responsible for a heightened racial consciousness while the women's movement raised gender consciousness. As Blacks and as women, the contributors brought a new level of personal and political awareness to the forefront of thinking and activism.

In a chapter of her volume *Conversations*, aptly titled "Between a Rock and a Hard Place: On Being Black and a Woman," Cole provides observations, analyses, and specific reasons for how feminism can be understood within a Black American cultural context.[69] Weaving together ideas rooted in history, popular culture, and sociocultural beliefs, Cole provides a useful framework for why feminism should not be viewed solely as a white woman's issue but rather as an ideology capable of encapsulating the experiences of Black women and other women of color. She posits that the issues addressed by feminist groups are ones that contribute to the welfare of all women. Commenting on the merits of the term *womanist*, coined by novelist Alice Walker,[70] Cole argues that the word has cultural roots that make it more embraceable by Black women than the term *feminist*.

What separates the two terms is not the common goal of enhancing women's lives but the social and historical realities that differentiate Black women's and white women's lives. These differences do not make the task of finding a cure for racism and sexism any less difficult, but they do require different strategies. When Black women describe and analyze cultures and societies with a gendered approach, using the variety of tools, methods, and theories at their disposal, the differing realities of women and men surface.[71] When the scholarship, lives, and experiences of Black women who are also anthropologists are examined using similar gendered understandings, the personal does become political. It is in the intensity and determination that these ancestors and elder directed toward finding a cure for racism that their work becomes a personal political act. When they entered a room, not only did the entire race enter but so did their womanhood and their anthropological expertise.

Women ancestors such as Day, Diggs, Dunham, Green, and Hurston can be claimed by those of us forging a Black feminist anthropology tradition because they had to contend with sexism as well as racism. Whether they chose to make the eradication of sexism a part of their activist scholarship is unimportant, given the historical period in which they lived and worked. Rather, what is most valuable is that even in the silence to which they were relegated by the discipline, the fact of their presence unlocked the door for subsequent generations of Black women intellectuals, trained as anthropologists and following in the African American vindicationist intellectual tradition, to enter the room and create their own place.

NOTES

I express my deep appreciation for the comments and opinions expressed by Black women anthropologists during interviews or in social settings, while I was gathering material for this chapter. Thanks also to the University of Maryland women's studies graduate assistants Suzanne J. Spoor and Claudia A. Rector, whose interest and technical talent made this work possible.

1. James Clifford and George E. Marcus, *Writing Culture: The Poetics and Politics of Ethnography* (Berkeley: University of California Press, 1986), and Micaela Di Leonardo, *Gender at the Crossroads of Knowledge: Feminist Anthropology in the Postmodern Era* (Berkeley: University of California Press, 1991) are good examples of recent "comprehensive" texts that make little mention of Black women anthropologists.

2. Margery Wolf, *A Thrice-Told Tale: Feminism, Postmodernism, and Ethnographic Responsibility* (Stanford: Stanford University Press, 1992). Wolf uses three perspectives to explore methodological issues.

3. The very presence of one nonwhite woman changed group dynamics, because most anthropologists were white males. The changes in the gender and racial dynamics were disruptive in departments and in universities in general.

4. Catherine Lutz, "The Erasure of Women's Writing in Sociocultural Anthropology," *American Ethnologist* 17, 4 (1991): 611–617. Lutz focuses on Euro-American women's scholarship. Work on selected Black women's scholarship was documented in A. Lynn Bolles, "Faceless and Voiceless: African American Anthropologists and the Citation Wars," paper presented at the American Ethnological Society, Los Angeles, Calif., April 1994. Comparing citations found in the *Social Science Index*, Bolles found that Black anthropologists were not cited by other anthropologists but by academics outside of the discipline, for example, in American studies, family studies, urban planning, and so forth.

5. Patricia Hill Collins, *Black Feminist Thought: Knowledge, Consciousness, and the Politics of Empowerment* (Boston: Unwin Hyman, 1990).

6. Johnnetta B. Cole, *Conversations: Straight Talk with America's Sister President*, 1st ed. (New York: Doubleday, 1993); Collins, *Black Feminist Thought*; Stanlie M. James and Abena P. A. Busia, *Theorizing Black Feminisms: The Visionary Pragmatism of Black Women* (New York: Routledge, 1993); and Rosalyn Terborg-Penn and Andrea Benton Rushing, *Women in Africa and the African Diaspora: A Reader*, 2nd ed. (Washington, D.C.: Howard University Press, 1996).

7. Francille Rusan Wilson, personal communication, 1998.

8. Leith Mullings, *On Our Own Terms: Race, Class, and Gender in the Lives of African American Women* (New York: Routledge, 1997), p. xii.

9. Ibid.

10. Mina Caulfield Davis, "Culture and Imperialism: Proposing a New Dialectic," in *Reinventing Anthropology*, ed. Dell Hymes (New York: Vintage Press, 1974).

11. A. Lynn Bolles, "Anthropological Research Methods for the Study of Women in the Caribbean," in *Women in Africa and the African Diaspora: A Reader*, 43–54.

12. Mullings, *On Our Own Terms*, xii.

13. Ibid.

14. Quoted in Mary Catherine Bateson, *Composing a Life* (New York: Plume Book, 1990), 63; Cole, *Conversations*, 19–20.

15. Mullings, *On Our Own Terms*, xiv

16. An example of a nonmainstream text is Zora Neale Hurston's *Mules and Men* (1935; reprint, Berkeley: Turtle Island Press, 1981), a study of rural, southern Black life in the 1930s. This ethnography is told through a compilation of folklore, personal narrative, and traditional medicinal remedies. Hurston was a true participant in her fieldwork, in contrast to the conventions of the time, which emphasized objective, scientific practice that placed the anthropologist at a distance from the people she studied.

17. Adele Logan Alexander, "Caroline Stewart Bond Day," in *Black Women in America* (New York: Carlson Publishers, 1993), 312.

18. St. Clair Drake, "Reflections on Anthropology and the Black Experience," *Black Scholar* 11, 7 (1980): 2–31.

19. Earnest A. Hooton, "Foreword," in Caroline Bond Day, *A Study of Some Negro-White Families in the United States* (Cambridge: Peabody Museum of Harvard University, 1932), iii–iv.; Lee D. Baker, in *From Savage to Negro: Anthropology and the Construction of Race, 1896–1954* (Berkeley: University of California Press, 1998), examines how anthropologists have addressed the issues of race historically and how the discipline influenced public discourse and policy on racial categories from the eighteenth to the mid-twentieth century. Baker documents how science and law played leading roles in the formation and perception of U.S. racial categories.

20. For example, earlier in the century, Arthur A. Fauset wrote about the contributions of Black people to the larger fabric of American society. During the Depression, anthropologist Allison Davis studied the impact of social inequality in education and co-authored *Children of Bondage* (see below). Montagne Cobb, a physical anthropologist, published "Race and Runners," *Journal of Health and Physical Education* 7, 1 (1936): 1–9, during the furor over the Olympic triumph of Jesse Owens, as a counterargument to biological determinism. Louis E. King's 1927–1931 research on migration and Black intelligence— "Negro Life in a Rural Community" (Ph.D. dissertation, Columbia University, 1951)— was used to challenge segregation laws in the landmark *Brown v. Board of Education* decision. See also Zora Neale Hurston's novels (e.g., *Their Eyes Were Watching God* [1937; reprint, Urbana: University of Illinois Press, 1978]) and Katherine Dunham's dance performances, such as "Rites de Passage" (first performed in 1938). Contemporary contributions such as Johnnetta B. Cole's work as president of Spelman College (1987–1998); Ruth Wilson and Moses Pound's "AIDS in African-American Communities and the Public Health Response: An Overview," *Transforming Anthropology* 4, 1–2 (1993): 9–16; and Helán Page's "Black Male Imagery and Media Containment of African American Men," *American Anthropologist* 99, 1 (1997): 99–111, continue the tradition of scholarship-activism that unsettles the status quo. See also Allison Davis, John Dollard, and American Youth Commission, *Children of Bondage: The Personality Development of Negro Youth in the Urban South* (Washington, D.C.: American Council on Education, 1940); and Arthur

Huff Fauset, *For Freedom: A Biographical Story of the American Negro* (Philadelphia: Franklin Publishing, 1927).

21. Bolles, "Faceless and Voiceless: African American Anthropologists and the Citation Wars."

22. Ibid.; Faye V. Harrison, "Ethnography as Politics," in *Decolonizing Anthropology,* ed. F. V. Harrison (1991; reprint, Arlington, Va.: Association of Black Anthropologists and American Anthropological Association, 1997), 88–109; Ira E. Harrison and Faye V. Harrison, *African-American Pioneers in Anthropology* (Urbana: University of Illinois Press, 1999). Ira Harrison and Faye V. Harrison, in their introduction to *African-American Pioneers in Anthropology,* present this argument in much greater detail. Of importance in all three of these works is that the authors are African American anthropologists and therefore citing and analyzing members of their own group, because no one else does.

23. Lila Abu-Lughod, *Writing Women's Worlds: Bedouin Stories* (Berkeley: University of California Press, 1993); Clifford and Marcus, *Writing Culture.*

24. Marvin Harris, *The Rise of Anthropological Theory: A History of Theories of Culture* (New York: Crowell, 1968); George W. Stocking, *The Ethnographer's Magic and Other Essays in the History of Anthropology* (Madison: University of Wisconsin Press, 1992). For example, Stocking's book is a collection of historiographical self-reflexive essays on ethnography since the 1960s; the ethnography of Africa and African Americans is mentioned, but only in terms of anthropologists (read: Caucasians) who did the scholarship. Only one African American anthropologist is listed in the bibliography. Harris's classic, *The Rise of Anthropological Theory,* also practices this trend.

25. Evelyn Beck, "Frida Kahlo," entry in *Lesbian Histories and Cultures,* vol. 1, of *Encyclopedia of Homosexuality,* 2nd ed., ed. Bonnie Zimmerman (New York: Garland Publishing, 2000). There has been a tremendous surge in interest in the work of Frida Kahlo, the renowned avant-garde Mexican artist and wife of muralist Diego Rivera. Kahlo's modernist, self-revealing work had been overlooked and much of the attention she received focused on her "bohemian" lifestyle, bisexuality, and radical politics.

26. For exceptions, see Deborah Gordon, "The Politics of Ethnographic Authority: Race and Writing in the Ethnography of Margaret Mead and Zora Neale Hurston," in *Modernist Anthropology,* ed. M. Manganaro (Princeton: Princeton University Press, 1990), 146–162; Graciela Hernandez, "Multiple Subjectivities and Strategic Positionality: Zora Neale Hurston's Experimental Ethnographies," in *Women Writing Culture,* ed. Ruth Behar and D. Gordon (Berkeley: University of California Press, 1995), 148–165; and Gwendolyn Mikell, "Feminism and Black Culture in the Ethnography of Zora Neale Hurston," in *African-American Pioneers in Anthropology,* 51–69.

27. Patsy Evans, a former staff director of minority affairs for the American Anthropological Association, confirms this list.

28. See Faye V. Harrison, "The Persistent Power of 'Race' in the Cultural and Political Economy of Racism," *Annual Review of Anthropology* 24 (1995): 47–74.

29. A. Lynn Bolles, field notes, n.d.

30. Harrison and Harrison, *African-American Pioneers in Anthropology,* 27–28.

31. During a life storytelling session on January 15, 1986, Johnnetta B. Cole explained that Herskovits did not approve of Black students conducting fieldwork in Africa. In his opinion, African Americans would not be objective enough to accomplish that work because they were "too close to the cultures." Herskovits gave blanket endorsement of her accompanying Robert Cole (her husband at the time), a white graduate student in economics and also affiliated with the African studies program that Herskovits directed. The couple went to Liberia, each collecting materials for their respective dissertations.

32. Robert E. Hemenway, *Zora Neale Hurston: A Literary Biography* (Urbana: University of Illinois Press, 1977), 105–107.

33. Sandra Morgen, *Gender and Anthropology: Critical Reviews for Research and Teaching* (Washington, D.C.: American Anthropological Association, 1989), 1.

34. Comparisons can be made between early and later editions of certain introductory anthropology textbooks. There are significant differences between the 1974 edition of Conrad Kottack's *Culture Anthropology* (New York: Random House) and the 8th edition (2000); or between the 1975 edition of John D. Haviland's *Cultural Anthropology* (Fort Worth, Tex.: Harcourt, Brace) and the 9th edition (1999). For an exception, see Johnnetta B. Cole, *Anthropology for the Nineties* (New York: The Free Press, 1988).

35. Lutz, *The Erasure of Women's Writing.* According to Lutz, recognition is demonstrated

when one's work is cited by others in the field and when students use that work during graduate education as a reputable resource.

36. Since the mid-1980s, the Association of Black Anthropologists and the Association for Feminist Anthropology have co-organized and presented workshops and panels on teaching and research as ways of understanding the mutual interests of the mutliple layers of racial, gender, and other differences.

37. Bolles, "Anthropological Research Methods."

38. For example, the Commission on the Status of Women in Anthropology of the American Anthropological Association sponsored a panel titled "Ethnocentrisms Within: Women of Color, Lesbians and Women with Disabilities" (November 23, 1996, in San Francisco) which included in the aforementioned format a woman with a disability.

39. A. Lynn Bolles, *Sister Jamaica: A Study of Women, Work, and Households in Kingston* (Lanham, Md.: University Press of America, 1996); idem, *We Paid Our Dues: Women Trade Union Leaders of the Caribbean* (Washington, D.C.: Howard University Press, 1996); Irma McClaurin, *Women of Belize: Gender and Change in Central America* (New Brunswick, N.J.: Rutgers University Press, 1996); Gwendolyn Mikell, *African Feminisms* (Philadelphia: University of Pennsylvania Press, 1997); Mullings, *On Our Own Terms*; Carolyn Martin Shaw, *Colonial Inscriptions: Race, Sex, and Class in Kenya* (Minneapolis: University of Minnesota Press, 1995); and Frances Winddance Twine, *Racism in a Racial Democracy: The Cultural Politics of Everyday Racism in Rural Brazil* (New Brunswick, N.J.: Rutgers University Press, 1998).

40. Cheryl Rodriguez, "African American Anthropology and the Pedagogy of Activist Community Research," *Anthropology and Educational Quarterly* 27, 3 (1996): 414–431; Harrison, "The Persistent Power of 'Race' in the Cultural and Political Economy of Racism"; and Page, "Black Male Imagery and Media Containment of African American Men."

41. Notable to this scholarship are Irma McClaurin-Allen, "Incongruities: Dissonances and Contradictions in the Life of a Black Middle Class Woman," in *Uncertain Terms: Negotiating Gender in America Culture*, ed. Faye Ginsburg and Anna Tsing (Boston: Beacon Press, 1990), 315–333; Johnnetta B. Cole, ed., *All American Women: Lines That Divide, Ties That Bind* (New York and London: Free Press and Collier Macmillan, 1986); Mullings, *On Our Own Terms*; Evelyn C. Barbee and Marilyn Little, "Health, Social Class and African American Women," in *Theorizing Black Feminisms: The Visionary Pragmatism of Black Women*, ed. Stanlie M. James and Abena P. A. Busia (New York: Routledge, 1993).

42. Mullings, *On Our Own Terms*; Bateson, *Composing a Life*, 45.

43. Rose M. Brewer, "Theorizing Race, Class and Gender: The New Scholarship of Black Feminist Intellectuals and Black Women's Labor," in *Theorizing Black Feminisms*, 13–30.

44. Collins, *Black Feminist Thought*.

45. Katherine Dunham, *Island Possessed* (1969; reprint, Chicago: University of Chicago Press, 1994), 4. *Island Possessed* is Dunham's account of the first of her many decades of research, observation, and admiration of the peoples of Haiti, beginning with her first encounters in Haiti in 1936.

46. A. Lynn Bolles and Yolanda Moses, "Vera Mae Green," in *Women Anthropologists*, ed. Ute Gacs (Urbana: University of Illinois Press, 1989), 127–132.

47. W.E.B. Du Bois, one of the most preeminent scholars of the century, was a professor of economics, history, and sociology at Atlanta University. He wrote what is considered his masterpiece, *Black Reconstruction in America, 1860–1885* (New York: Russell and Russell, 1935), and with Diggs cofounded *Phylon: A Review of Race and Culture*, the first social science journal with articles by Black scholars about Black people.

48. A. Lynn Bolles, "Ellen Irene Diggs: Coming of Age in Atlanta, Havana and Baltimore," in *African-American Pioneers in Anthropology*, 160. Fernando Ortiz, a British-trained ethnographer, focused on Cuban culture, and particularly African influences in that society. He interpreted Cuba's transculturalism as a balancing act among cultural components of European, African, and indigenous origins, maintained by colonial and neocolonial formations firmly grounded in a historical framework. His seminal work, *Cuban Counterpoint* (first American edition, New York: A. A. Knopf, 1947), used sugar and tobacco as symbols of societal interplay between cultural forms and material conditions, to suggest creolization as a fluid process.

49. Although Diggs never voiced regrets, it appears that lack of funding was a major obstacle to continuing her field research. See Bolles, "Ellen Irene Diggs."

50. St. Clair Drake, the seminal historiographer of anthropology's relationship with Black intellectuals, was a major figure in African and African Diaspora studies. Among his publications are his historic ethnography about Black Chicago, co-written with Horace Cayton, *Black Metropolis: A Study of Negro Life in a Northern City* (New York: Harcourt, Brace and Company, 1945), and the landmark volumes *Black Folk Here and There*, vols. 1 and 2 (Los Angeles: Center for Afro-American Studies, University of California, 1987 and 1990).

51. Charles Wagley was a leading Latin Americanist of the day whose pioneering work in Brazil, Guatemala, and Plantation America are considered classics in anthropology. Elena Padilla, a Puerto Rican by birth, is a medical anthropologist interested in the influence of culture on health, illness, and health care delivery systems among urban Latino populations. Gene Weltfish specialized in Native American cultures and was a scholar activist concerned with social justice and inequality. Weltfish lost her job at Columbia during the McCarthy era for her supposed communist sympathizing. Vera Green led the student protest of the university's actions against Weltfish.

52. Oscar Lewis, *La Vida: A Puerto Rican Family in the Culture of Poverty—San Juan and New York* (New York: Random House, 1966). Lewis used what has come to be called a life story methodology to describe and explain the perpetuation of poverty among the poor in Mexico and the United States. He is the source of the often-quoted phrase "the culture of poverty," and he constructed a checklist to note what constitutes poverty and the intergenerational aspects of poor families. *La Vida*, an ethnography written like a novel, sparked a storm of criticism from scholars in all branches of the social sciences, especially from those who saw other sources aside from culture as reasons for a peoples' impoverishment. A subsequent text, *A Study of Slum Culture: Backgrounds for La Vida* (New York: Random House, 1968), provided the scientific data to support the claims of *La Vida*, but the controversy continued. The culture of poverty is still the basis for public policy concerning poor families.

53. Franz Boas, the "father" of American anthropology at Columbia, was convinced that important cultural knowledge was found in folklore and other customs. These customs had to be studied using a "new historical method," which would afford meaning along with an accurate understanding of what led to the customs in the first place. See Baker, *From Savage to Negro*, 105.

54. Anthropometry was a theory that tried to show a correlation between sizes of the cranium and other physical features such as breadth of brow and nose; intelligence; and other aspects of culture such as religion and ethnicity.

55. Hemenway, *Zora Neale Hurston*. Hemenway's literary biography provides much detail of Hurston's position in this literary movement. See Alice Walker, ed., *I Love Myself When I Am Laughing . . . And Then Again When I Am Looking Mean and Impressive: A Zora Neale Hurston Reader* (New York: Feminist Press, 1979), which gives samples of Hurston's literary and social commentary on the period and its figures.

56. According to letters from the Zora Neale Hurston collection at the University of Florida, she was offered academic positions but turned them down. Perhaps her unsatisfactory experience as a drama teacher (1939–1940) at North Carolina College for Negroes (now NCCU, North Carolina Central University) kept her away from the classroom. Her comments about her year at NCCU appeared in an essay titled "The Rise of the Begging Joints" in the March 1945 issue of *American Mercury*. In the article she took her revenge on the president of the college and referred to the institution as "a one horse religious school."

57. Zora Neale Hurston, *Tell My Horse: Voodoo and Life in Haiti and Jamaica*, with New Foreword by Ishmael Reed (1938; reprint, New York: Harper and Row, 1990).

58. Hurston's *Mules and Men* addresses the reader in three voices—first person singular, first person plural, and third person—depending on the action and setting. For example, Hurston says, "Hello boys, I hailed them as I went in neutral" (p. 23). Later, when explaining a Hoodoo rite, Hurston places herself in the middle: "That night we held a ceremony in the altar room on the case. We took a red candle and burnt it just enough to consume the tip. Then it was cut into three parts and the short lengths of candle were put into a glass of holy water. Then we took the glass and went at midnight to the door of the woman's house and the Frizzly Rooster held the glass in his hands and said, 'In

the name of the Father, in the name of the Son, in the name of the Holy Ghost'" (p. 271).

59. Hurston, *Tell My Horse*, 77–78.

60. A. Lynn Bolles, interview with Irene Diggs, October 17, 1981; and idem, interview with Vera Green, December 1977.

61. An example of Green's support was the "Women and Work" workshop at Rutgers University, held in spring 1978 and organized by Helen Safa, M. Fernandez Kelly, and Lynn Bolles at the Latin American Studies Center, the workshop's official host. Participants included Karen Brodkin (Sacks), Dorothy Remy, and Louise Lamphere. See Dorothy Remy and Karen Brodkin, *My Troubles Are Going to Have Trouble with Me: Everyday Trials and Triumphs of Women Workers*, Douglass Series on Women's Lives and the Meaning of Gender (New Brunswick, N.J.: Rutgers University Press, 1984).

62. Joyce Aschenbrenner, "Katherine Dunham: Anthropologist, Artist, Humanist," in *African-American Pioneers in Anthropology*, 147.

63. W.E.B. Du Bois, *The Souls of Black Folk: Essays and Sketches* (1903; reprint, New York: Signet Clasics, 1982), 54. Du Bois was prophetic in asserting that in the United States, the problem of the twentieth century was race relations. His analysis still holds true at the beginning of the twenty-first century.

64. Mullings, *On Our Own Terms*, xiv.

65. Drake, *Black Folk Here and There*, 191–212. Drake used the term *vindicationist* in *Black Folk Here and There* to identify Black scholars who study racist ideas and behavior. According to Willie Baker, a Drake biographer, vindicationists correct distorted interpretations of the African or African American past or they develop counter ideologies for coping with the present. They may also take direct action, for example, giving up an otherwise comfortable existence in the interest of destroying racist beliefs and behaviors. Willie Baker, "St. Clair Drake: Scholar and Activist," in *African-American Pioneers in Anthropology*, 193.

66. Harrison and Harrison, *African-American Pioneers in Anthropology*, 13.

67. Rosalyn Terborg-Penn, *African American Women in the Struggle for the Vote, 1850–1920* (Bloomington: Indiana University Press, 1998).

68. Mullings, *On Our Own Terms*, xviii; Bateson, *Composing a Life*, 45 (quoting Johnnetta B. Cole).

69. Johnnetta B. Cole, "Between a Rock and a Hard Place: On Being Black and a Woman," in *Conversations*, 81–108.

70. Alice Walker, *In Search of Our Mothers' Gardens: Womanist Prose* (New York: Harcourt Brace, 1983), 10.

71. For example, there is a tendency to shift the center of authority from the inquiring anthropologist outside the culture to ordinary "drylongso," that is, the everyday, taken-for-granted people under study. See John Langston Gwaltney, *Drylongso: A Self-Portrait of Black America*, 1st ed. (New York: Random House, 1980). This is a classic ethnography of working-class, middle-class, and poor Black people of a town in New Jersey in the 1970s.

2

IRMA MCCLAURIN

THEORIZING A BLACK FEMINIST SELF IN ANTHROPOLOGY
Toward an Autoethnographic Approach

SELF AND THE "NEW" ANTHROPOLOGY

My entrance into the field of anthropology coincided with what George Marcus and Michael Fischer call an experimental moment.[1] Since that time, anthropology has expanded to include ethnographies of the particular,[2] "native" anthropology,[3] ethnographies that record lives and challenge borders,[4] ethnographies that seek to be truly reflexive, dialogic, and polyvocal,[5] "ethnography without tears,"[6] and "anthropology that makes you want to cry."[7]

Such changes speak well of the efforts of activist anthropologists—who are feminist, Black, progressive—to redirect the trajectory of the discipline away from its colonial and racist origins. Yet, despite such changes, some perspectives remain marginal, even to this experimental discourse, not because they do not speak out but because often their ideas and words are appropriated, reformulated, and rewritten or because they do not have the political status to warrant attention. I cite the often-quoted statement of James Clifford and George Marcus in their introduction to *Writing Culture* that "feminism had not contributed much to the theoretical analysis of ethnographies as texts."[8] This statement speaks deeply of the entrenched nature of authority in anthropology. Even as the discipline seeks to realign itself and challenge its own authoritativeness, it reproduces the very thing it sets out to destroy. Thus, Clifford and Marcus's defense of their omission of feminists—and absolutely no mention of "native" anthropologists' contributions— rings shallow, indicating that the same old hegemonic game is being played in a different (experimental/postmodern) guise. Their exclusionary discourse reveals the ease with which hegemonic practices become reified through knowledge production:

> We decided to invite people doing "advanced" work on our topic, by which we understood people who had already contributed significantly to the analysis of ethnographic textual form. . . . We invited participants well known for their recent contributions to the opening up of ethnographic writing possibilities, or whom we knew to be well along on research relevant to our focus.[9]

What should be evident from this passage is that those who are "authorized" to speak on what constitutes innovation in the discipline are those already recognized as authorities (by, of course, the editors themselves).[10] Therefore, Blacks and feminists, ever marginal to the authoritative discourse, cannot sit at the dining room table because they were never invited—having been hidden in the kitchen (to borrow an image from Langston Hughes), waiting to be called upon (as needed) for their "anecdotal" opinions; nor will they be recognized by the hosts, who base their guest lists on their own exclusive criteria.

Ironically then, the postmodern "authority" on ethnicity and ethnography is Michael M. J. Fischer, a member of an unmarked ethnic group, while marked ethnics are absent and silent.[11] As if anticipating critiques such as this one, Clifford and Marcus momentarily concede, in a footnote, that their omissions may derive from the politics of institutional power that make it dangerous for "women or people of color" to indulge in experimentation.[12] Having made such a concession, however, they still ignore the very real ethnographic contributions of Black anthropologists such as Zora Neale Hurston and John L. Gwaltney.[13]

In her critique of Clifford and Marcus's omission, bell hooks offers a cogent analysis of the contradictory and highly political nature of such gatekeeping and its implications (the construction of what she calls "an absent presence") for scholars on the edge of the discipline. She writes:

> Despite the new and different directions charted in this collection [*Writing Culture*], it was disappointing that black people were still being "talked about," that we remain an absent presence without voice. The editors state at the end of their introduction that "the book gives relatively little attention to new ethnographic possibilities emerging from non-Western experience and from feminist theory and politics." They also give no attention, no "play" as we would say in black vernacular speech, to the anthropologists/ ethnographers in the United States who are black, who have either been "indigenous ethnographers" or who entered cultures where they resemble the people they are studying and writing about. Can we believe that no one has considered and/or explored the possibility that the experiences of these non-white scholars may have always been radically different in ways from their white counterparts and that they possibly had experiences which deconstructed much old-school ethnographic practice, perhaps reaching conclusions similar to those being "discovered" by contemporary white scholars writing on the new ethnography?[14]

It is from such silent, absent, and "native"/community-authorized positions that Black feminist anthropologists speak. We are rarely cited, although our ideas (and our experiences) may be appropriated and used without permission. And even when permission is granted, our ideas and words receive more attention when used as examples simply because the speaker is well positioned, if not as white male then as white woman.[15] For the most part, despite the rise of innovative approaches and styles of ethnography, as well as a flood of critiques about the racist and colonialist history of anthropology, minority scholars (Black, Native American, Latino/a, gay, and others, including some women) still struggle for credibility in the discipline; we battle a rising tide as our attempts to speak as situated anthropologists are viewed with "objective" suspicion or dismissed as "essentialist."[16]

At what is perceived to be the experimental moment in anthropology, within which considerable attention is paid to "the new ethnography," "feminist anthropology," "postmodern anthropology," it may strike some as odd, essentialist, and definitely unpostmodern for some of us to make Self and subjectivity, and their relationship to inequality and power relations, our focal point. In our defense, and as a direct challenge to Clifford and Marcus's belief that we have contributed nothing new to ethnographic innovation, I invoke three viewpoints, which—representing diverse, political, and non-anthropological perspectives—elucidate the value of strategic essentialism for Black women as a productive standpoint strategy. Each of these perspectives touches on specific points germane to Black feminist scholars, for whom issues of Self and subjectivity are never secondary but are intricately woven into the direction, content, analysis, praxis, and materiality of our scholarship.

Elizabeth Fox-Genovese, a historian, argues that while concerns with subjectivity may be passé for white male scholars who have had the historic luxury of defining "self" and who have been positioned such that they also determine who has it, for Black women who speak out of what Foucault calls "subjugated discourses," the issues (of Self and subjectivity) are still pertinent. Thus, despite the embracement of multiple subjectivities as a reference point for identity among postmodernists, Black women are still attempting to construct an understanding of an essentialist subjective identity, all the while embracing its constructiveness through the multiple lenses of gender, race, and class. Fox-Genovese observes in "To Write My Self: The Autobiographies of Afro-American Women":

> The death of the subject and of the author may accurately reflect the perceived crisis of Western culture and the bottomless anxieties of its most privileged subjects—the white male authors who had presumed to define it. Those subjects and those authors may, as it were, be dying. But it remains to be demonstrated that their deaths constitute the collective or generic death of the

subject and the author. There remain plenty of subjects and authors who, never having had much opportunity to write in their own names or the names of their kind, much less in the name of the culture as a whole, are eager to seize the abandoned podium.[17]

The second voice I evoke in defense of an "essentialist" standpoint position is that of Nancy Hartsock. In an important essay titled "Foucault on Power: A Theory for Women?" Hartsock questions the relevance of postmodernist theory for feminists and other subjugated groups. She cogently argues:

> Poststructuralist theories such as those put forward by Michel Foucault fail to provide a theory of power for women. . . . Thus, postmodernism, despite its stated efforts to avoid the problems of European modernism of the eighteenth and nineteenth centuries, at best manages to criticize these theories without putting anything in their place. For those of us who want to understand the world systematically in order to change it, postmodern theories at their best give little guidance.[18]

Hartsock, unlike the postmodernists she challenges, does more than merely deconstruct the problematics of postmodernism; rather, she offers solutions. Her recommendation is that feminists and others use their subjective knowledge as the cornerstone of not only resistance but transformation:

> That is, a theory of power for women, for the oppressed, is not one that leads to a turning away from engagement but rather one that is a call for change and participation in altering power relations.
>
> The critical steps are, first, *using what we know about our lives* as a basis for critique of the dominant culture and, second, creating alternatives. When the various "minority" experiences have been described and when the significance of these experiences as a ground for critique of the dominant institutions and ideologies of society is better recognized, we will have at least the tools to begin to construct an account of the world sensitive to the realities of race and gender as well as class.[19]

It is the incorporation of personal experience into the theoretical and the validation of the marginal/minority perspective to which this chapter addresses itself by postulating a strategy by which Black feminist anthropologists might achieve their own (and Hartsock's) vision of social transformation.

The final words I draw upon to vindicate what will certainly be criticized as an anachronistic position and problematic identity in this experimental moment of anti-essentialism, and post-every-thing, are those of Black poet Nikki Giovanni, who states quite sim-ply that there is a general assumption that "the self is not part of the body politic." According to Giovanni, "There's no separation."[20] What I think Giovanni is referring to here is the fact that there is a materiality (derived from political and economic relationships and fields of power) to identity that must be acknowledged. For her, and I concur, notions of the self are intricately woven into the body politic of American culture.

Moreover, while postmodernists and poststructuralists demand the demise of Master Narratives and Grand Theories, the place of subjugated narratives and marginal/minority/"native" perspectives in theory building remains unclear and tenuous. And so, while cat-egories and rhetoric have shifted, power relations in everyday life remain enmeshed in identity politics as constituted within a mod-ernist and essentialist cultural worldview. As Hartsock points out, it is difficult to see how the eradication of subjectivity can be po-litically deployed in the shaping of a new world order. She argues that

> rather than getting rid of subjectivity or notions of the subject, as Foucault does, and substituting his notion of the individual as an effect of power relations, we need to engage in the historical, political, and theoretical process of constituting ourselves as sub-jects as well as objects of history. We need to recognize that we can be the makers of history as well as the objects of those who have made history. Our nonbeing was the condition of being of the One, the center, the taken-for-granted ability of one small seg-ment of the population to speak for all; our various efforts to con-stitute ourselves as subjects (through struggles for colonial independence, racial and sexual liberation struggles, and so on) were fundamental to creating the preconditions for the current questioning of universalist claims.[21]

Hartsock goes on to argue that marginalized people are less likely to create totalizing discourses simply because they will never mistake themselves for "the universal 'man.'" Similarly, I argue that the notion of the subject and multiple identities are not mutually exclusive formulations. Black women, and other marginalized subjects, always have had to contend with what W.E.B. Du Bois called "double consciousness" [22]—multiplicity—as a manifest part of our construction of the Self. This is an important point, for as marginalized people find themselves floundering in how to fashion political identities (that move beyond simply having theoretical saliency) and transformative strategies within a deconstructionist mode, their efforts to engage notions of the Self and subjectivity are met with accusations of narcissicism, "navel-gazing," essentialism, and counterproductivity. In the end, they/we continue to speak from below, purveyors still—even within this supposedly open deconstructionist arena—of subjugated discourses. And it is these discourses that are still not recognized by those who embrace the notion of multiple subjectivities but deny the historical reality that those of us who live on the margins of society have always embodied multiple roles, straddled multiple social arenas, negotiated multiple effects of power, and fashioned multiple identities to survive.

In this respect, identity remains a contested and negotiated arena in which we struggle to fashion transformative strategies that allow us to "name and describe our diverse experiences."[23] Such strategies must produce or accommodate self-expression, cultural translation, representation, and activism. To represent these complex processes, we have in fact—despite Clifford and Marcus's belief to the contrary—engaged in "unconventional forms of writing" and praxis, and have most certainly produced our share of "developed reflection[s] on ethnographic textuality."[24]

For Black feminist anthropologists, elders such as Zora Neale Hurston, Katherine Dunham, and Pearl Primus form the genealogical foundation of innovative approaches,[25] sometimes disparagingly referred to in the discipline as examples of native anthropology, but more frequently, simply not named or mentioned at all in the anthropological canon—an absent presence. In dance and writing forms, in art and ethnography, these scholars/teachers/sistah anthropologists provide a lineage that resonates both consciously and unconsciously with forms of subjectivity and reflexivity, identity politics and theoretical formulation—unconventional and risky during their time. Even the act of leaping into the air was, for Pearl Primus, a politicized action, a way of symbolizing the complexities of her identity as a Black American woman: "Yes, they like my jumps, . . . but I didn't leap just for leaping's sake. I had something to say in movement at all times. I wanted to show white people that there is respect due this culture. And I danced to show black people that this is a great heritage."[26] Black feminist anthropology, then, derives its political identity and its praxis from this intellectual heritage of innovation and implicit critique, from the fusion of art and politics, theory and poetics, from the interplay between identity and ethnography to produce an anthropological legacy of

> concrete multiplicity . . . as seen from the margins . . . [designed] to expose the falseness of the view from the top and . . . transform the margins as well as the center . . . [, in which we] develop an account of the world which treats our perspectives not as subjugated or disruptive knowledges, but as primary and constitutive of a different world.[27]

And it is from this historically grounded sense of difference/*differance* that I propose we, who self-identify as Black feminist anthropologists, continue to fashion unique and efficacious ethnographic strategies of data collection, analysis, and representation (i.e., knowledge production) as our contribution to the contemporary scholarly tradition of anthropology. Notwithstanding Hartsock's caveat that power impedes the creation of alternatives,[28] I nonetheless propose that autoethnography is a viable form through which Black feminist anthropologists may theorize and textualize our situated positions and elevate our subjugated discourses to levels recognized by both margins and center of the discipline.

SELF AND ANTHROPOLOGY

It has been almost thirteen years since I (voluntarily) entered the field of anthropology, and still I find myself grappling with the same questions that plagued me initially: what is my place in the discipline's intellectual discourse, and how do I talk about my "situated identity"? These questions remain salient so many years after my induction primarily because anthropological graduate training fails to provide opportunities or information that enable us to answer them; Lila Abu-Lughod suggests it is because anthropologists are "still . . . reluctant to examine the actual situatedness of their knowledge." Yet, as she points out, this is an inescapable feature of identity, for "every view is a view from somewhere and every act of speaking, a speaking from somewhere."[29] This idea of situatedness is one that resonates heavily with Black feminism's standpoint position based on Self and subjectivity. In other words, what draws Black feminists together is a collective belief in the materiality of racism and patriarchy, notwithstanding the constructed nature of race, that impinges on the lives of Black women globally in constraining and oppressive ways, and must be critiqued, described, and ultimately ameliorated. "In my view," says Johnnetta B. Cole, "to be a Black feminist anthropologist means to bring into one's inquiry about the human condition, an analysis that is informed by a sense of the importance of 'race' and of gender. And it means to participate in some way in the struggle against racism, sexism and all other systems of inequality."[30]

Predicated on the existence of this collective vision of the world and the very real position of Black women within it, Black feminist anthropologists, whose primary research tool is *participant* observation, are faced with the task of fashioning a research paradigm that decolonizes and transforms—in other words, one that seeks to alleviate conditions of oppression through scholarship and activism rather than support them. To do so means directly confronting the way in which our identities (always informed by race, class, and gender) are implicated in the research process and in the very way in which we relate to the discipline of anthropology.

In the past, leading scholars have prevailed in their belief that we ("native" anthropologists) engage the discipline no differently than our white counterparts.[31] That is, they presumed that our anthropological training eradicated all vestiges of indigenous cultural identity, and so according to them, the "native" anthropologist ceases to retain a critical perspective on the hegemonic culture and inevitably (or so they claim) loses the ability to identify with the very people from whom she came. In effect, they argue—and it is a position that has held considerable sway in the discipline, since no one has challenged it—that by virtue of our training as anthropologists, we indigenous/native anthropologists are destined to lose our cultural otherness. Marcus and Fischer articulate this long-held belief about the inability of "the Other" to remain critical or deconstruct the canon after training:

> A long-time fantasy among Anglo-American anthropologists has been that some day there would be Trobriand, Bororo, or Ndembu anthropologists who would come to the United States and provide a reciprocal critical ethnography (as Tocqueville is conventionally said to have done) from the point of view of the radically cultural other. By the time such others are trained as anthropologists, however, they of course are no longer radically other.[32]

John Aguilar advances a similar observation in his 1981 essay, "Insider Research: An Ethnography of a Debate," in which he asserts that professional Western training (an acculturative process) affords the native anthropologist the opportunity to partially transcend what he calls "the insider perspective" and thus eliminate what he presumes is an inherent bias that must be discarded to create the distance necessary for scientific inquiry. In these thoughts, Aguilar actually anticipates the previously cited observation of Marcus and Fischer by several years, when he claims that "the insider's socialization into the ideology of the professional community and the necessity of meeting the intellectual requirements of colleagues may combine to neutralize one of his or her principal advantages."[33]

I contend that Aguilar, supported later by Marcus and Fischer, promulgates an ideological and ethnographic conundrum for "native" anthropologists—many of whom are not simply insiders but former colonial subjects now conducting research among their own or similarly oppressed people. The conundrum they construct resides in their belief that although our view from the bottom of the colonial heap constitutes a critical lens through which we see the world as "native"/colonized, they claim that this view is inevitably erased through our acculturation as scholars/anthropologists. Albert Memmi, in his insightful discussion of the constitution of colonial oppression, *The Colonizer and Colonized*, calls this viewpoint "the myth of the colonized" and explains its significance to the colonialist project:

> Just as the bourgeoisie proposes an image of the proletariat, the
> existence of the colonizer requires that an image of the colonized
> be suggested. . . . But the favored image becomes a myth pre-
> cisely because it suits them too well. . . . What is more, the traits
> ascribed to the colonized are incompatible with one another,
> though this does not bother his prosecutor. He is depicted as
> frugal, sober, without many desires and, at the same time, he
> consumes disgusting quantities of meat, fat, alcohol, anything. . . .
> At the basis of the entire construction, one finally finds a com-
> mon motive: the colonizer's economic and basic needs, which he
> substitutes for logic, and which shape and explain each of the
> traits he assigns to the colonized.[34]

I think Memmi's analysis has value for anthropology. I suggest that
the refusal to attribute any radical or transformative capabilities to
"native" anthropologists creates a kind of disciplinary colonialism
in which "native" anthropologists are forever subjugated to an
acculturative place within anthropology. Contrary to Marcus and
Fischer's assumption that we lose our critical insight when we become trained as anthropologists, I argue that we cannot form the
voices of critique they so desire primarily because the discipline does
not want to hear us—and so, many of us languish in silence, hid-
ing our critiques.

> Finally, the colonizer denies the colonized the most precious right
> granted to most men: liberty. Living conditions imposed on the
> colonized by colonization make no provision for it; indeed, they
> ignore it. The colonized has no way out of his state of woe—nei-
> ther a legal outlet (naturalization) nor a religious outlet (conver-
> sion). The colonized is not free to choose between being colonized
> or not being colonized.[35]

The inevitability of the colonialist project to create the colonized
and effectively to disempower her, no matter what, resonates in
the work of Aguiliar, Marcus and Fischer, and other scholars who,
intentionally or not, fall back on a belief in the primordial power
of Western ideology, which, when confronted by the critical voices
of the "natives," overwhelms and silences them. This results in the
presumption that once trained (or assimilated) as anthropologists,
or as any Western intellectual, "natives" are forever implicated in
the colonialist project. Certainly, it is presumed that we dare not
challenge it! As Memmi reminds us: "In order for the colonizer to

be the complete master, it is not enough for him to be so in actual fact, but he must also believe in its legitimacy. In order for that legitimacy to be complete, it is not enough for the colonized to be a slave, he must also accept his role."[36]

Although assimilation/acculturation theories have had a powerful hold on the anthropological imagination (as well as on American social practice and policy making as a way of grappling with the processes by which formerly colonized or minority people can be incorporated into the state), they are only one way of reading the text of American culture in particular and colonialist interactions in general.[37] Further, they remain unsatisfactory as explanatory devices because they forestall the possibility of resistance and simultaneity. Predicated on the view of culture as all consuming and totalizing, the idea of acculturation presupposes that two distinct cultures cannot co-reside—thus, the notions of biculturalism (double vision), or double consciousness,[38] become more imagined states of intersubjectivity than real. Aguilar explains the hegemonic disavowal of biculturality, nativeness, and double-consciousness or double-vision in the following way: "Unless the bicultural individual can effectively compartmentalize each of the two perspectives (that of his own culture and that of the dominant culture), each will function to block the other."[39] To counter this Western totalizing discourse, I argue that "native" anthropologists in general have created scholarship (and new ethnographic interventions) in which our difference, our otherness, serve as valuable points of reference.[40] Black feminist anthropologists, in particular, embody several traditions, all of which emanate from what Foucault calls "subjugated discourses." That is, Black feminist anthropologists derive their inspiration from the traditions of women-centered, feminist, African American, vindicationist, and "native" scholarship that are inherently reflexive and oppositional, and that seek to challenge the historical foundations of anthropology.

Clearly then, the route to constructing Black feminist anthropological standpoints is not an exclusionary one—guidance is sought from multiple sources along the way. For example, my own work[41] takes guidance from the ideas of "halfie" anthropologists such as Lila Abu-Lughod,[42] who interrogates the anthropological identity conundrum mentioned earlier from the perspective of someone who has lived it as an Arab-American woman studying Arab women. She opines that we must learn to "write against" the concept of culture, thereby creating a new genre, which she calls the "ethnography of the particular."[43]

Such ethnographies require a delicate balance of boundary blurring. They require us as ethnographers to continuously move back and forth between personal histories, local communities, global transactions,[44] and ethnographic responsibilities.[45] By exchanging the totalizing, predictive ethnographies of the past for this new form of particularized ethnographies,[46] Abu-Lughod argues that we produce works in which people are "confronted with choices, struggle with others, make conflicting statements, argue about points of view on the same events, undergo ups and downs in various relationships and changes in their circumstances and desires, face new pressures, and fail to predict what will happen to them or those around them."[47] In other words, we construct a complex ethnographic world from our data, our field experiences, our knowledge as "natives," halfies, woman, other, that is contradictory, multilayered, engaged, and as close to representing the social reality of the people we study as we can get. This strategy not only reshapes ethnographic practice but transforms it into ethnographic praxis (action). It is to this direction, I think, that Black feminist anthropologists have and must continue to devote ourselves. As Leith Mullings reminds us, the task at hand for Black feminists in general, and Black feminist anthropologists in particular, is not a daunting one; we must simply "illuminate the experiences of African American women and theorize from the materiality of their lives to broader issues of political economy, family, representation, and transformation."[48]

BLACK FEMINISM(S) AS SUBJUGATED DISCOURSE(S)

Before articulating autoethnography as a particular methodological strategy for Black feminist anthropology that allows us an arena within which to bring together identity, scholarship, and knowledge production, I wish to digress momentarily. My goal is to critically reflect on how best to articulate the common and diverse standpoints from which Black feminist anthropologists should and do speak. Doing so mandates a clear understanding of what constitutes Black feminism as a coherent, yet heterogeneous way of seeing and interpreting the social world and the role of Black women in that world.

In the process of defining, one inevitably elides nuances to highlight important features. Before proceeding, I make no claims to a definitive definition or description of Black feminism, for like all cultural domains, it is one filled with contestation, conflicts, and contradictions, and it is ever-changing. Having provided this caveat, I shall elucidate some of the core concepts that I think enable Black feminists, in our studies and discussions of women of Africa and the African Diaspora, to find common ground.

Rose Brewer, in a key essay, suggests that a central (unifying) concept that underlies Black feminism is "reconstructing the lived experiences, historical positioning, cultural perceptions and social constructions of Black women who are enmeshed in and whose ideas emerge out of that experience, . . . [as well as] developing a feminism rooted in class, culture, gender and race in interaction as its organizing principle."[49] Similarly, Stanlie James argues that another crucial (unifying) component of Black feminist theorizing is its recognition of the simultaneity of oppression in Black women's lived experience. She posits that the particular way Black feminists theorize then is directly linked to our experience of multiple and contemporaneous oppressions, our activism, and our desire for social transformation. She grounds her observations in the belief that

> theorizing by Black feminists develops out of Black women's experiences of multiple interrelated oppressions including (but not limited to) racism/ethnocentrism, sexism/homophobia and classism. While reflecting the diversity of its many adherents it also struggles to embrace contradictions. Thus Black feminist theorizing reflects a proactive/reactive stance of pragmatic activism which addresses those issues deemed deleterious to the well-being of Black women.[50]

In these two passages, both Brewer and James locate the validation of Black women's "lived experience" as a crucial component of Black feminist epistemology.[51] Acceptance of this feminist/vindicationist tenet forms the coherent thread of what James and Busia term Black feminists' "visionary pragmatism." Borrowing then from these ideas of Brewer and James and Busia, I would like to operationalize my understanding of Black feminism for the remainder of this discussion. Acknowledging that Black feminism has an epistemological basis as well as an ontological dimension, I define it as *an embodied, positioned, ideological standpoint perspective that holds Black women's experiences of simultaneous and multiple oppressions as the epistemological and theoretical basis of a "pragmatic activism" directed at combating those social and personal, individual and structural, and local and global forces that pose harm to Black (in the widest geopolitical sense) women's well-being.* In the context of this definition then, Black is both a descriptive and political term that recognizes the unequal distribution of material resources in the world and the resulting unequal relations of power. It is a term that is transhistorical, transracial, transgeographical, and transnational,[52] while feminism is conceptualized as an ideology that continuously interrogates the nature of women's relation to the social world from a variety of geocultural, historical, personal, and structural standpoints. Black feminism, as a politicized standpoint theory, weaves together these three concepts grounded in epistemology, political identity, and gender. It is upon this foundation that Black feminism, as I understand and practice it, is predicated, and upon which we as Black feminist anthropologists can establish an applied theoretical and ethnographic tradition—one that preserves culturally specific (i.e., racial/ethnic) and materially based (i.e., class) "gender consciousness and identity"[53] and is directed toward political mobilization and unity, the creation of an alternative vision within the domain of anthropology, and the formulation of an activist ethnographic praxis in the field.

TOWARD A THEORY OF SELF IN ANTHROPOLOGY: SITUATED NARRATIVES AND AUTOETHNOGRAPHY

Having defined what I mean by Black feminism as an embodied theoretical standpoint that derives its formulations from the lived experiences of Black women's lives and social positions in the world, I have come to my final concern in this chapter, which is to argue for ethnographic textualizations that permit us as Black feminist anthropologists to speak with our own voices in the ethnographic enterprise and to make heard the voices of the populations we study, especially those of Black women.

I suggest that autoethnography both as a stylistic form to textualize the ethnographic experiences of Black feminist anthropologists and as a theoretical lens through which we can interpret how we do what we do provides the vehicle for a transformative ethnographic knowledge production. I hope to demonstrate that these two dimensions of autoethnography (as style and praxis) are necessary, for as feminist anthropologist Deborah D'Amico-Samuels reminds us, "the connections between what we describe as social scientists and who we are personally and structurally need to be part of the way we design our methods as well as the way we analyze our data."[54] This observation by D'Amico-Samuels, I strongly assert, resonates with the statement of Nikki Giovanni quoted earlier, that Self (one's personal history/auto) is and must be an integral component of one's politics, creativity, and scholarship.

DEFINING AUTOETHNOGRAPHY

To explain why I embrace the strategy of autoethnography and all that it embodies requires an autobiographical digression. My first encounter with the term came in 1976 at the American Anthropological Association conference, where I listened to two emerging Black anthropologists—Kimberly Eison Simmons and David Simmons—use their student experiences at a midwestern, predominantly white college as a point of departure for talking about anthropological issues of subjectivity, otherness, and the production of ethnography.[55] I was captivated by their presentation for two reasons: I also had attended that college "somewhere" in Iowa, and I had, I think, mildly influenced their choice of anthropology as an area of study. Most intriguing about their exploration of identity and experience, however, was the label they attached to it—autoethnography.

At that moment, I was convinced that something powerful had taken place in their presentation both for them and for the audience, and I found myself drawn to the idea that self (auto), collective/nation (ethno), and writing (graphy) offered possibilities for scholars such as myself in that I am always in search of a theory, a concept, an innovation that will allow me to describe and interpret the kind of anthropology I do.

As far as I can tell, the first use of the term is attributed by Jennifer Brown to D. M. Hayano, who defined it as the "cultural study of one's own people."[56] In 1986, in her Ph.D. dissertation, Françoise Lionnet uses the term to discuss the works of four writers, including Nietzsche and Toni Morrison, and resurrects it again in a 1990 essay on Zora Neale Hurston.[57] It is Lionnet's application of the term to Hurston's work that intrigues me as an anthropologist. When Lionnet uses the term to describe Hurston's work, she sees autoethnography as "the defining of one's subjective ethnicity as mediated through language, history, and ethnographic analysis."[58] Drawing upon the same relational tenets between autoethnography, identity, and subjectivity, Ruth E. Trotter White uses the term as a theoretical frame through which to explicate the fiction of Toni Morrison. She politicizes autoethnography as a "concept . . . [that] focuses on righting the ways in which a culture can be misrepresented and distorted by another that is outside—dominating or colonizing."[59]

Trotter White's deployment of autoethnography as a critical, reflexive, strategic weapon owes much to Mary Louise Pratt, who discusses autoethnography as an intervention by "natives" who, having acquired cognitive and linguistic dexterity in the "master's tools," uses them to speak on behalf of their colonized brothers and sisters.[60] In Pratt's reading of colonial texts, autoethnography is a form "in which people undertake to describe themselves in ways that engage with representations others have made of them."[61]

In this respect, autoethnography is dialogical in that it represents the speaker/writer's subjective discourse, but in the language of the colonizer. In speaking the colonizer's language, the "native" demonstrates her capacity to be both like the colonizer and unlike him. In deploying autoethnography, the "native" serves as cultural mediator. Pratt invokes the historical example of Guaman Pomo, who uses two languages (the master's Spanish and his own indigenous Quechua) to mediate a clash of worldviews and possibly open a door of understanding. The conflict to be mediated is between Spanish colonial culture and Inca ideals and worldview. Autoethnography becomes Pomo's strategic device to represent the latter (and himself) to the Spanish king. In Pratt's view, this autoethnographic intervention involves a "selective collaboration with and appropriation of idioms of the metropolis or the conqueror. These are merged or infiltrated to varying degrees with indigenous idioms of self-representations intended to intervene in metropolitan modes of understanding."[62] Pomo's agenda, according to Pratt's reasoning, is to address two audiences—the metropolis and "the speaker's own community." Pratt, like Lionnet and Trotter White, views the authoethnographic author as interlocutor and translator—one who stands juxtaposed (for action, and sometimes passive) between two diverse audiences—forever the Janus, facing two directions that are diametrically opposed.

Alice Deck differs from Pratt in her view of authoethnography as she applies it to Zora Neale Hurston and Noni Jabavi, a South African journalist, although eventually the two viewpoints converge again.[63] I intentionally call upon Hurston here because, although she is well known in literary circles, her contributions to mainstream anthropology have been largely ignored by the discipline.[64] Yet Hurston's deployment of autoethnography marks the beginning of reflexive and dialogic ethnographic forms in the discipline— forms later to become central to what is called interpretive anthropology. Deck acknowledges the view of autoethnography as cultural mediation but chooses to focus on the *auto* (i.e., individual/subjective) dimensions of the concept, which she views as constituting a conversation with self and memory. That is, authors rely on their "native" ethnographic knowledge to assemble a portrait that is a combination of personal memories (autobiographical) and general cultural descriptions (ethnography).

In reference to Hurston, whose work figures as an ideal illustration of autoethnography, Deck sees her text as "an intricate interplay of the introspective personal engagement expected of an autobiography and the self-effacement expected of cultural descriptions and explications associated with ethnography."[65] What makes Deck's explication of Hurston valuable is the attention she gives to Hurston's anthropological training, which is frequently glossed over in many literary explications of Hurston's work. By focusing on the ethnographic dimensions of Hurston's work, Deck affirms that even in literature, Hurston's goal is indeed "anthropological" in the purest sense of the word. As an auto*ethnographer* then, Deck argues, Hurston seeks "to demonstrate the basic humanity of . . . [her] peoples to an audience of readers living outside of the particular communities under scrutiny."[66] In this reading of Hurston's autoethnographic texts, Deck comes full circle to Pratt's perspective that autoethnography functions as a type of cultural mediation and as a repository of cultural memory.

AUTOETHNOGRAPHY VERSUS REFLEXIVITY

How then is autoethnography distinctive from reflexive ethnographies? Although this may appear to be nothing more than the proverbial splitting of hairs, I suggest that Deck effectively demonstrates some critical distinctions between Hurston's work and Vincent Crapazano's *Tuhami* and Marjorie Shostak's *Nisa*.[67] One fundamental difference is that Deck sees Hurston's ethnographic authorization as self-endowed. That is, it derives from her indigenous status and enables her to "promote . . . [her] interpretations of . . . [her world] as authentic without the validation of other social scientists. With all due respect to René Descartes, Hurston's authenticity and "native" authorization emanate from an amalgamation of self and community. Her work resonates with the belief—THEY ARE BECAUSE I AM/I AM BECAUSE THEY ARE! As Deck points out, non-"native" anthropologists, like Shostak and Crapazano, must rely on other "anthropological and historical studies" to verify their observations. As a result, their portraits "read like hierarchies of voices; those of the academic outsiders serv[ing] to validate those of the indigenous characters Nisa and Tuhami."[68] Because Hurston consciously chooses to study a community of which she is a "native"/native (Eatonville, Florida), her work resonates with reflexivity grounded in a social reality of which she is both a product and a producer:

> And now, I'm going to tell you why I decided to go to my native village first. I didn't go back there so that the home folks could make admiration over me because I had been up North to college and come back with a diploma and a Chevrolet. I knew they were not going to pay either one of these items too much

mind. . . . I hurried back to Eatonville because I knew that the town was full of material and I could get it without hurt, harm, or danger.[69]

Hurston seeks out her community not only because it is a significant source of folk data and safe, but because there she cannot pretend to be anything other than what she is—in her hometown, the appellation "Anthropologist" has no social capital.[70]

AUTHOETHNOGRAPHY AND AUTOBIOGRAPHY: SIX OF ONE OR HALF DOZEN OF THE OTHER?

Another difference I wish to briefly clarify is the distinction between autoethnography and autobiography. On this issue, Deck asserts that autoethnography is less concerned with chronicling events, and so de-emphasizes certain details and dates, although it relies on memory and indigenous knowledge. Accordingly, Hurston's and Jabavu's texts are autoethnographical because they contain

> a layering of autobiographical double consciousness (myself in the past compared to myself at the present moment of narration), along with the two-dimensional ethnographic awareness, on the one hand, of the self "in the field" (their native villages) among family and friends that constitute the objects of their study and on the other hand, of the object's experiences of themselves (which Hurston and Jabavu could only observe) and their experiences of Hurston and Jabavu as "visiting daughter."[71]

This layering and use of experience as a critical point of departure for both the production of the text and the interpretation of ethnographic data can also be found in Faye Harrison's discussion of her ethnographic research in Jamaica and in my own study of women in Belize.[72] Harrison specifically identifies autobiographical encounters as the source for her impetus to study Jamaica. In doing so she implicitly raises questions about the artificial divisions we are trained to make between Self and scholarship. She writes:

> I decided to undergo my rite of passage into professional anthropology in Kingston largely because of Jamaica's political climate during the 1970s. . . . My goal was to enlist anthropological analysis into the struggle for Caribbean transformation.
> This political and intellectual concern developed out of my ear-

lier experiences—as a child growing up in the South, in the midst of the Civil Rights Movement; as a university student involved in the campaign to exonerate and free political prisoners such as Angela Davis.[73]

Harrison's autobiographical memory authenticates an autoethnographic research rationale. I would assert then that all autoethnography, which I view as not simply a highly reflexive form but as a particular kind of reflexive form, is simultaneously autobiographical and communal, as the Self encounters the Collective. Further, the legitimation of data (or its validation) resides not in conventional scholarly requirements and standards but in self-referencing. Harrison's work reflects this engagement of Self-validation to which I alluded earlier in the chapter. Deborah E. Reed-Danahay, in her seminal anthology on autoethnography, affirms this important interplay between autobiography and auto-ethnography:

> The term [autoethnography] has a double sense—referring either to the ethnography of one's own group or to autobiographical writing that has ethnographic interest. Thus, either a self (auto) ethnography or an autobiographical (auto) ethnography can be signaled by "autoethnography." . . . When the dual nature of the meaning of autoethnography is apprehended, it is a useful term with which to question the binary conventions of a self/society split, as well as the boundary between the objective and the subjective.[74]

Throughout her description of her fieldwork experience, Harrison implicitly and explicitly relies on her commonsense self/folk knowledge and her potential membership in the community to navigate the tricky, and sometimes dangerous, waters of Jamaican politics in the 1970s. One example of this "introspective personal engagement" (a quality Deck sees as central to autoethnography) can be found in Harrison's discussion of rape. Although Harrison recognizes that rape may be a real possibility and hears the community's cautions about her safety, the certainty with which the potential for rape is presented to her as an inherent characteristic of and threat from lower-class Jamaican men arouses her suspicion and provokes critical reflection. In disregarding the warnings of middle-class Jamaicans, Harrison aligns herself on the basis of politics rather than class, resorting to personal knowledge, deeply rooted in cultural memory, and a Black southern worldview of how the rape myth has been used historically to maintain Black men in their place (the rope functioning as the equalizer of all Black men). Moreover, the specter of the Black Man as Rapist myth continues to divide and preclude alliances among such groups as white feminists and Black men.[75]

Harrison makes this observation about the connection between the Jamaican version of this myth and her own encounters with it in a post-segregated America: "Although it appears that political terrorists did at times use rape as a weapon against their party's opponents during the late 1970s, the representation of the ghetto man as a rapist reminded me of the myth of the Black rapist in the U.S. South."[76] Throughout her fieldwork in Jamaica, such autobiographical issues surface and become an integral part of the ethnographic experience. As a result, Harrison's anthropological posture, like Hurston's, is informed more by this gossamer of cultural memory than by methodological conventions learned in courses on research methods; it shapes her nonconventional responses, orients her interpretations of Jamaican culture, and gives rise to a diasporic perspective.

CONCLUSION

In the realm of politics, the feminist movement validated and inscribed for future generations a belief in the axiom that "the personal is political." In the realm of poetics, Black autobiography, most notably the slave narratives, chronicled ethnographically the horrors of slavery as a way of informing the white public. It also served as a venue through which slaves could validate their experiences, support the cause of abolition, and assert their humanity. In laying claim to the personal, feminism mandated that introspection and reflection become part of the political process. In highlighting the cruelty of slavery, slave narratives resisted the conventional poetics of autobiography and shaped a tradition of Black autobiography in which poetics and politics were inseparable and in which the individual self and the collective were indistinguishable. Thus, despite the paucity of slave narratives by women, Linda Brent's (a k a Harriet Jacob) *Incidents in the Life of a Slave Girl* is all the proof we need to convince us of Jacob's personal pain and to serve as documentation of the collective pain of all Black slave women.[77]

Anthropology's contribution to our understanding of human life has been its emphasis on detailed descriptions of the workings of the collective—societies, communities, and other groups. The discipline's sometimes frozen/static ethnographic representations of cultures and society at particular moments in time have indeed salvaged for us views of the past that, for all their problems, still have value because of their holistic approach and intense detail.

Blending the grounded, detailed descriptions that come from ethnography with the poetics of autobiography to create autoethnography offers Black feminist anthropologists a suitable genre through which we may express ourselves and our experiences as "natives" in the field among our communities (both locally and in the Diaspora). It is also a form through which we can meaningfully interpret and theorize about the unique ways in which we engage with anthropology. In following this path, like those who traveled before us, such as Zora Neale Hurston and even W.E.B. Du Bois,[78] we are able to explicate the subtleties of our culture, and by delving into and using the subtleties of our personal expression, we may "reveal exactly how things stand with the 'inner life' of . . . [our] communities."[79]

Admittedly, autoethnography and other literary or textualization forms can never be the exclusive "property" of any one group—nor should they be. Rather, they are innovative strategies of knowledge production that allow Black feminist anthropologists, and other speakers of subjugated discourses, if they so choose, to "defin[e] . . . [our] subjective ethnicity [race, class, and gender] as mediated through language, history, and ethnographical analysis."[80] In doing so, we are on the way to establishing our own comfort zone in the contested domain of anthropology, and on our way to developing a theory of Self, scholarship, and praxis through the formation of Black feminist anthropology that is simultaneously innovative, reflexive, and transformative.

NOTES

1. George E. Marcus and Michael M. J. Fischer, *Anthropology as Cultural Critique* (Chicago: University of Chicago Press, 1986).
2. Lila Abu-Lughod, "Writing against Culture," in *Recapturing Anthropology: Working in the Present*, ed. Richard G. Fox (Santa Fe: School of American Research Press, 1991).
3. Dorinne K. Kondo, *Crafting Selves: Power, Gender, and Discourses of Identity in a Japanese Workplace* (Chicago: University of Chicago Press, 1990); José E. Limon, "Representation, Ethnicity, and the Precursory Ethnography: Notes of a Native Anthropologist," in *Recapturing Anthropology*, 115–135; idem, *Dancing with the Devil: Society and Cultural Poetics in Mexican-American South Texas* (Madison: University of Wisconsin Press, 1994); Irma McClaurin, *Women of Belize: Gender and Change in Central America* (New Brunswick, N.J.: Rutgers University Press, 1996).
4. Ruth Behar, *Translated Woman: Crossing the Border with Esperanza's Story* (Boston: Beacon Press, 1993), 373.
5. McClaurin, *Women of Belize,*
6. Paul Roth, "Ethnography without Tears," *Current Anthropology* 30, 5 (1989): 555–561.
7. Ruth Behar, *The Vulnerable Observer* (Boston: Beacon Press, 1997).
8. James Clifford and George E. Marcus, eds., *Writing Culture: The Poetics and Politics of Ethnography* (Berkeley: University of California Press, 1986), 20.
9. Ibid.
10. How this institutionalized power works and enables the discipline of anthropology to construct the "native" anthropologist as the Other is illustrated by the life of Francis La Flesche. In what can be described as nothing less than a battle over the humanity of the Other, Roger Sanjek and Garrick Bailey, in a series of letters to the editor in the December 1994 issue of *Anthropology Newsletter*, indict the American Anthropological Association for its complicity in continuing to perpetuate colonialist views of native anthropologists. Roger Sanjek in "Racist Past Is Racist Present" and Garrick Bailey in "Francis La Flesche, Anthropologist" respond to the newsletter's reprinting of a "doctored" photo of La Flesche that originally appeared in the obituary column of the 1933 *American Anthropologist* in which La Flesche was dressed in a buffalo robe. According to Sanjek, this "obituary photograph was retouched to remove his usual attire, leaving only the buffalo robe he had once been persuaded to don over his jacket and tie for a single shot." Sanjek concludes that "even in death, his Indian identity was seen as superseding his professional accomplishments." Bailey's letter covers the same terrain as Sanjek's and asserts that "in death the anthropological world recreated La Flesche as they wished him to be, a 'helpful native' and not a colleague." Moreover, Bailey reminds us that La Flesche's ideas about American Indian culture were "dismissed in the obituary as 'sentimental accounts,'" and although he published more than three thousand pages of articles and books, alone or in collaboration, only those works for which he was sole author were acknowledged as belonging to him, suggesting that "in the company of a 'real' anthropologist, he was merely the informant." Bailey concludes that "Non-Euro-Americans in anthropology continue to exist in an academic twilight zone somewhere between 'native informant' and 'professional colleague.'"
11. Michael M. J. Fischer, "Ethnicity and the Post-Modern Arts of Memory," in *Writing Culture*, 194–233.
12. Clifford and Marcus, *Writing Culture*, 21. For a discussion of the politics of inclusion / exclusion in academic writing, see Catherine Lutz, "The Erasure of Women's Writing in Sociocultural Anthropology," *American Ethnologist* 17, 4 (1991): 611–617; and A. Lynn Bolles, "Faceless and Voiceless: African American Anthropologists and the Citation Wars," paper presented at the American Ethnological Society, Los Angeles, Calif., 1994.
13. I contend here that Zora Neale Hurston, in *Mules and Men* (New York: 1935, reprint, Indiana University Press, 1978), and John L. Gwaltney, in *Drylongso: A Self-Portrait of Black America* (New York: Vintage Books, 1980), are two African Americans engaged in ethnographic research practices or writing strategies that called into question the dominant conventions of their time. My current research is a study of Zora Neale Hurston as a precursor of ethnographic innovation.
14. bell hooks, "Culture to Culture: Ethnography and Cultural Studies as Critical Interven-

tion," in *Yearning: Race, Gender, and Cultural Politics*, ed. bell hooks (Boston: South End Press, 1990), 126.

15. Bolles, "Faceless and Voiceless." For a cogent discussion of how white privilege operates, see Peggy McIntosh, "White Privilege and Male Privilege: A Personal Account of Coming to See Correspondences through Work in Women's Studies," in *Race, Class, and Gender: An Anthology*, ed. Margaret L. Andersen and Patricia Hill Collins (Belmont, Calif.: Wadsworth Publishing), 1992; and Karen Brodkin, *How Jews Became White Folks* (New Brunswick, N.J.: Rutgers University Press, 1999).

16. For reviews that critique me for being essentialist, see Michael Stone, "Review of Irma McClaurin, *Women of Belize: Gender and Change in Central America*," H-LatAm, H-Net reviews, January 1997, URL: http://wwwh-net.msu.edu/reviews/showrev.cgi?path= 15734854903612; and Donna Bonner, "Review of Irma McClaurin, *Women of Belize: Gender and Change in Central America*," *American Anthropologist* 99 (December 1997).

17. Elizabeth Fox-Genovese, "To Write My Self: The Autobiographies of Afro-American Women," in *Feminist Issues in Literature Scholarship*, ed. Shari Benstock (Bloomington: Indiana University Press, 1987), 161–180.

18. Nancy Hartsock, "Foucault on Power: A Theory for Women?" in *Feminism/Postmodernism*, ed. Linda J. Nicholson (London: Routledge, 1990), 157–175.

19. Ibid., 172.

20. Nikki Giovanni, cited in Fox-Genovese, "To Write My Self," 164 (my emphasis).

21. Hartsock, "Foucault on Power," 170–171.

22. W.E.B. Du Bois, *The Souls of Black Folk* (1903; reprint, New York: New American Library, 1969).

23. Hartsock, "Foucault on Power," 171.

24. Clifford and Marcus, *Writing Culture*, 21. For historical ethnographic examples, see Hurston, *Mules and Men*; idem, *Tell My Horse: Voodoo and Life in Haiti and Jamaica* (1938; reprint, New York: Perennial Library, 1990), 311; and John L. Gwaltney, *The Thrice Shy: Cultural Accommodation to Blindness and Other Disasters in a Mexican Community* (New York: Columbia University Press, 1970); idem, "On Going Home Again—Some Reflections of a Native Anthropologist," *Phylon* 30 (1976): 236–242. For an excellent analysis of Zora Neale Hurston's methodological contributions to anthropology, see Gwendolyn Mikell, "Feminism and Black Culture in the Ethnography of Zora Neale Hurston," in *African-American Pioneers in Anthropology*, ed. Ira E. Harrison and Faye V. Harrison (Urbana and Chicago: University of Illinois Press, 1999), 51–69. For more recent examples, see Tony Whitehead, "Identity, Subjectivity and Cultural Bias in Fieldwork," *Black Scholar*, September–October 1980; A. Lynn Bolles, "Doing It for Themselves: Women's Research and Action in the Commonwealth Caribbean," in *Perspectives and Resources: Integrating Latin American and Caribbean Women into the Curriculum and Research*, ed. Edna Acosta-Belén and Christine E. Bose (Albany: Center for Latin America and the Caribbean [CELAC] and Institute for Research on Women [IROW], 1991); Faye V. Harrison, "Ethnography as Politics," in *Decolonizing Anthropology: Moving Further toward an Anthropology for Liberation*, ed. Faye V. Harrison (Washington D.C.: Association of Black Anthropologists, American Anthropological Association, 1991), 88–109; Irma McClaurin-Allen, "Incongruities: Dissonance and Contradictions in the Life of a Black Middle-Class Woman," in *Uncertain Terms: Negotiating Gender in American Culture*, ed. Faye Ginsburg and Anna Tsing (Boston: Beacon Press, 1990); and McClaurin, *Women of Belize*.

25. For an analysis of Dunham's and Hurston's contributions, see, respectively, Jane Aschenbrenner, "Katherine Dunham: Anthropologist, Artist, Humanist," 137–153, and Mikell, "Feminism and Black Culture in the Ethnography of Zora Neale Hurston," 51–67, in *African-American Pioneers in Anthropology*. Pearl Primus was not included in this volume, and writings about her work are scarce. My inclusion of Primus is based on my association with her during her tenure in the Afro-American studies department at the University of Massachusetts. Although I was not an anthropologist at the time, I knew she was considered by colleagues in the department and in the dance community to be innovative in her blending of anthropology and dance. See Patricia Wright, "The Prime of Miss Pearl Primus," *Contact: A Publication of the University of Massachusetts at Amherst* 10, 3 (February 1985): 13–16. In this article, Wright refers to Primus's blending of dance and anthropology as a form of "translation," while Primus describes her efforts as push-

ing "the sociological envelope," guided by her desire to "speak of the dignity, the beauty, and the strength of black people" (p. 14).

26. Wright, "The Prime of Miss Pearl Primus," 15.
27. Hartsock, "Foucault on Power," 171.
28. Ibid.
29. Abu-Lughod, "Writing against Culture," 141.
30. Kamela Heyward-Rotimi, "Perspectives of Black Feminist Anthropology: An Interview with Dr. Johnnetta B. Cole," *Voices* 2, 2 (May 1998): 4; *Voices* is a publication of the Association for Feminist Anthropology.
31. John L. Aguilar, in "Insider Research: An Ethnography of a Debate," and Donald Messerschmidt, in "Introduction," both in *Anthropologists at Home in North America: Methods and Issues in the Study of One's Own Society*, ed. Donald Messerschmidt (Cambridge: Cambridge University Press, 1981), speak of the native/colonized experience and the insider/settler experience as if the two are exactly the same. In folding the one experience into the other, specifics of geography and national origins are made to stand for the same thing as the social, economic, and political exclusion faced by historical minorities. Although it is true that everyone is a native of someplace, "native" in the context in which I use the term refers to individuals or groups whose specific identity is implicated with colonial and neocolonial projects, systematic political, social, and economic marginalization, and constructed negative cultural identifiers attributed to race and ethnicity. In this sense, while I agree that everyone is an insider in some culture, I take issue with the idea that everyone is a "native." To differentiate my use of "native" from the concept of native as it is bandied about by Messerschmidt, Aguilar, and Freilich (Morris Freilich, ed., *Marginal Natives at Work: Anthropologists in the Field* [New York: Schenkman Publishing, 1977]), I mark its uniqueness through the use of quotation marks that both distinguish it from other uses of native and show its constructed nature. Finally, "natives" are made, not born. In this respect, I speak to those individuals who may derive from a group whose ancestral or personal experience is one of marginalization but who no longer see themselves as linked to that experience or to their group. Whether their shedding of minority identity is the result of false consciousness or acculturation is not the point of this chapter; rather, my point is that "native" is a highly politicized assumed identity that presupposes an understanding of colonist/postcolonial history and the dynamics of race and gender global politics, and requires a political commitment to reveal through praxis how social inequality in any form is produced and reproduced.
32. Marcus and Fischer, *Anthropology as Cultural Critique*, 156.
33. Aguilar, "Insider Research," 24.
34. Albert Memmi, *The Colonizer and the Colonized*, with an Introduction by Jean-Paul Sartre and an Afterword by Susan Gilson Miller, expanded ed. (Boston: Beacon Press, 1965), 79–83.
35. Ibid., 85–86.
36. Ibid., 88–89.
37. See Robert L. Bee, *Patterns and Processes: An Introduction to Anthropological Strategies for the Study of Sociocultural Change* (New York: The Free Press, 1974), for an overview of the development of acculturation theories in anthropology.
38. Du Bois, *The Souls of Black Folk*.
39. Aguilar, "Insider Research," 20.
40. For examples of others who share this viewpoint, see Kondo, *Crafting Selves*, and Limon, *Dancing with the Devil*, 115–135. Perhaps Nancy Hartsock best captures my point here when she states that we must use what we know as the basis for formulating our critique. Hartsock, "Foucault on Power," 172.
41. McClaurin, *Women of Belize*.
42. Lila Abu-Lughod, *Veiled Sentiments: Honor and Poetry in a Bedouin Society* (Berkeley: University of California Press, 1988).
43. Abu-Lughod, "Writing against Culture."
44. Caroline B. Brettell, ed., *When They Read What We Write: The Politics of Ethnography* (Westport, Conn.: Bergin and Garvey, 1993).
45. Cf. Diane L. Wolf, ed., *Feminist Dilemmas in Fieldwork* (New York: Westview Press, 1996).

See also Warren Perry, "Dimensions of Power in Swaziland Research: Coercion, Reflexivity, and Resistance," *Transforming Anthropology* 7, 1 (1998): 2–14; Whitehead, "Identity, Subjectivity and Cultural Bias in Fieldwork"; and Tony Whitehead, Larry Conaway, and Mary Ellen Conaway, eds., *Self, Sex, and Gender in Cross-Cultural Fieldwork* (Urbana: University of Illinois Press, 1986).

46. For example, see McClaurin, *Women of Belize.*
47. Abu-Lughod, "Writing against Culture," 154.
48. Leith Mullings, *On Our Own Terms: Race, Class, and Gender in the Lives of African American Women* (New York: Routledge, 1997), xi.
49. Rose M. Brewer, "Theorizing Race, Class and Gender: The New Scholarship of Black Feminist Intellectuals and Black Women's Labor," in *Theorizing Black Feminisms: The Visionary Pragmatism of Black Women,* ed. Stanlie M. James and Abena P. A. Busia (London: Routledge, 1993), 16.
50. Stanlie M. James, "Introduction," in *Theorizing Black Feminisms,* 2.
51. See also McClaurin-Allen, "Incongruities," 316.
52. My ideas about identity and the global nature of blackness are influenced by Steward Hall, "Cultural Identity and Diaspora," in *Colonial Discourse and Post-Colonial Theory,* ed. Patrick Williams and Laura Chrisman (New York: Columbia University Press, 1994), 392–394; and Andrée Nicola McLaughlin, "Black Women, Identity, and the Quest for Humanhood and Wholeness: Wild Women in the Whirlwind," in *Wild Women in the Whirlwind: Afra-American Culture and the Contemporary Literary Renaissance,* ed. Joanne Braxton and Andrée Nicola McLaughlin (New Brunswick, N.J.: Rutgers University Press, 1990), 147–180.
53. Susan Bordo, "Feminism, Postmodernism and Gender-Scepticism," in *Feminism/Postmodernism,* ed. Linda J. Nicholson (London: Routledge, 1990), 153.
54. Deborah D'Amico-Samuels, "Undoing Fieldwork: Personal, Political, Theoretical and Methodological Implications," in *Decolonizing Anthropology: Moving Further toward an Anthropology for Liberation,* 73.
55. David Simmons and Kimberly Simmons, "Homeplaces, Dispersions, and Passages: (Re) Claiming and (Re) Constructing African American Identity on a Predominantly White College Campus," paper presented in "Changing as They Are Changed: Conceptualizing the Global African Diaspora," a session at the annual meeting of the American Anthropological Association, San Francisco, Calif., November 20–24, 1976.
56. Jennifer S. H. Brown, "Ethnohistorians: Strange Bedfellows, Kindred Spirits," *Ethnohistory* 38, 2 (1991): 121n.
57. Françoise Lionnet-McCumber, "Autobiographical Tongues: (Self-) Reading and (Self-) Writing in Augustine, Nietzsche, Maya Angelou, Marie Cardinal, and Marie-Therese Humbert (Metissage, Emancipation, Female Textuality, Self-Portraiture, Autoethnography)," Ph.D. dissertation, University of Michigan, Ann Arbor, 1986; Françoise Lionnet, "Autoethnography: The An-Archic Style of *Dust Tracks on a Road,*" in *Reading Black, Reading Feminist: A Critical Anthology,* ed. Henry Louis Gates, Jr. (New York: Meridian, 1990), 382–414.
58. Lionnet, "Autoethnography," 383.
59. Ruth E. Trotter White, "Autoethnography and the Sense of Self in the Novels of Toni Morrison," Ph.D. dissertation, University of Iowa, 1992, 12.
60. Audre Lorde has questioned whether hegemonic tools can be disciplined to suit revolutionary or subversive purposes; she writes: "It is learning to take our differences and make them strengths. *For the Master's tools will never dismantle the Master's house. They will allow us temporarily to beat him at his own game, but they will never enable us to bring about genuine change*" (emphasis in original). Lorde, *Sister Outsider: Essays on Speeches* (Trumansburg, NY: Crossing Press, 1984), 112.
61. Mary Louise Pratt, "Arts of the Contact Zone," in *Ways of Reading: An Anthology for Writers,* 4th ed., ed. David Bartholomae and Anthony Petrosky (Boston: Bedford Books of St. Martin's Press, 1996), 531.
62. Ibid.
63. Alice A. Deck, "Autoethnography: Zora Neale Hurston, Noni Jabavu, and Cross-Disciplinary Discourse," *Black American Literature Forum* 24, 2 (1990): 237–256.
64. Zora Neale Hurston is the subject of my current research project, tentatively titled *Zora*

Neale Hurston and Anthropology: Challenging the Old, Forging the New (An Intellectual Biography). Although Hurston is never mentioned in any of the standard histories of anthropology, notable and recent examples of efforts to resurrect and illuminate her ethnographic contributions are Mikell, "Feminism and Black Culture in the Ethnography of Zora Neale Hurston"; Graciéla Hernández, "Multiple Subjectivities and Strategic Positonality: Zora Neale Hurston's Experimental Ethnographies," in *Women Writing Culture*, ed. Ruth Behar and Deborah A. Gordon (Berkeley: University of California, 1995), 148–165; bell hooks, "Saving Black Folk Culture: Zora Neale Hurston as Anthropologist and Writer," in *Yearning*, 135–143; and Gwendolyn Mikell, "The Anthropological Imagination of Zora Neale Hurston," *Western Journal of Black Studies* 7, 1 (1983): 27–35.

65. Deck, "Autoethnography," 238.
66. Ibid., 247.
67. Vincent Crapazano, *Tuhami: Portrait of a Moroccan* (Chicago: University of Chicago Press, 1980); Marjorie Shostak, *Nisa: The Life and Words of a !Kung Woman* (New York: Vintage Books, 1981).
68. Deck, "Autoethnography," 247, 246.
69. Hurston, *Mules and Men*, 3–4.
70. Pierre Bourdieu defines social capital as "the aggregate of the actual or potential resources which are linked to possession of a durable network of more or less institutionalized relationships of mutual acquaintance and recognition—or in other words, to membership in a group—which provides each of its members with the backing of the collectively-owned capital, a credential which entitles them to credit, in the various senses of the word." Bourdieu, "The Forms of Capital," in *Handbook of Theory and Research for the Sociology of Education*, ed. John G. Richardson (1983; reprint, Westport, Conn.: Greenwood Press, 1986), 248.
71. Deck, "Autoethnography," 249.
72. Faye V. Harrison, "Ethnography as Politics," in *Decolonizing Anthropology*. See also idem, "Auto-Ethnographic Reflections on Anthropology in Peripheral Vision," paper presented at Practicing Anthropology, a forum on elitism and discrimination, 1994. McClaurin, *Women of Belize*.
73. Harrison, "Ethnography as Politics," 91.
74. Deborah Reed-Danahay, "Introduction," in *Auto/Ethnography: Rewriting the Self and the Social*, ed. Deborah E. Reed-Danahay, Explorations in Anthropology (Oxford: Berg, 1997), 2.
75. On how feminism continues to promulgate the Black Male as Rapist stereotype, see bell hooks, "Representations: Feminism and Black Masculinity," in *Yearning*, 68.
76. Harrison, "Ethnography as Politics," 100.
77. Harriet Jacobs, *Incidents in the Life of a Slave Girl* (New York: Oxford University Press, 1988).
78. Hurston, *Mules and Men*; idem, *The Sanctified Church: The Folklore Writings of Zora Neale Hurston* (Berkeley, Calif.: Turtle Island, 1981); and idem, *Tell My Horse*, 311. Du Bois, *The Souls of Black Folk*.
79. Deck, "Authoethnography," 255.
80. Ibid., 383.

3

KIMBERLY EISON SIMMONS

A PASSION FOR SAMENESS

Encountering a Black Feminist Self in Fieldwork in the Dominican Republic

To understand and explicate multiple forms of oppression, one needs a dynamic model of the experience of social inequalities within which race, class, and gender are accepted as interactive realities that assert themselves to varying degrees in complex and contradictory ways. The model must also attend to how individual identities are formed within the historically and culturally specific contexts of these structures of social inequality.

—Irma McClaurin-Allen, "Incongruities: Dissonance and Contradiction in the Life of a Black Middle-Class Woman," 1990

Black feminist thought consists of specialized knowledge created by African-American women which clarifies a standpoint of and for Black women. In other words, Black feminist thought encompasses theoretical interpretations of Black women's reality by those who live it.

—Patricia Hill Collins, *Black Feminist Thought: Knowledge, Consciousness, and the Politics of Empowerment*, 1991

Recent scholarly work has focused on Black women's experiences and the ways in which theories are generated from such experiences.[1] From their early involvement in the abolitionist and suffrage movements to their activism during the Civil Rights movement, Black women have been at the center of the struggle for liberation for all Black people.[2] Despite Black women's presence and contribution to the larger women's movement and the Civil Rights movement, however, they have been mostly invisible in feminist research designed to document and illuminate women's lives and histories, mainly because the focus of the research has been on the experiences of White women—women being coterminous with White.[3]

This same conflation can be found in the discipline of anthropology, where, as Faye V. Harrison reminds us, "in spite of varying attempts at revision and reform, . . . [it] remains overwhelmingly a Western intellectual—and ideological—project that is embedded in relations of power which favor class sections and historical blocs belonging to or with allegiances to the world's White minority."[4] And it is out of these two inauspicious beginnings that Black feminist anthropology emerges as a transformative and oppositional approach to research, methodology, and analysis.

In this chapter, I critically examine Black feminist anthropology as a form of "decolonized" anthropology of the kind that Harrison advances. In addition, I postulate that it is an intellectual enterprise that uses an engaged scholarly activism and praxis to (1) reclaim the centrality of sameness—against a backdrop of difference—as a point of entry for Black feminist anthropology; and (2) (re)focus attention in anthropology on the critical importance of race and racial constructions of gender and class.[5]

UNDERSTANDING SAMENESS AND DIFFERENCE IN BLACK FEMINIST ANTHROPOLOGY

Sameness as a critical starting point of analysis for Black feminist anthropologists is not unique in the history of anthropological studies of women by women. In fact, early feminist anthropology, drawing from the numerous disparate strands of the then-nascent feminist studies, also theorized from a position of sameness.[6] This conceptualization of sameness, importantly, began with an assertion of the universality of women's experience as constituted by their biological status as female. Soon, however, it became apparent—largely as a result of the critiques of minority and Third World women activists and scholars—that the unifying analytical theme of biology and its presumed cross-cultural applicability was conceptually and politically problematic. Because many White feminist anthropologists occupied racial and class positions different from those of the women they studied, the disjuncture between their lives and those of their subjects was often crystallized in relationships formed in the fieldwork experience.[7]

The cumulative effect of such disjunctures, and close reflection and meditation on issues of positionality and power, has meant an ontological shift from analyses of sameness to those of difference in much contemporary feminist anthropology. An example of this shift is the current focus on explaining variation in the cultural status of women throughout the world, using the intersection of gender, race, and class as a point of departure.[8] Increasingly, feminists must contend with the fact that women is a heterogeneous category, as the epigraph by Irma McClaurin-Allen suggests.[9] This shift from the idea of a singular feminism to the acknowledgment of different feminisms was and is crucial to this change.[10] Further, as feminist anthropology continues to explore how unequal power relations are created in the dynamics of anthropological research, women anthropologists can no longer afford to ignore the differences of education, resources, and mobility between themselves and their women subjects.[11]

Despite this turn toward an acknowledgment of difference, the silence of Black women in anthropology is analogous to their invisibility in the broader feminist movement.[12] Such marginalization is the result of an insular and incomplete interrogation of difference as it is constituted by race, gender, and class analyses by some White feminist anthropologists. Along similar lines, Henrietta L. Moore posits that "it forces us to reformulate the privileging of the woman ethnographer with regard to the women she studies, and to acknowledge that the power relations in the ethnographic encounter are not necessarily ones which are erased simply by commonalities of sex."[13] Notwithstanding the contributions traditional feminist anthropology has made to our understanding of women and gender, I contend that Black feminist anthropology leads us on a different trajectory, where sameness and race are relevant and critical variables that define our research questions, determine our site selection, and influence our analyses as Irma McClaurin, Faye V. Harrison, and A. Lynn Bolles have each articulated.[14]

SITUATING MYSELF AS A BLACK FEMINIST ANTHROPOLOGIST

The 1970s emerge as a critical period in the development of a conscious effort by Black women to examine race, gender, and class from a similarly situated standpoint, crystallized in the anthology *The Black Woman*, edited by Toni Cade Bambara.[15] It is this perspective that gave way to the formulation of what we now call Black feminism, with its emphasis on the simultaneous production of race, gender, and class inequality.[16] It is Black feminism's conscious and purposeful linking of theory and practice that enables us as scholars to place U.S. African American women and African and African Diaspora women at the center of a conceptual framework that holds as central their lived experiences, histories, and the alliances they create. As a result, Black feminism stands at the crossroads of engaged scholarship, responsibility, and activism. It encompasses sisterhood in Africa and the African Diaspora, where ideas are exchanged, associations are formed, and coalitions are established because of similarities in experiences of class oppression, racism, and sexism emanating from intersecting histories of colonialism, slavery, and neocolonialism.[17]

Building on these tenets, Black feminist anthropology moves beyond an interest in merely compiling data to confirm the existence of gender, racial, and class oppressions to a position that highlights Black women's testimonials, the life lessons that have emerged in the context of oppressive religious, economic, political, and social conditions, and their varied strategies of survival and resistance. With such a focus, Black women's experiences and voices become central to the construction of a theory of Black feminist anthropological inquiry and analysis. Using this approach, I have come to position myself with women subjects who, like me, wish to create alliances with other women in the African Diaspora around the problematics of race/color and gender in their lives.[18]

It is this very coupling of an engaged Black feminist theory with identity issues that determined my dissertation research on an Afro-Dominican feminist group, Identidad (Identity), in the Dominican Republic. Much more than a pure scholarly pursuit, my work with and for Identidad became, and continues to be, the primary means by which I integrate my identity as an African American woman and my activist, intellectual, and Black feminist agenda.[19]

Yet, I must strongly emphasize that the road to embracing a Black feminist anthropology was not direct or self-consciously traveled. As an African American woman in the United States, I was living Black feminism long before it found conscious expression through my anthropological praxis. This is a central point: that it was in and through the process of preparing for and conducting fieldwork—the synergistic merging of intellectual, activist, and emotional endeavor—that for me Black feminist anthropology found its greatest realization and actualization.

IDENTITY, ANTHROPOLOGY, AND THE FIELD

During her fieldwork on gender and culture in Belize, Central America, Black feminist anthropologist Irma McClaurin encountered a complex situation based on a profound acceptance of her by those she studied:

> My greatest personal benefit came from a sense of belonging, a sense of place. People often insisted that I must have a Belizean ancestor somewhere in my past; when I denied this, they settled upon the idea that our ancestors must have come from the same area in Africa but ended up on ships with different destinations. Most ethnographers yearn for some degree of acceptance by those they study. Like them I too had hoped to become well regarded by my consultants, but I experienced more. I found an extension of solidarity based on color, common roots of oppression, and often gender.[20]

This complex situation is very similar to my own experiences in the Dominican Republic, where I found myself absorbed into the collective Dominican body and often referred to in terms that Dominicans used to describe themselves—*la clarita* or *india clara* (light-skinned). Such terms stand in stark contrast to the words typically used to describe Americans of European descent—*gringo/a* or *Norte Americano/a* (North American)—language that automatically marks them as outsiders and interlopers. To me these terms—*la clarita, india clara*—signify an acceptance of my phenotypic similarity, which for many Dominicans means that I have to *be* Dominican. Importantly, these words are used by Dominicans to describe other Dominicans and serve to reinscribe, among other things, who is a Dominican and what they look like. Such terms are seldom, if ever, used to describe White Americans, and this labeling process has important implications for the degree to which Dominicans allow foreigners access to their inner lives.

My incorporation into Dominican society was neither seamless nor complete, of course, but these encounters highlight the complexity of Dominicans' notions of themselves. Because I spoke Spanish with an English-language accent, for example, people queried me about whether I was *de aqui o de alla* "from here or from there" (meaning the United States).[21] The construction of *here* and *there* is the way Dominicans conceptualize and acknowledge the presence of a Dominican diaspora and classify relationships between Dominicans on the island and Dominicans in the United States. This construction may also be viewed as a narrative of authenticity, for within it is contained a clear delineation of who is Dominican and who is a "Dominican Dominican."[22]

Often, Dominicans born *alla* are thought of as less Dominican, as watered-down versions of the original, a concept that had important implications for me. Because I was viewed as being a Dominican from "there"—the United States, a place known locally for its racist practices—many Dominicans who had never traveled to the United States would ask me about my experiences as a Dominican woman with racism. Consequently, and interestingly, during the research experience, I came to realize that there was a mutual positioning taking place—I was positioning Dominicans within the context of the African Diaspora, while they were positioning me within a Dominican Diaspora—recognizing both similarities and differences.

Like the experiences McClaurin describes that affirmed the sense of kindredness she felt with her collaborators in Belize,[23] my early attempts to self-define as African American or Black were often met with looks of disapproval and expressions of disbelief. I was told that I needed to be proud of my Dominican heritage, of who I was and where I came from, even if I was born *alla*. This contestation over my identity and origins usually persuaded me to assume an *india clara* (and sometimes a *mulata*) identity in the Dominican Republic, especially because this is how others defined me in relation to themselves.[24] Moreover, protestations to the contrary were met with bewilderment and alarm.

Such encounters, with their feelings of shared similarity—phenotypic, cultural, historical—prompt a mutual positioning and generate a kindredness between researcher and subject that may be unique to Black feminist anthropology. While on the one hand, there is an imagined shared history linked to the formation of what scholars refer to as the African Diaspora,[25] there is also the reality of tremendous heterogeneity in social location, place-specific particularities, global processes, and personal histories. The perpetual tensions between sameness and difference of place, position, personal identity, history, and global processes are critical points of entry for understanding and making sense of ethnographic particularities by any anthropologists, but they become even more determining for Black feminist anthropologists. Toward this end, the personal histories and experiences of Black feminists doing anthropology serve as crucial starting points for the exploration of issues that pivot around identity, race, gender, class, and nation.

In fact, it is my own history and experiences as a light-skinned Black woman that shaped my early interest in identity formation and the construction of racial categories.[26] For as long as I can remember, I recall people asking: "What are you?" This question, often posed by strangers waiting in line at a grocery store or some other public place, was always raised with great curiosity. Explaining "what I was" entailed providing a brief family background and condensed history lesson about race and Blackness in the United States. Occasionally, I would reverse the scenario and ask the curious person to guess, to which they would respond: "Puerto Rican," "Egyptian," "Mexican," "Indian," and sometimes simply "mixed." Experiences with race and color outside the United States simply reinforced the vagary of identity and race for me. In Europe, people described me as "North African" or "Surinamese," in Nigeria and

Ghana, I was referred to as "half-caste," whereas in Zimbabwe I was considered a "Colored Indian."[27] The Dominican Republic, however, is the only place I have been where I was thought to be *from there* and where local socio-racial terms that are used to describe the majority of the population were also used to describe me.

Although my interest in race and identity stems from direct interactions with people asking me "what I am," my interest in women's issues and organizations is ancestral, linked to the generational importance of women's organizations in my own family. My mother is a member of Delta Sigma Theta Sorority, Inc. (Delta), a prominent community service sorority in the Black community composed of "college-educated" women and founded in 1913 by twenty-two Black women students at Howard University. As it has been recounted to me, their goal was twofold: (1) to formalize a sense of sisterhood and (2) to confront racism in the women's suffrage movement: "[Delta Sigma Theta Sorority's] primary focus, then, has been on transforming the individual. At the same time, however, its founding in 1913, a time of both racial and feminist ferment, also imbued it with a secondary purpose: to have an impact on the political issues of the day, notably the woman suffrage movement."[28] Here, the duality of sisterhood and activism, in the face of racism, is expressed as a foundational issue and rallying point. The founding of Delta was timely because the needs of Black women were not addressed by larger women's organizations as the result of racism and, in many cases, classism. Delta has emerged as one of the largest Black women's organizations in the world, with chapters in the United States, Africa, and the Caribbean—creating a sisterhood throughout the African Diaspora.

Like my mother, my maternal grandmother was a member of a Black women's organization, the Order of the Eastern Star, whose teachings were based on the Bible and whose aims were charitable; they are considered the sister organization to the Masons, a secret men's society dating back to slavery. Both my mother and grandmother were very active in their organizations, volunteering their time and working on various community service projects. As a child, I witnessed firsthand the importance of women's organizations and coalition building in the Black community. In 1994, I became a member of Delta, and joined my mother, sister, mother-in-law, and a host of aunts and cousins in the sisterhood and their commitment to community service. This emphasis on sisterhood, community service, and women's organization has shaped my perspective—my passion for sameness (which builds on points of commonality)—as a Black feminist anthropologist.

Through personal/autoethnographic experiences, and from a sense of shared experiences in the African Diaspora as its foundation, I see Black feminist anthropology as linking theory, lived experiences, and praxis to create its own unique analytical perspective.[29] Applying this Black feminist perspective and drawing on information derived from earlier reflections and writings about my ethnographic research in the Dominican Republic, I elaborate on what it means to be a U.S. Black feminist anthropologist working with an Afro-Dominican feminist organization. I hope to convey a strong sense of Black feminist anthropology in practice through an analysis of my fieldwork and personal experiences with the women of La Casa por la Identidad de la Mujer Afro (The House for Afro-Dominican Women's Identity), a group known locally as Identidad.[30]

IDENTIDAD: THE PRACTICE OF BLACK FEMINIST ANTHROPOLOGY

I first arrived in the Dominican Republic in the summer of 1993 to conduct research for my master's thesis. My project goal was to analyze the construction of gender roles and its implication for women, social relationships, and identity. I also conducted related research on race and color in the Dominican Republic with the women participants in my study.[31] Although I had maintained a scholarly and personal interest in race, my research agenda's overwhelming emphasis on gender to the exclusion of race, I see in retrospect, was driven by the funding I had received from women's studies and the research interests of my adviser and the women's studies committee.

A contributing factor to the invisibility of race in my initial research project was my discovery of the dearth of literature on race and contemporary racialized identities in the Dominican Republic.[32] In other parts of the Caribbean and Latin America—Venezuela and

Brazil especially come to mind—an ideology of "racial democracy" is espoused.[33] Assuming that this scholarly inattention to such issues reflected the reality "on the ground," I postulated that there was no literature on Dominicans' conceptions of race and racism because Dominicans simply did not talk about such issues. It was not a part of their lived experience. Moreover, I did not want to import or impose U.S. views of race and racism on Dominicans. To the extent that it is possible for researchers to shed their own cultural baggage, I set my own considerations about race and racism aside.

During this initial field experience in 1993, my host mother/friend, Maria,[34] told me about Identidad and her friend, Nica, its director. Because up to this moment, I had focused my research ostensibly on how Dominican society understood gender and performed gender roles, I knew very little about the racial politics of the day. Identidad, I learned from Maria and Nica, organized not only around issues related to gender and class—topics definitely relevant to my master's thesis—but they incorporated the twin issues of race and color. These two elements, I was to discover, were extremely controversial and contentious topics among Dominicans.

Not long after my introduction to Nica, through various arrangements that built upon my research and personal network, I was invited to attend a meeting of Identidad in the capital city of Santo Domingo. Prior to this meeting, I was completely unaware that anyone organized locally around these issues or felt compelled not only to challenge racism and sexism but also to publicly lay claim to Black, Afro-Dominican, or any other African Diasporic identities. To do so in the Dominican Republic was to assume a radical oppositional stance to both national and folk identity politics.[35]

IDENTIDAD: THE ORGANIZATION AND ITS OBJECTIVES

Identidad is a nongovernmental organization composed of approximately twenty core members. Although the organization is located in Santo Domingo, most of its members reside in the capital; a few live in Santiago, where I conducted my research, and the remainder live in other parts of the Dominican Republic. According to census data, Santo Domingo has always had a larger number of Black Dominicans compared with Santiago and other areas in the north. The group's meetings were not regularly scheduled due in part to members' schedules[36]—these women often traveled to the United States to work or visit family and sometimes to attend conferences and conduct research. They also traveled internationally to facilitate workshops, which provided a forum for them to reflect and discuss topics related to race, color, and gender.[37] Identidad members in Santo Domingo frequently traveled to Santiago and other cities to bring these ideas to women. By conducting workshops with women throughout the country, Identidad reaches out and raises awareness across social class. In this way, the desire to claim a Black identity, and later an Afro-Dominican identity, was not just a middle-class concern but one that reached from the grassroots up, having an impact across social class lines.

My own history of involvement in women's organizations as well as my interest in how Dominicans negotiated identity within the interconnecting webs of race, class, and gender are what drew me to become involved in Identidad. When I asked the group how I could support their work, I was told they were interested in African American women's popular magazines from the United States. They translated the articles on career opportunities, education, health, motherhood, and fashion and used them as points of departure in focus groups and workshops. I left with them the copies of *Essence* magazine I had brought with me from the United States. Little did I realize the impact this popular Black women's magazine that addresses issues from dating to health to how to "dress for success" would have on Identidad. When I returned in 1995 for further research, they were using the image of Susan L. Taylor (the editor-in-chief of *Essence*) on the cover of their newsletter.[38] The new director of Identidad explained that to them, Taylor (more likely her cornrowed image) represented their ideal of beauty and strength.[39]

Increasingly Identidad became the focal point of much of my interrogation of Dominican society and culture. And increasingly my research interests shifted away from a solitary concern with gender to one that looked at the nexus of race, class, and gender in the performance of Dominican life and identity, both here and in the United States. So when I returned in 1995, this time I had come to study Identidad, an organization that lists five objectives as crucial to their political agenda: (1) to promote a broad process of reflection that serves as a premise in the search of identity; (2) to help other women become aware of the relationship between racial and gender discrimination and oppression; (3) to reveal the contributions of the Black woman in the formation of the nation; (4) to demythologize the dominant stereotypes about the Black woman; and (5) to convey ideas that advance accurate models of identity with regard to the Black woman.[40]

As I learned during the course of my research, Identidad's formation did not have an easy history. As the members grappled with notions of changing identity, larger societal tensions around race and color especially surfaced in the group. In 1995, a rupture occurred around the organization's name and the terms it used to describe women's experiences within the group. In particular, a small contingent of lighter-complexioned women questioned the exactness and accuracy of using the appellation *Negra* (Black) in the organization's name. In the Dominican Republic, *Negra* is a word usually reserved for Haitians, Africans, and extremely dark-complexioned Dominicans. The label is fraught with contentious historical and contemporary meanings, and as such it became the battleground for what was to be a protracted conflict over identity politics. Other traits used to signify race, such as hair and its style, also were called into question. Much like those who participated in the Black nationalist movement of the 1960s, some members of Identidad embraced an oppositional identity predicated on rejecting "normative" behaviors. Thus, some advocated rejecting the use of hair relaxers and straighteners and wore their hair "natural" (in forms such as afros, braids, and curly locks, for example).

Color as a distinguishing feature was also reinvented in such a way that light-skinned members of Identidad were made to feel that they were not "Black enough."[41] And ironically, those light-skinned Dominican women in the group who chose to define themselves as Black sometimes met with disapproval or encountered confusion from the darker-skinned women in the group. In the end, a new, albeit short-lived, organization, Café con Leche (Coffee with Milk), was born. The organization espoused a new interpretation of race mixture, color, and gender in the Dominican Republic, one distinct from Identidad. Not having a large membership, Identidad was profoundly impacted when some of its original members formed Café con Leche; in effect, the coexistence of the two groups divided these Dominican feminists into Black and *mulata* camps. After what was termed a "period of reflection," Identidad underwent reorganization and redefinition, and replaced the controversial nomenclature "Black" with "Afro-Dominican." The goal was to re-create a more inclusive Identidad and reunite the group by bringing women from Café con Leche back into Identidad—which is precisely what happened. Identidad re-formed around a new direction—with a woman who was both a founding member of Identidad and a former member of Café con Leche as the new director.

Along with a reorganization came a new mission and revised objectives:

> Es una organización de mujeres de origen afro que enmarcamos nuestro trabajo en la transformación de las estructuras sociales y políticas reproductoras y transmisoras de ideologías que fomentan los prejuicios raciales y por condición de género. . . . La misión de Identidad es enfrentar todo tipo de discriminación étnico racial, rescatar y promover los aportes de la cultura afro a nuestra conformación social. Los lineamientos estrategicos parten de: (a) empoderar a las mujeres negras en el rescate de su identidad afro a traves de lo simbólico, lo artistico, y lo religioso; (b) la denuncia de todo tipo de discriminacion a cualquier persona por su condición étnico racial o de género; (c) la investigación; d) la articulación—para combatir el racismo y el sexismo.

> [It is an organization of women of African origin that frames our work in the transformation of the social structures and political reproducers and transmitters of ideologies that evoke the racial prejudices and for the condition of gender. . . . The mission of Identidad is to confront all types of racial/ethnic discrimination, to rescue and promote the contributions of the African culture to our social fabric. The strategic boundaries consist of: (a) empowering Black women in the rescue of their Afro-identity through the symbolic, the artistic, and the religious; (b) denouncing all types

of discrimination of any person based on their racial/ethnic status or gender; (c) doing research; (d) speaking out against racism and sexism.][42]

These objectives highlight the point that it is necessary for Domini-cans to "rescue" or recover their Afro-Dominican identity—an identity that has been buried in the historical memory. In its or-ganizational objectives, Identidad links this recovery with a mission to combat sexism and racism while combining research and action.

These events and new objectives capture the complex and con-tested process of identity formation and negotiation within the Dominican Republic and the emergence of a transhistorical iden-tity as the most effective means of political mobilization for Identidad. The result was that the organization moved away from Black as color and racial marker to a stance that privileged culture, heritage, and ancestry. In defining themselves as Afro-Dominican, the women of Identidad reclaimed an African heritage and em-braced the Afro-American culture that the Black Atlantic experience has produced.[43] They also connected themselves, through ances-try, to a Diasporic sisterhood with other women of African descent in the Americas and around the world. As Carmen, the new leader, explained: "We began to question the significance of Black as a de-scriptive category and decided, after a period of reflection, that we were of African descent with mixture, and it was important to claim an Afro-Dominican identity which includes all mulatto and Black Dominican women."[44]

At present, Identidad works to raise awareness in the Domini-can Republic about racism and sexism. Its Afro-Dominican femi-nist agenda is one that asserts the necessity of race and gender, along with class and sexuality, as significant points in their research and articulations of Dominicanness[45]—which I define as their sense and experience of being Dominican. An important aspect of this new identity is that as Afro-Dominicans, and as women of the Diaspora, they align themselves with Haitian women and others in the African Diaspora who experience the political, sexual, and economic marginalization that they have experienced in the Do-minican Republic, and which Ruth Simms Hamilton argues are de-fining features of the African Diaspora:

The African diaspora represents a type of social grouping characterized by a historical patterning of particular social relationships and experiences. As a social formation, it is conceptualized
as a global aggregate of actors and subpopulations, differentiated in social and geographical space, yet exhibiting a commonality based on historical factors, conditioned by and within the
world ordering system.[46]

Similar African Diasporic views were articulated when I attended a
public forum that Identidad organized titled "Que Somos Etnicamente las Dominicanas y los Dominicanos" (What We Dominicans
Are Ethnically). During the course of the discussion, Carmen explained why Identidad is advancing an Afro-Dominican identity:[47]

Cómo definirla etnicamente, sea un proceso de construcción, sea
una cuestion de que estrategicamente sea más válido asumir
certa categoría u otra? Yo me inclino evidentemente por la
propuesta Afro-Dominicana en el sentido de que para mi, y yo
no soy una estudiosa del tema, sino que es una opción más sentimental y militante que otra cosa; la propuesta de la categoría
Afro-Dominicana me resuelve la mezcla, es decir lo dominicano
es una construcción historica de mezclas de culturas: hispana,
africana e indígena—aunque por opción política optamos por
destacar aun que otra o eliminar una y otra. Ahora bien yo creo
que hay un predominio de la cultura africana que se ha adaptado
a los tiempos. Aqui, y hay evidencias, el elemento afro es fundamental—por eso Identidad de las Mujeres Afro.

[How to define someone ethnically—is it a process of construction, a question of what category is more strategically valid to
assume? I am inclined to lean toward the proposed Afro-
Dominicana in the sense that for me, and I am not an expert on
the topic, but rather it is a sentimental and militant option more
than anything else; the proposal of the category Afro-Dominicana
resolves for me the mixture, that is to say that Dominican is a
historical construction of mixtures of cultures: Spanish, African
and indigenous—although for political preference we opt to highlight one over another. Now, I believe that there is a predominance of the African culture that has adapted over time. Here,
and there is evidence that the African element is fundamental—
for that reason [we call ourselves] Identidad of the Afro Women.]

Identidad's adoption of the prefix Afro—as a way of reclaiming and
embracing African ancestry is a radical departure in the Dominican

Republic, because the prevailing idea of mixture is one that has developed without any reference to Black or African ancestry; in fact, many Dominicans distance themselves from the idea that Blackness or African ancestry figures in any part of their identity and past; most embrace the concept of "whitening," achieved largely by "marrying up." The preferred marriage partners in the Dominican Republic then are those who most resemble the *mulata* (mulatto) or who are *blanco* (white). Hair texture, skin color, economics, education, and the like are indexes of how "white one is."[48]

For Identidad, the decision to embrace both Blackness and feminism, unpopular topics in the Dominican Republic, places the organization in the unenviable position of having to continuously defend itself and its perspectives.[49] The group's perceived radicalism largely has to do with its alliance with Haitian women and the complex history of the Dominican Republic's relationship with its neighbor Haiti. Dominicans and Haitians live in close proximity to each other and have developed their ideas about nationality, race, and peoplehood in relation to each other. For Dominicans, this means constructing the *indio* identity as a defining characteristic of Dominicanness, which differentiates them from the Black identity that they see as signifying Haitianness.[50] Thus, in the Dominican Republic, the socio-racial category White is used to classify a person of Spanish ancestry, while Black is used to classify someone of African ancestry. In this local/national racial taxonomy, White and Black are conceptualized as "pure" categories, and most Dominicans view themselves as somewhere in the middle. They are *mixed* people, a mixed nation betwixt and between these White and Black categories. In this identity discourse, which has evolved over centuries, mixture refers to Dominicans—the *liga* (combination) or *mezcla* (mixture)—enabling them to maintain a real and symbolic distance from anything Black, especially Haitians.

Only recently has the state used any socio-racial category that denotes African/Black ancestry to classify a population that perceives itself as composed only of persons who are *mixed*. I found in my 1998 research that even the classic term *mulato* (which is used elsewhere in the Caribbean and African Diaspora to mark mixture), emerged only recently, in 1998, on the *cédula* (the national identification/election card), as an official state-sanctioned category.

All previous census reports classified the Dominican Republic's mixed population as *mestizo*.[51]

The sociocultural meanings that Dominicans attach to the socio-racial categories of *mestizo* and *indio* have their roots in national myths about the Taino Indians (the inhabitants of the island before the arrival of Columbus), the ensuing interactions between them and the Spaniards, and the skin color variation produced as a result of that contact.[52] Textbooks and present-day conversations invoke a memory and mourning of the Taino and assert reverence for the Spanish, for their language and religion, among other practices. This suggests that despite tangible evidence of Africanisms (most easily observed in foods, dance, and music) in the Dominican Republic, there has been a deliberate, state-inspired attempt to erase the African presence. As a result, African origins, cultural production, and identity have been omitted to promulgate and maintain a *mestizo* or *indio* identity. Identidad's efforts have been significant in helping to challenge this erasure, along with the efforts of other organizations, revisionist historians, and Dominican scholars, who are literally rewriting the nation's history and redefining Dominicanness.

BLACK FEMINISM AND AFRO-DOMINICAN WOMEN

Without a doubt, adopting a Black feminist standpoint has been an unpopular move for Identidad. One reason is that it places the organization in direct conflict with CIPAF, the country's leading feminist research and activist organization, which does not deal with the topics of race and racialized experiences.[53] Rather, CIPAF has chosen to focus on broad gender issues such as the free trade zones (women as workers in the factories), female-headed households, machismo,[54] abortion rights, and the use of nonsexist language in Spanish (e.g., using *los Dominicanos* and *las Dominicanas* in the same sentence to denote gender).[55] All of this is done, however, without any interrogation of race and the implications it has for any of these issues. Thus, Identidad has concluded quite critically that CIPAF fails to represent their interests, despite being the leading feminist organization. Although CIPAF and Identidad have overlapping concerns around gender issues, their relationship directly mirrors that in the United States between White feminists and Black/Third World feminists, who struggle over using middle-class White women's experience to reflect the experience of all women. Whereas U.S. White feminists have undergone a process in which recognition of difference in gender experiences is a given, Dominican feminists have yet to reach such an agreement.

Where Identidad and CIPAF seem to converge is over the importance of women's organizations in the lives of its members. The ensuing solidarity (sisterhood) that results from women coming together around common goals is unique to feminist praxis and especially has marked the experiences of Black feminist anthropologists like myself, McClaurin, and Bolles. This is largely because the communities in which we conduct our fieldwork resemble our own communities in many respects, and we find ourselves coming to work with and for the women's groups we encounter. Both McClaurin and Bolles describe similar fieldwork experiences in Belize and Jamaica, respectively.[56] In describing the power of women's organizations in Belize as a catalyst for social action, McClaurin observes: "In a community of kindred spirits, . . . [women] have found a source that motivates each of them to some level of personal action as well as community concern. Women's groups in Belize, as elsewhere in the world, are often the catalyst that some women need in order to become agents in their own lives."[57] I found similar examples of kindredness as well as individual and collective agency among the women in Identidad and CIPAF, while my relationship to Identidad was one of kinship rather than researcher/informant.

FULL CIRCLE: EXPERIENCE, BLACK FEMINISM, AND ANTHROPOLOGICAL PRAXIS

It has been my own experiences with color/colorism in the United States and the necessity of having to answer the "what are you" question most of my life that have figured prominently in my choice of research topics. My interest in anthropology in identity construction does not derive from the acquisition of knowledge through coursework but is inspired by my personal history with its legacy of activism and involvement in women's organizations.

My choice of topic, the location of my fieldwork, and the rapport and commitment I established with Identidad are not accidental but emerge from my own desire to live and practice a Black feminist agenda.

Working with the women in Identidad enabled me to combine my personal history with my scholarship, sisterhood, and activism. While I cannot claim that my experiences as a Black woman in the United States directly reflect those of women in Identidad, there were sufficient points of convergence around ancestry, color experience, and feminist ideas to provide a bridge of sisterhood. On a personal level—and scholarship is always informed by the personal—I found my engagement with Identidad satisfying as we struggled to understand and organize around concerns of race, class, gender, and positioning. As I came to understand the politics of identity in the Dominican Republic, the politics of identity in the United States and throughout the African Diaspora have been further illuminated.

On this basis, I realize now that my connection as a Black feminist anthropologist to the Black feminists in Identidad represents a union of possibilities in which we are all able to contribute to the reconstruction and articulation of Black women's identity in its immensely varied forms and to work to affect macro-structural changes through activism. At the local level, Identidad makes claims and assertions and engages in political praxis that can impact the racial system in the Dominican Republic. In the intellectual arena, Black feminist anthropologists make similar claims and assertions and also engage in political praxis that we hope will impact the discipline of anthropology, (re)position the centrality of gender, class, and race, and create a useful space in which to explore the validity and significance of *sameness*—as I have explained it here— in anthropological research.

Despite some scholars' critiques of essentialism and eschewing of similarities in a postmodernist framework, I think I have made a compelling case for the inclusion of the centrality of sameness as a point of analytical departure in my own Black feminist anthropological framework. Such a perspective, I recognize, is counterintuitive in the present moment, primarily because embracing notions of sameness and convergence as starting points is not part of the anthropological discourse. My own encounters with White women social scientists during my stay in the Dominican Republic clearly revealed this, and much more.

During the early stages of my fieldwork in the Dominican Republic, I met another graduate student, and over the course of a few days, we discussed our research interests and shared our experiences in the Dominican Republic. At some point, she expressed her sense of limitation as a White person because no one seemed willing to talk with her about color and race. Her experience was not unique. Almost four years later, as I prepared to return to the Dominican Republic in 1998 to finish my dissertation research now explicitly focused on race, identity, and gender, I was informed by a sociologist and an anthropologist, both White women, in a manner clearly meant to discourage me, that "Dominicans don't talk about color." The authority to make such a claim was based on their own previous experiences, which they never questioned—each presented their observations/conclusions to me matter-of-factly and as normative.

My experience, however, contrasted greatly with what they described. It was the norm for me to have conversations with Dominicans about color in the Dominican Republic; such discussions were common, everyday practice. Further, we did not confine our conversations to how we, as similarly positioned Others, experienced color in the Dominican Republic; we also examined the discourses surrounding color and race issues in the United States as they pertained to me and to Dominicans who migrated.

My point is this—in the same way that in early feminist studies, *women* meant *White* women, and thus White women's experiences were accepted as the norm, so too among feminist anthropologists, White women's experiences in the field are taken to be normative. It is in the context of such authoritative, ethnocentric, and racist presumptions—that if Dominicans did not talk about color with them, then it must mean that Dominicans do not talk about color with any researchers—that much ethnography about "racial democracy" in the Dominican Republic and other Latin American countries has been promulgated. It is the experiences of Black feminist anthropologists, including myself, and native anthropologists in the field that have recently come to challenge such axiomatic think-

ing. This is not to suggest that there are not differences of education, class, and power that interrupt the field dynamics of Black
feminists and native anthropologists, but rather that frequently our
personal history of otherness provides a bridge that is not necessarily accessible to White anthropologists.

I would argue strongly that the difference between my field
experience and what I was told to anticipate is the result of a sense
of sameness generated by phenotypic similarity, a participation in
the history of the Americas that aligns me in certain contexts more
closely with subjects in the field, and a link to a real and imagined
African Diaspora. The rapport I established as a Black woman/femi-
nist and my ability to effectively conduct anthropological research
with women cultural consultants in the Dominican Republic is the
result, in part, of our mutual recognition of historical, racial, political, and gendered sameness.

NOTES

I acknowledge and thank my husband and colleague, David S. Simmons, for reading
different versions of this essay and for providing support, feedback, and important insights, and for suggesting the title, "A Passion for Sameness." I especially thank the
editor of this volume, Irma McClaurin, for working closely with me and giving me
critical comments, and for her encouragement and mentorship. I express my gratitude
to my mother, Ludia R. Eison, my sister, Kamika Eison Wheatley, my daughter, Asha D.
Simmons, and all of the women in my family, for the legacy and promise of sisterhood,
and to my father, Wilson Eison, Jr., and my entire family for love, support, and prayers.
I also thank all of my cultural consultants in the Dominican Republic, especially the
women in Identidad. Ruth Simms Hamilton provided me with helpful suggestions on
an earlier draft, for which I am grateful. I also acknowledge the support received from
my dissertation guidance committee: Scott Whiteford, Laurie Kroshus Medina, Judy Pugh,
Ann Millard, and Ruth Simms Hamilton. I completed my dissertation research under
the Martin Luther King–Cesar Chavez–Rosa Parks Future Faculty Fellowship, a State of
Michigan program administered by the graduate school at Michigan State University.

1. For a more in-depth discussion of Black feminist theorizing, see Patricia Hill Collins,
   Black Feminist Thought: Knowledge, Consciousness, and the Politics of Empowerment (1990;
   reprint, New York: Routledge, 1991); bell hooks, *Feminist Theory: From Margin to Center*
   (Boston: South End Press, 1984); and Stanlie M. James and Abena P. A. Busia, eds., *Theorizing Black Feminisms: The Visionary Pragmatism of Black Women* (London and New York:
   Routledge, 1993).
2. Ula Taylor, "The Historical Evolution of Black Feminist Theory and Praxis," *Journal of
   Black Studies* 29, 2 (1998): 234–254; and Leith Mullings, *On Our Own Terms: Race, Class,
   and Gender in the Lives of African American Women* (New York and London: Routledge,
   1997).
3. Gloria T. Hull, Patricia Bell Scott, and Barbara Smith, eds., *All the Women Are White, All
   the Blacks Are Men, but Some of Us Are Brave: Black Women's Studies* (Old Westbury, N.Y.:
   Feminist Press, 1982); and bell hooks, *Feminist Thought*.
4. Faye V. Harrison, "Anthropology as an Agent of Transformation: Introductory Comments and Queries," in *Decolonizing Anthropology: Moving Further toward an Anthropology
   for Liberation*, ed. Faye V. Harrison (1991; reprint, Arlington, Va.: Association of Black
   Anthropologists and American Anthropological Association, 1997), 1.

5. Elizabeth Higginbotham, "African-American Women's History and the Metalanguage of Race," *Signs: Journal of Women in Culture and Society* 17, 2 (1992): 253–254.

6. See Sherry Ortner, "Is Female to Male as Nature Is to Culture?" in *Woman, Culture and Society* (Stanford: Stanford University Press, 1974), 67–88; Michelle Z. Rosaldo, "Theoretical Overview," in *Woman, Culture and Society*, 17–43; and the collection as a whole, edited by Michelle Z. Rosaldo and Louise Lamphere, for examples of issues of *sameness*.

7. Ruth Behar, *Translated Woman* (Boston: Beacon Press, 1993); and Kamala Visweswaran, "Histories of Feminist Ethnology," *Annual Reviews of Anthropology* 26 (1997): 591–621.

8. For a history of feminist anthropology, see Henrietta L. Moore, *Feminism and Anthropology* (Minneapolis: University of Minnesota Press, 1988); and Micaela di Leonardo, ed., *Gender at the Crossroads of Knowledge: Feminist Anthropology in the Postmodern Era* (Berkeley: University of California Press, 1991).

9. See Irma McClaurin-Allen, "Incongruities: Dissonance and Contradiction in the Life of a Black Middle-Class Woman," in *Uncertain Terms: Negotiating Gender in American Culture*, ed. Faye Ginsburg and Anna Tsing (Boston: Beacon Press, 1990), 315–333, for a discussion of woman as heterogeneous category.

10. Di Leonardo, *Gender at the Crossroads*; and Visweswaran, "Histories of Feminist Ethnology."

11. See Henrietta L. Moore, *A Passion for Difference: Essays in Anthropology and Gender* (Bloomington: Indiana University Press, 1994), and di Leonardo, *Gender at the Crossroads*, for a more thorough discussion of the shift from sameness to difference along the lines of power.

12. See bell hooks, *Ain't I a Woman? Black Women and Feminism* (London: Pluto Press, 1982); and Harrison, "Anthropology as an Agent of Transformation."

13. Moore, *Feminism and Anthropology*, 9.

14. Cf. Irma McClaurin, *Women of Belize: Gender and Change in Central America* (New Brunswick, N.J.: Rutgers University Press, 1996); Faye V. Harrison, "Persistent Power of 'Race' in the Cultural and Political Economy of Racism," *Annual Review of Anthropology* 24 (1995): 47–74; and A. Lynn Bolles "Anthropological Research Methods for the Study of Women in the Caribbean," in *Women in Africa and the African Diaspora*, 1st ed., ed. Rosalyn Terborg-Penn, Sharon Harley, and Andrea Benton Rushing (Washington, D.C.: Howard University Press, 1987), 65–77.

15. Toni Cade Bambara, ed., *The Black Woman: An Anthology* (New York: Penguin, 1970).

16. Collins, *Black Feminist Thought;* Paula Giddings, *When and Where I Enter: The Impact of Black Women on Race and Sex in America* (Toronto: Bantam Books, 1984); bell hooks, *Feminist Theory;* Barbara Smith, ed., *Home Girls: A Black Feminist Anthology* (New York: Kitchen Table Press, 1983); Hull, Scott, and Smith, *All the Women Are White, All the Blacks Are Men, but Some of Us Are Brave;* and Johnnetta B. Cole, *All American Women: Lines That Divide, Ties That Bind* (New York: The Free Press, 1986).

17. For a conceptualization of the African Diaspora, see Ruth Simms Hamilton, "Introduction and Overview," in *Creating a Paradigm and Research Agenda for Comparative Studies of the Worldwide Dispersion of African Peoples*, Monograph No. 1 (East Lansing: African Diaspora Research Project, Michigan State University, 1990). See also Filomina Chioma Steady, ed., *The Black Woman Cross-Culturally* (Cambridge, Mass.: Schenkman, 1981); and Terborg-Penn, Harley, and Rushing, *Women in Africa and the African Diaspora*.

18. McClaurin, *Women of Belize*.

19. Bolles, "Anthropological Research Methods."

20. McClaurin, *Women of Belize*, 16.

21. See Glenn Hendricks, *The Dominican Diaspora: From the Dominican Republic to New York City-Villagers in Transition* (New York: Teachers College Press, Columbia University, 1974); Eugenia Georges, *The Making of a Transnational Community: Migration, Development, and Cultural Change in the Dominican Republic* (New York: Columbia University Press, 1990); Sherri Grasmuck and Patricia R. Pessar, *Between Two Islands: Dominican International Migration* (Berkeley: University of California Press, 1991); and Jorge Duany, *Quisqueya on the Hudson: The Transnational Identity of Dominicans in Washington Heights*, Dominican Research Monographs (New York: CUNY Dominican Studies Institute, 1994), for more on the history of Dominican migration to the United States.

22. The idea of a "Dominican Dominican" emerged during interviews as a way of talking about a person who has not emigrated and has ancestral ties in the Dominican Republic that can be traced back over generations.

23. McClaurin, *Women of Belize*, 16.
24. My husband, David, had very similar experiences and was defined by "local" terms as well. Like me, he was considered to be Dominican and from "there" (the United States). And our daughter, Asha, was often referred to as *la Dominicanita* (the little Dominican girl). Their experiences helped corroborate my own.
25. Benedict Anderson, *Imagined Communities: Reflections on the Origin and Spread of Nationalism* (New York: Verso, 1991).
26. See Kathy Russell, Midge Wilson, and Ronald Hall, *The Color Complex: The Politics of Skin Color among African Americans* (New York: Harcourt Brace Jovanovich, 1992), for a historical overview of the politics of skin color and phenotypic variation in the African American community in the United States.
27. I accompanied my husband, David, to his field site when he was conducting research in Nigeria and in Zimbabwe.
28. Paula Giddings, *In Search of Sisterhood: Delta Sigma Theta and the Challenge of the Black Sorority Movement* (New York: William Morrow, 1988), 6.
29. Simms Hamilton, "Introduction and Overview."
30. My M.A. thesis (1994) was based on research in the Dominican Republic and was titled "Dominican Women: The Cultural Construction of Gender and Female Identity" (Iowa State University). I have also given many conference papers, based on ongoing research in the Dominican Republic, dealing with race, color, and gender identities. The papers in order of presentation are as follows: "Matrifocality and Marianismo in the Dominican Republic: A Look at Traditional and Changing Gender Roles," paper presented at the Society for Applied Anthropology Meetings, Cancun, Mexico, April 13–17, 1994; "The Cultural Construction of Gender and Female Identity: Dominican Women within a Cultural Context," paper presented at the National Women's Studies Association Conference, Iowa State University, June 15–18, 1994; "Becoming Afro-Dominicanas: (Re)Negotiating Indio in the Company of Sistahs," paper presented at the 94th Annual Meeting of the American Anthropological Association, Washington, D.C., November 15–19, 1995; "Las Mujeres Negras: A Grassroots Approach to Collective Identity in the Dominican Republic," paper presented at the 118th Annual Meeting of the American Ethnological Society, San Juan, Puerto Rico, April 18–21, 1996; "Becoming Afro-Dominican: The Role of International Migration, Race, and Gender in (Re)Constructing a Black Identity," paper presented at the National Black Graduate Student Association Conference, Claremont, Calif., May 1996; and "India, Black, and Afro-Dominican(a): Negotiating and (Re)Constructing Identities in the African Diaspora," paper presented at the IMGIP/ICEOP-KCP Joint Fellows Conference, Northbrook, Ill., November 7–9, 1997. All of these papers frame the issue of race, color, and gender in the Dominican Republic; this chapter is based on these earlier papers.

    When Identidad formed in 1989, they were known as El Movimiento por la Identidad de la Mujer Negra (The Black Women's Identity Movement). I later heard talk about the division in the organization around issues of color and a subsequent reorganization to include all women of African descent (*mulata* and *Negra*) in the Dominican Republic.
31. I use *race/color* when I am addressing issues of race and color simultaneously.
32. Although there was very little on contemporary racial identities, work focusing on earlier periods, involving the Caribbean in general or the Dominican Republic in particular, was helpful in formulating ideas about race in the Dominican Republic. See Harry Hoetink, *The Dominican People, 1850–1900: Notes for a Historical Sociology* (Baltimore: Johns Hopkins University Press, 1982); Sidney W. Mintz and Richard Price, *The Birth of African-American Culture: An Anthropological Perspective* (Boston: Beacon Press, 1976); Harry Hoetink, "'Race' and Color in the Caribbean," in *Caribbean Contours* (Baltimore: Johns Hopkins University Press, 1985), 55–84; idem, "The Dominican Republic in the Nineteenth Century: Some Notes on Stratification, Immigration, and Race," in *Race and Class in Latin America* (New York: Columbia University Press, 1970), 96–121; Magnus Mörner, *Race Mixture in the History of Latin America* (Boston: Little, Brown, 1967); and Peter Wade, *Race and Ethnicity in Latin America* (London: Pluto Press, 1997).
33. See France Winddance Twine, *Racism in a Racial Democracy: The Maintenance of White Supremacy in Brazil* (New Brunswick, N.J.: Rutgers University Press, 1998); and Winthrop R. Wright, *Café con Leche: Race, Class and National Image in Venezuela* (Austin: University of Texas Press, 1990), for a discussion of the "myth of racial democracy."

34. All of the names of participants and cultural consultants have been changed to pseud-onyms.

35. I attended subsequent meetings and activities when they occurred either in Santo Domingo or Santiago.

36. McClaurin, in *Women of Belize*, makes a similar observation about group meetings in Belize.

37. Identidad hosted the first meeting of Black Latin American and Caribbean women in the summer of 1992. They also participated in the Cross-Cultural Black Women's Stud-ies Summer Institute, in Venezuela, in 1993. Most recently, they held a feminist work-shop in Santiago in May 1998, which I attended, and they used this forum to discuss plans for an upcoming meeting of Latin American and Caribbean feminists in 1999. In 1998 they also sponsored a workshop on combating racism.

38. In concert with my own Black feminist agenda, I offered to be an ally and to help them tell their story, to facilitate the visibility of Identidad in the Dominican Republic and in the United States, and to assist them in ways that would contribute to their growth and sustainability as an organization (e.g., identifying funding sources, participating in work-shops, donating magazines that deal with African American women's issues, and so forth).

39. Nica, the previous director, had moved to the United States.

40. Author's translation of objectives from early Identidad publications, excerpted from the AAA and AES papers cited in note 30.

41. This is another similarity between Dominicans and African Americans.

42. In Casa por la Identidad de las Mujeres Afro, "Memorias del taller sobre estrategias y metodologias para combatir el racismo" (Memories of a presentation about strategies and methodologies to combat racism) (Santo Domingo, 1998). This list of objectives, excerpted from a larger set of issues and objectives, represents the organization's main objectives. Author's translation.

43. See Paul Gilroy, *The Black Atlantic: Modernity and Double Consciousness* (Cambridge: Harvard University Press, 1993), where he advances the idea of a Black Atlantic. He asserts that peoples of African descent have much in common, despite "artificial" barri-ers and borders. He is critical of hybridity and categories that further divide Black people, stressing that the experiences that resulted and continue to result from the slave trade and Middle Passage allow us to talk about a Black Atlantic experience that is common to the descendants of slaves in the Americas.

44. Translation from an interview with Carmen.

45. In earlier literature, the organization defined its members as Black feminists. Recently, it published a collection of essays titled *Movimiento feminista y de mujeres: Contextualización histórico y elementos claves para su comprehensión* (Feminist movement and women's movement: Historical contextualization and elements for your comprehension) by Yuderkys Espinosa, Lusitania Martínez, Lourdes Contreras, Cristina Castillo, and Ochy Curiel (Santo Domingo: Organized Commission of the 8th Feminist Meeting, 1998). In this document, the authors define the women's movement as "those organizations, groups, collectives of women—professionals, laborers, housekeepers, mothers—that mobilize around the issues that affect women on a daily basis" (e.g., lack of water and electricity), and the feminist movement is characterized as "the organized action of women in the struggle to combat the subordination of women." These are my transla-tions of definitions taken from the description of their goals on page 5 of the above-mentioned publication.

46. Simms Hamilton, *Creating a Paradigm and Research Agenda for Comparative Studies of the Worldwide Dispersion of African Peoples*, 18. Hamilton conceptualizes the African Diaspora as a global social formation and advances a conceptual framework to explore the lived experiences, histories, movements, and identities of peoples of African descent. The African Diaspora emerges as a conceptual tool and way of understanding the history (e.g., slave trade and Middle Passage) and lifeways of peoples of African descent (e.g., settlement and migration) as well as the identities that emerge and the relationships to host countries, homelands, and Africa.

47. This event was held in July 1998, at the public library, in Santo Domingo. Although I taped the panel discussion, Identidad also taped it and provided me with a transcription.

48. See Verena Martinez-Alier, *Marriage, Class and Colour in Nineteenth-Century Cuba; A Study of Racial Attitudes and Sexual Values in a Slave Society* (London: Cambridge University Press, 1974). Also, the *Americas* (1994) video series has a segment on the politics of skin color in the Dominican Republic.

49. Blackness is not a popular concept in a country that continues to define Haitians as Black and Dominicans, in relation to them, as a non-Black, albeit mixed people. Mixture has been articulated in different ways over time (*mestizo, Indio,* and most recently, *mulato*).

50. See Frank Moya Pons, *The Dominican Republic: A National History* (New Rochelle, N.Y.: Hispaniola Books, 1995); Hoetink, *The Dominican People;* idem, "'Race' and Color in the Caribbean"; and idem, *The Dominican Republic in the Nineteenth Century,* for a discussion of Dominican–Haitian relations over time. In general, there have been long-standing tensions between the Dominican Republic and Haiti. From 1822 to 1844, Haiti and the Dominican Republic were under Haitian rule—this period is referred to as the "Haitian Domination." In interviews, participants referred to this as the "browning" period—the *mixing* of Haitians and Dominicans over time. The dictator Rafael Leonidas Trujillo (1930–1961) generated fear and created anti-Haitian sentiment that continues today based on what he termed the "Haitianization" of the Dominican Republic. Trujillo encouraged immigration from Europe and discouraged immigration from Haiti and surrounding Caribbean nations to increase the number of Whites while decreasing the number of Blacks in the Dominican Republic. Influenced by the racist ideology of Adolf Hitler, in 1937 Trujillo ordered the *matanza* (massacre) of thousands of Haitians residing in border communities; a few years later, he invited Jewish refugees to settle along the northern coast of the Dominican Republic with the hope that they, along with other Europeans, would mix with Dominicans and contribute to the whitening process. This was part of his "biological" strategy.

51. I was in the Dominican Republic from May through November 1998 finishing research for my dissertation, which examines the ways in which Dominicanness is tied to race and nation and how it has changed over time due to transnational migration and ideas of both a Dominican and African Diaspora. These data are part of a historical chapter on how race was defined and articulated from 1900 to 1961. In addition to ethnographic research, I also conducted archival research. The information in this section involving categories is based on early census reports that were used to classify the population.

52. Silvio Torres-Saillant, "The Dominican Republic," in *No Longer Invisible: Afro-Latin Americans Today* (London: Minority Rights Publications, 1995), 132–133.

53. CIPAF, which stands for Centro de Investigación para la Accion Femenina (Research Center for Feminine Action), is an NGO (nongovernmental organization) and self-defined feminist organization based in the capital, Santo Domingo. I receive CIPAF's monthly newsletter by subscription.

54. In general, *machismo* refers to *macho* behavior and the ideology of physical and intellectual superiority of men; its "counterpart," *Marianismo,* refers to the Virgin Mary and the ideology of spiritual and moral superiority of women. These competing ideologies are prevalent throughout Latin America. See Helen I. Safa, *The Myth of the Male Breadwinner: Women and Industrialization in the Caribbean* (Boulder, Colo.: Westview Press, 1995), for a discussion of *Marianismo,* female-headed households, and women's roles in the family.

55. Typically, in Spanish, *los Dominicanos* and *los niños* mean "the Dominicans" and "the children," respectively. However, feminists in the Dominican Republic (from CIPAF, Identidad, and other organizations) consider this language sexist because the masculine form is used to represent both men and women. For that reason, Dominican feminists undertook a campaign to educate people about nonsexist language. This was a major campaign for CIPAF.

56. McClaurin, *Women of Belize;* and A. Lynn Bolles, *Sister Jamaica: A Study of Women, Work, and Households in Kingston* (Lanham, Md.: University Press of America, 1996).

57. McClaurin, *Women of Belize,* 166.

4

CAROLYN MARTIN SHAW

DISCIPLINING THE BLACK FEMALE BODY
Learning Feminism in Africa and the United States

Coming of age in a black segregated community in Virginia in the 1950s, I felt out of step with the world around me, but I knew that I was with my people, that my ship would rise or fall with the tide of black folk. I was not good at verbal games or physical games, I hated going to church, and while I liked music and dancing, I could not carry a tune and my dancing was more enthusiastic than polished. Although I joined social clubs and civic organizations, became a spokesperson for my school and community, and was praised for my academic achievement, I still felt bad because I was not good at what so many others could do with easy pleasure. Not having the cultural competencies that could comfort me as a representative of black culture, yet clearly being a part of the community, I did not think of being black as I do now as related to the specific heritage of black American culture. I saw race primarily in terms of the black body and of racism, racism based on the abnegation of the black body—color, form, face, and hair. From outside my community, my body was racialized in pernicious ways. Inside the black community, it was again the body that defined me—this time in terms of gender and sexuality. Management of the black female body was at the core of my identity.

For me, the care and discipline of the body were established interculturally, through the multiple and overlapping discourses and communities or "part societies" of which I was a member. For example, in 1957 when I was twelve going on twenty, the Soviet Union's launching of its *Sputnik* satellite pushed me to pit mind versus body as I studied science and craved a soft feminine vulnerability in the shadow of Marilyn Monroe. At the same time, I ran away from the images of savage Africans that were exploding in mass media, especially the Mau Mau in the colonial uprising in Kenya, and embraced racial uplift through education and civic duties. At home my family profited from the gains of blacks in organized labor unions, and in my social life I flirted with boys as I confronted the evils of sexuality. My subjectivity, my sense of myself as a person, and my existence as a subject in the world were constructed through the conjunction of ideas, meanings, images, discourses, and actions emanating from different social and cultural domains.

This conjunction or intersection I call interculturality—a way of describing the borderland, but not only between different communities and "part societies." Interculturality also refers to the intersection of different forms of knowledge and experience, and deployments and effects of power. Using this term is a recognition that society and culture can be fragmentary, multivocal, and emergent and that contradictions and tensions are continually negotiated and manipulated by actors in society. The individual, the social agent or actor, is a product of culture and produces culture. An individual's subjectivity is determined by that which he or she is subject to (such as laws, language, and stories) and that which he or she is subject of (such as personal decisions, actions, and stories). What holds together fragmentary cultures and part societies? I find the term *discourse* useful for thinking about linkages and articulations within and across "part societies."[1]

Part societies I think of as the space beyond the borderlands, where the center does, if only momentarily, hold. The idea is that there may be some degree of coherence in fragmented social fields. For me, discourse is a way of talking about social and cultural processes that link disparate ideas, resources, rules, persons, and institutions in an open interactional field, constituting the field, defining the elements of the field, the range of accepted behavior as well as the modes of resistance, and emphasizing the reality of power in the construction of what is and can be done and known. Fragmented planes of human interaction, interactional fields, intersect. Whatever unity is achieved must come through various kinds of linkages and articulations. Surely, violence and coercion play a part in the maintenance of loosely integrated systems, as do hegemonic consent, media, communications technology, transportation systems, and social inertia. The state of the world's economy, military and trade alliances, wars and treaties, ecological and ethnic group movements can be forces for change and for conservatism. There are many different kinds of articulations, not all of them compatible, that pull together fragments and partial societies; discourse analysis is but one method of finding connecting threads.

This chapter is an opportunity for me to look back on my own process as a black feminist anthropologist, to show how my early experiences influenced my work as an anthropologist and how my work as an anthropologist influenced my feminism. I categorize my work as black feminist anthropology because I allow my consciousness as a black woman to influence how I think through research problematics regarding gender. It is not just gender consciousness that makes my work feminist but a commitment to understanding and undermining sexism. Sexism goes hand in glove with other inequalities in society, and my work seeks to bring to light the intersection of inequalities through an examination of discourses of subordination and domination, showing how gender distinctions are created with and through wide-ranging power differentials, especially in regard to race, sex, and class.[2]

I am indebted to issues raised early in the development of feminist anthropology for directing the questions that I ask: Michelle Rosaldo's caution that the status and power of women must be seen in relation to the forms of inequalities that men suffer and Eleanor Leacock's insistence that the mode of production regulates women's status and power greatly influenced my approach to feminist anthropology.[3] In the decades that followed these works, feminist anthropologists have turned from production to consumption, from status to performance, and from essentialist notions of the female body to social constructions of gender. Feminist anthropologists, for whom gender is defined by power differentials in competing and overlapping sociocultural domains, have studied the different ways men's and women's bodies signify race, suffer capitalist exploitation, perform sexually, and are inscribed by the powers of the state. In this chapter, I discuss my early adolescence, showing the ways in which intersecting domains or discourses contributed to my own bodily discipline.[4] In truth, that meditation on my life has been so constructed because of what I learned using a similar approach in the study of colonial discourse in Kenya.

When I first went to the field in Kenya in 1971, I was prepared to find individuals caught between competing demands derived from their cultural and social systems, to understand internal diversity, and to note the influences from outside the community and the nation. Curiously, what I was not prepared for was how important gender differences were. My grappling to understand the differences it made to see Kikuyu society from a woman's perspective was as crucial to my becoming a black feminist anthropologist, as were my determination for equal rights for women and my sense of outrage at male domination. For me it took a discovery of gender in the field to uncover my own subjugated knowledge, and it took feminist scholarship to help me articulate the intersections of race and gender in shaping who I am and the theories that I choose.

Feminist anthropology helped me grasp that it is the social construction of gender that is at stake in production and reproduction, and that gender, like kinship, emerges from an interactional field in which biology is just one of the constraining and empowering resources.[5] Feminist scholars underscored that women must be apprehended through gender plus race, class, and sexuality.[6] I was especially interested in understanding the power of sexuality in shaping the person and society. Too often sexuality is understood as a subset of gender, obscuring the ways in which sexual categories and practices contravene notions of gender and blocking apprehension of the role of sexuality in itself in the social construction of the person. During the consciousness-raising seventies, like many women I also came to see that private experiences had public consequences: construing the personal as political, we broke down the barriers separating private hurts and social norms.

What I present here is an autoethnography, an ethnography of myself, or a psychosocial history. Like any history, it is teleological. I am looking back to explain the present moment—my existence as a feminist anthropologist—and with that in mind I highlight those moments of the past that seem most relevant to the present. This does not mean that I will find everything that went into making me a feminist anthropologist or that what I find is actually the most significant. My story, like any life history, could be told in many different ways. What I leave out in this process of selection, reinterpretation, remembering, and forgetting may actually carry weight equal to or more than what is included here—I am not sure that I am the best interrogator of my own life. Ten years from now in a different historical and theoretical moment, my story might look quite different. And so, in this chapter, for this moment, I address how I was constructed through intercultural processes, discuss my becoming a feminist anthropologist, and reflect on my work with African women.

MARILYN MONROE, MAU MAU, "SPUTNIK," AND ME

When I was a girl, I dreaded playing the dozens. Growing up in the 1950s in a black community in the Tidewater area of Virginia, I was not afraid that the game of escalating insults would turn into a physical fight. I was afraid that I would not be quick enough with a retort. Fortunately I was not often called on or "called out" in this game. But it was not just the dozens, but "signifyin'," hand clapping games, jump rope games—a whole repertoire of verbal skills and athletic abilities that eluded me. I did not have the cultural competencies often taken for granted in the black community. Friends and relatives, adults and children teased me for being awkward and uncoordinated. I was "big for my age," "goose-necked," and had a "liar's gap" in my teeth. While teachers praised me as bright and articulate, I had no street smarts, and I was a disaster on the playground. In elementary school, I achieved distinction as everybody's friend, a good public speaker, and an "A" student. The body was important, but I could not win with it.

My world was made up of black people. Racial segregation was the law of the land: all of my schools in Virginia were segregated, and Jim Crow laws regulated access to public facilities and accommodations. Although there was a drugstore run by whites not far from my house, most of the white people I saw were on television. Most of my neighbors had working-class families like my own, but there were a few schoolteachers and nurses in my immediate community. My mother and father both worked. My father was a longshoreman, and his union card placed him in an elite blue-collar category that never failed to distinguish me as privileged.

Most of the women I knew were working mothers, and their older children had considerable responsibilities for younger brothers and sisters. We went to black doctors and lawyers, but some people speculated that white lawyers would be less likely to cheat you and that maybe white doctors were better trained. Feelings that we were second-class citizens getting the worst from the United States competed with a sense of ourselves as a strong community, lifting ourselves up from being field hands and tenant farmers, enjoying the prosperity of the United States. The intersection of the domain of rights, codified in legal, political, and civil rights and expressed through discourses of racial subordination and resistance, and the domain of wealth shaped by the strength of the economy and the differential access to and control over economic resources created the bumpy terrain that we traversed daily.

When I went to junior high school, my world widened. I came into contact with a broader range of black people—boys and girls living on one of the last plantations in Virginia, children of the black middle and upper classes, teachers who had gone to school with whites in the North, and school principals and guidance counselors determined to prove that we were as good as or better than any white person. When the Soviet Union launched *Sputnik I*, I was twelve years old in the eighth grade. Shortly thereafter my segregated high school began dividing students into "tracks," and I was put on the college prep track. The goal of the United States—a goal so pervasive that funds to support it trickled down to a black high school in the South—was to build the country's math and science resources so that it could never be bested by the communists again.

This tracking led to my getting an enriched education and constant attention from teachers and guidance counselors. When I wanted to drop out of typing because I was hopelessly awkward, my parents were called to school and told the importance of my knowing how to type when I went on to college. In the school cafeteria, when I struggled with using a knife and fork to cut my chicken, my geometry teacher quietly showed me how. When I came to school in a tight sweater with a heavy pendant nestled between my breasts, the guidance counselor called me into his office to tell me that I, especially, should not wear revealing and sexy clothes. As I developed into a woman, the staff at school worried that I would be lost to sexuality and pregnancy. And well they should have worried.

Around the same time that I was helping increase the United States' math and science war chest, my own chest was growing. I was alternately thrilled and embarrassed. For me, mind and body were in opposition, as they also had been for my mother: my grandmother had yanked her out of school in the eighth grade after my mother had had her first gentleman caller—"You can't see boys and go to school," my grandmother had said. I had shown through my awkwardness, my total lack of athletic skills, that body was not my thing; would I as a teenager rebel and find sex the one physical area for easy pleasure? No, I didn't want to be loose, but I did want to be attractive, to be alluring, with a teenage intensity unmatched by any in adulthood.

Could I be smart and sexy? To answer that question, I had all the images and representation of women around me. The image of Marilyn Monroe was everywhere, sporting a soft pink come-hitherness that I knew was out of my reach but fantasized about. Another "double M," Moms Mabley, a raunchy and raw black comedienne whose records we secretly enjoyed, was more available as a cultural type. What I wanted to know as a young black girl was whether I had to trade the sense of myself as soft and vulnerable for the hard-edged raunchiness that the popular mainstream media and we ourselves often associated with black women. In contradistinction, Dorothy Dandridge, an icon of brown-skinned beauty in the fifties, was one of my idols. Magnificent in *Carmen Jones*, she was smart, sexy, but tragically brought down by her own pleasures. Eartha Kitt seemed cut from the same mold. Only recently in thinking back over this time period did I realize that Lena Horne was also an available role model. And when I think about this, I realize that it was easier to pretend to be Marilyn Monroe than to envy the icy beauty of Lena Horne. In doing that I would be admitting that I wanted light skin and entry into the black upper classes—that was nothing to play with. Lena Horne's almost white beauty was a real impossibility, too painful to imagine.

My sense of myself as a woman was not constructed only through mass media. But if I were looking in my community for women who thought of themselves as good women and as sexual, then my task was once again well nigh impossible. I had before me in my community many positive role models and some equally eloquent negative role models of what it meant to be a woman. On the plus side were the mothers of the church, the working mothers, the teachers, the scout leaders, the women of the lodges and secret societies, and the storytellers, entertaining us well into the night. On the negative side were the drunks, the women who ran off with other women's husbands, the women who stayed with men who beat them, the women who gave all their money to men, and the women who stayed at home and did not have paid employment. This last group—I only knew one—was acting like they were white, we thought. What black woman with any gumption would just stay at home? Good women worked, I knew that, but were good women also sexy? Did good women enjoy sex? I knew that they had children, but what about sexual pleasure?

Given the heavy doses of sexuality in rhythm and blues music popular in my community at the time, it was not as though sex were hidden. But rather that sex was naughty, downright bad. Some women rejoiced in that badness, but in my family, sex was the original sin, one of the ways that evil is expressed in the world.

The closest I ever came to knowing what ecstatic enjoyment was, was in the church when floods of emotion would overtake women as they "got happy" during a sermon or hymn: their hands and feet would fly in all directions, their bodies would arch, and then they would collapse in exhaustion. It was expected (all in the passive voice) that girls would not have sex until after they married, but if they did and got pregnant, they were never turned out. In fact, with motherhood, they were likely to be accepted into the family as adults and their children treated as though they were their brothers and sisters. One way of thinking about this is that sex was represented through two opposing discourses: the first, sex is dangerous—destructive of the moral fiber—and the second, sexual intercourse is inevitable, and the products of sex, children, are loved and valued.

Discipline of the black female body brought together contradictory discourses from many domains, including religious ideas about original sin, the sanctity of marriage and the blessing of children, and popular representations of the black women as sexually available and as workhorses. Anthropologist Zora Neale Hurston, in her novel *Their Eyes Were Watching God,* pits the black woman as mule against woman's desire for tenderness and sexual fulfillment.[7] The interactional field in which the black female body is disciplined includes the limitations on women's social and physical mobility as well as racial segregation. This field includes women's economic and psychological constraints and resources and the push and pull of hegemonic and counter-hegemonic forces.

With sexuality constructed through contradictory and incompatible discourses, actors must navigate their own way. Normalizing tendencies help define core sexual relations as legal, monogamous, heterosexual, and fruitful, but the margins include expression of dissident sexualities, including but not limited to gay and lesbian, commercial, nonmonogamous, single motherhood, and celibacy.[8] While I wanted to be sexy and alluring, I was constrained by my need for social approval in the black community and by my fear of mistreatment at the hands of whites who would see me as a workhorse or a whore. This demanded dignified, circumspect dress and public demeanor. In private, "A" student that I was, I found ways of resisting the control of my body as representative of the race and the use of my body for political statements about the goodness of black-skinned women.

Modesty and virtue are masked by dark skin. Harryette Mullen in her work on American slave narratives suggests that it is the inability of dark skin to redden in a blush that, from a white perspective, denies modesty, virtue, and innocence to the darker races.[9] A recent documentary film on the racist Aryan white power movement in the United States uses the phrase "blood in the face" as its title, connoting the importance placed on reddened skin as a sign of the honor of whiteness. This is particularly crucial to women whose honor is vested in control of the body, in maintaining an inviolate body. With slavery and the rape of enslaved black women as originary or foundational in the production of African Americans, the skin of the black women in the context of the slave master's sexual violation showed no signs of modesty. (Enslaved women's bodies often bore marks of the lash but no demure blush.) The white veneration of modesty and its display in young women were underscored in a study of blushing in Charles Dickens's *Our Mutual Friend*, where one can find "a narrative event in the coming of a blush," revealing what a young woman knows of love and the expectations of marriage.[10]

The face should show what is on the inside. Black American composer Fats Waller aptly captures the problematic for blacks of the relationship between the inside and the outside in his composition "Black and Blue," which asks, "What did I do to be so black and blue?" The reply: "I'm white, white inside, but that don't help my case, cuz I can't hide what is on my face." What is on my face? Political statements and moral precepts written in skin color and facial features. What is on my face? Eyes (bulging or squinting), nose (big, wide, open), teeth (gapped, bucked), jaw (protruding, square), forehead (sloping, wide)—all make statements about sensuality, poverty, intelligence, brutality, and honesty. Racial aesthetics are a part of discourses of domination and subordination through which black bodies, male and female, are disciplined.

While I was imagining a soft, seductive femininity in black, popular media presented the figure of the black man as dangerous or a dupe. In 1957, Virginia was in the midst of "massive resistance" to school integration; public schools were shut down to avoid racial integration. Editorials condemning the Civil Rights movement, said to be communist-inspired, filled white newspapers in my hometown. National media based in the North self-righteously decreed that the South had a problem with race, while right there in national magazines like *Newsweek* and *Time* were representations of Kenyan "tribesmen" as, at first, dupes of communists and then as Mau Mau savages.[11] The Kenyan Mau Mau movement contained many contradictions, but it was essentially an anticolonial movement that started after World War II and was crushed by the British military even as Kenya moved toward independence. American discourse on Mau Mau joined together three great fears of white America in the fifties: blacks who did not stay in their place, the incursion of communism, and unbridled sexuality.

In the U.S. print news media during 1952–1960, Mau Mau synedochically stood for all black people, and especially for American blacks as we began to make moves to change the status quo—from integration of the armed forces to school desegregation to the Civil Rights movement. Discourses on Mau Mau resonated with competing American tropes on the naturalness of racial hatred, the communist threat to racial harmony, the inferiority of the Negro, and the limits of education. As the American press took up the colonialists' cause in the fight against Mau Mau in the 1950s, racial and cold war politics merged to construct Mau Mau as a threat to the civilized world of Western democracies, coming from the dissatisfied lower classes and races who were stirred up by communist agitators. The representation of Mau Mau as degenerate, violent, oversexed, concentrating on bloody Mau Mau oaths instead of political analysis—all point to the image of "the Negro" as essentially primitive, despite the best intentions of Western civilization.

I came to know Kenya during this period, and I got the message that the progress that had been brought to Africa by British education and civilization was halted by the senseless, superstitious violence of Mau Mau. White America was worried that education, even in integrated schools, would not go deep enough to touch the licentiousness of black women or the savagery of black men.

While a member of a segregated black community and a young "lady" who tried to live up to that community's strict codes for a good and moral person, I was also constructed as scientist and savage, vulnerable and hard, American and suspect. These various constructions of self emanated from discourses of competing and overlapping domains of society. I was, in effect, a member of several local communities and "part societies," crisscrossing black and white America. As I grew older, my experiences within black communities, in the South, in the North, in the Midwest and on the West Coast, on city streets and in suburban homes, in lesbian and heterosexual groupings, and in Muslim and Christian gatherings—experiences as a "bookish" outsider in almost all these environments—have directed my theoretical attention to the internal diversity within black communities and the crosscurrents of contradictory beliefs and ideas that are continually renegotiated in social interactions.

There are varieties of black cultures in the United States; as black communities differ, so will black culture. The amazing similarities of blacks in the United States are as much a result of the impact of the social and cultural domination of whites as of the cultural identities forged in those communities. Persisting throughout the variation of black cultures are contradictory beliefs and ideas that individuals negotiate in conjunction with equally contradictory beliefs and ideas from outside those communities. As a young woman, I viscerally felt what it was like to be at the nexus of competing discourses and social expectations. In Kenya I sympathized with individuals similarly caught between worlds.

GENDER IN THE FIELD AND FEMINISM IN THE SEVENTIES

I chose to study the Kikuyu in Kenya for two main reasons: because I wanted to understand the other side of the people who brought the world Mau Mau, and because I wanted to see the effects of racism in a former white settler colony. During my first extended ethnographic fieldwork during 1971–1972, I lived among the Kikuyu about fifty miles north of Nairobi, Kenya. My dissertation research focused on the relationship between kinship and politics in this community that had given the world the fierce image of Mau Mau anticolonialists in the 1950s. My book, *Colonial Inscriptions: Race,*

Sex, and Class in Kenya, gives a fuller development of that research and of some of the theoretical, historical, and ethnographic material contained in this chapter.[12]

Briefly, the Kikuyu, one of the major ethnic groups in Kenya, live primarily in villages and towns in the foothills of Mt. Kenya, although many men and women have for generations lived in Nairobi and other urban centers in the country. An area with long-established labor migration, the rural countryside, where women work family farms, is overwhelmingly populated by married women, children, and older men. Before the colonial period, Kikuyu were polygynous, patrilineal, with a predominant pattern of patri-virilocality, although tenancy with distant relatives and nonrelatives was widely practiced.[13] In the past, clan ties and age grades based on male and female initiation ceremonies brought these widely scattered people together.[14]

Today, for women, income-generating cooperatives, community-building organizations, and social clubs, and for men, political parties and local beer halls perform some of the same integrative functions. Although Kikuyu men and women jointly participated in some activities, and either men or women could hold certain leadership positions, Kikuyu conceived of their system as one in which women were excluded from political decision-making. Women were expected to defer to their husbands, to contribute to family subsistence, to cook and participate in the maintenance of home, to provide primary child care, and to conduct themselves with dignity so as to honor their natal and marital lineages.

Concentrating on an analysis of social processes, my research endeavored to elucidate the effects of the involvement of Kikuyu in wider political and economic networks, to reveal the variability and openness of African communities, and to assess structural and incidental change over time. This Marxist-influenced problematic led to queries about conflict, contradiction, dialectics, economic determination, and social transformation. Processual analysis deals with the relationship between structure and agency, but it focuses on the social system.[15] In this approach, people are thought to be pulled in multiple directions by competing organizing principles such as kinship loyalty and patron–client relationships. As people literally and metaphorically make decisions, they are shaped by and help reconfigure their social systems.

In 1971, I did not go into the field looking to understand gender relations. What surprises me as I reflect on that period of my life was my ability to keep my awareness of gender as a major force in my life separate from my interest in understanding organizing principles that shaped society in Kenya. A story I often tell about my fieldwork is that I learned about gender in the field, at twenty-six years of age. I learned about the importance of gender from trying to come to grips with an obstreperous daughter-in-law in the family I lived with. I'll call her Eunice. Eunice was a nurse, trained wholly in Kenya, and a young mother who continually upset everyone's expectations of her as a kinswoman. She always went outside the expected norms to achieve her ends. Presenting herself as a "modern" woman, Eunice was disrespectful to her mother-in-law; she was disloyal to her own mother; she argued publicly with her husband; and she was exploitative of the young women from her mother's family who took care of her house and child. I did not like her.

Having been trained to look for individual negotiations within systemic variation, I was not surprised to find that Eunice, the daughter-in-law, could manipulate cultural rules and understandings. The daughter in the family I lived with also had her own way of doing things. A high school graduate, she had had a child out of wedlock, and her parents were, she believed, greedily holding off on the wedding until the bridewealth transactions were completed. This daughter had no qualms about using covert methods to achieve her ends, including involving me in surreptitious appeals to her father and father's brother to speed up the bridewealth negotiations. She would massage the system to get what she wanted. Eunice was different—her actions protested the unfairness of her situation, and she loudly proclaimed when she was mistreated as a wife, daughter, or daughter-in-law. This daughter-in-law was not just being the obstinate bride trying to get her way. Eunice was asserting a right for self-determination within her marriage and within her natal and her husband's families. One New Year's Eve it all came to a head, when Eunice broadcast this cutting remark to her husband in front of a crowd at a local nightclub: "Who are you to tell me what to do? I have money." Once they got home, he beat her and she left him—they reconciled after a few weeks. I interviewed women who had seen the incident and knew of its consequences, asking them who was in the wrong and what was at stake in the argument.

Most women believed that Eunice was in the wrong, that she should not have embarrassed her husband in public. She should have shown him more respect; he was right to beat her. But even in these statements supporting patriarchal authority, women told of their own power and how they, often in private, could shape family and community decisions. My observations of the daughter-in-law bothered me and stayed with me once I returned from the field. Not classifying Eunice as a feminist or a proto-feminist, because she did not articulate or even imply a position that was of and for women, I nonetheless saw that central to the tensions and anxieties that motivated her was her sense of the possibility that she could be equal to her husband and that her treatment as a woman was unfair. Eunice, the obstreperous daughter-in-law, was demanding the right to make her own choices. Years later, when I was working in Zimbabwe, a black Zimbabwean sociologist articulated a vision of "women's liberation" that spoke to Eunice's standpoint. In Zimbabwe, Rudo Gaidzanwa, in a review of women's fiction from the colonial period to independence, argued that liberated women are ones who exercise choice, act creatively, exploit opportunities, and maximize options.[16] She agreed, however, that drastic changes needed to take place in society and culture to free women's options, so that choice creatively exercised would not condemn women to reproduce a cultural system that devalues them.

Back from the field, teaching at the University of California, Santa Cruz, I developed a course on African women, which I taught for the first time in 1974. This was the beginning of my positioning myself as a feminist, influenced by my reflections on my Kenya fieldwork, my reading of the literature on African women, my membership in an anthropology department that had an equal number of women and men, and my residence at an interdisciplinary college that had instituted one of the first women's studies programs in the United States. My theoretical position had also changed: although I was not at that time using the term *intercul-turality*, the idea, then greatly influenced by the women's movement and academic women's studies, was beginning to develop. After Kenya, my belief in cultural and social holism was much shaken, and I came to see gender as more than just one of the organizing principles of society that could be negotiated in an open interactional field. I saw gender as central in shaping social and cultural worlds. Later, especially through feminist writings, including those of bell hooks, I agreed with the idea that gender is constructed in the matrix of race, class, and sexuality.[17]

How could it be that it took my experiences in Kenya to teach me to foreground gender, when I grew up smarting from having to take care of my older brothers, being told what I could and could not do because I was a girl, and seeing women struggling to support families, husbands, and lovers? Why had I not asked anthropological questions about gender? Compartmentalization? Not wishing to be doubly marginalized? At some level, I was obsessed by what it means to be female and on another I did not take up the issue. There was a disjuncture between my knowledge as a woman and my learning to foreground that knowledge. This unbidden knowledge can be thought of as subjugated knowledge.[18]

Subjugated knowledge includes understandings that are obscured by hegemonic theories and practices as well as by subaltern theories and practices themselves. I also use the phrase to mean knowledge that can be retrieved through personal excavation of the sort that I am undertaking in this chapter. As I see it today, my earlier theoretical approach obscured the centrality of gender by making it one among many variables. My personal concern about status and advancement in the university made me shy away from topics that would further marginalize me, topics such as women and children. And my own anger at gender inequality was suppressed so that I could function smoothly at work and at home.

The women's movement put an end to all that, especially to peace at home. I had married during my senior year in college and had given birth to my daughter eight years later, while I was writing my dissertation and teaching at the university. With the birth of my daughter, my workload trebled, and I grew resentful of my professor husband, then a Black Muslim, follower of the Honorable

Elijah Muhammad, who believed that men should have nothing to do with children younger than twelve years old. I was too tired to cater to him as I had done before. He had also introduced a young woman into our home, a student at the university, a potential convert to Islam, but one who stirred up my anger and passion. In the late 1970s, I began to meet with graduate and undergraduate students, mostly white women, in writing groups that also functioned as consciousness-raising groups. In that context, I learned to see the personal as political, to speak bitterness, and to examine my own choices and desires. A few years later, I left my husband and embraced lesbian feminism. Not until now, when I am once again married to a man, have I written about the influence of my lesbianism on my theory.

Being a woman-identified woman freed me in many senses—I more fully accepted myself. In my thirties, I wanted to relive my childhood—read children's books, ride bicycles, play games, run, dance, join a gym, exercise my body. I wanted to claim my body as a site of pleasure in ways that I had not done as a girl. My life was full of possibilities, and this sense of abundance spread into my theory, which concentrated on the transformation of political and economic structures for women's liberation and human fulfillment. I resisted cultural feminism, quite popular on my campus, that celebrated female difference, inscribing the body with deterministic powers. I embraced socialist feminism, wanting to understand how capitalism structures male dominance and how male dominance is organized by the capitalist division of labor, with my goal being undermining these structures for radical social change.[19]

Living a transgressive lifestyle made radical social change seem possible. Joining the battle for the Equal Rights Amendment, for abortion rights, for affirmative action, against sexual harassment, for equal funding of women's sports, for welfare rights, for recognition of women's unpaid labor, and for comparable pay for comparable worth in women's employment was not only liberating but exhilarating. In black communities, I found many people with fellow feelings, but I did not necessarily come out to them as a lesbian. Black lesbians and feminists were sometimes challenged to declare which side they were on, with black people or with women.

Being taunted with the specter of a government armed and turned against blacks, we were reminded that being black meant that we could not hide among white women or in predominantly white gay and lesbian communities. In social and political encounters with other black people and in classrooms made up mostly of white students, I took pains to be inclusive, to deal forthrightly with the pervasive power of racism, to develop class analysis, and to not come across as man-hating (which I was not). My revolutionary zeal has died down since that time; I believe less in the possibility of radical social change. But that I associated the possibility of such changes in social life with the opening up of my personal life is undeniable. One thing I know for sure is that my resistance to the disciplines of the black female body to which I had consented before was crucial in my approach to black feminist anthropology.

MORE LESSONS FROM AFRICA

Despite my concern to ameliorate the condition of women in the United States, my research focuses on African women. In that research I maintain an interest in the body and in sexuality. In a recent book on African feminisms, Gwendolyn Mikell states that experiences of exploitative political leaders and of economic restructuring have "pushed women toward greater boldness in addressing the economic and political elements that determine and affect their status."[20] Mikell contrasts the political and economic concerns of African feminists with Western debates about essentialism, the female body, and radical feminism, accurately characterizing African feminism as "distinctly heterosexual, pro-natal, and concerned with many 'bread, butter, culture, and power' issues."[21] It is the stark contrast between Western concerns with the female body and African concerns with the body politic that I object to and that my research addresses. I want to underscore the ways in which the effects of power are felt in everyday experiences and how the body is material for the expression of discourses of domination and subordination.

Historian Achille Mbembe, in a study of Cameroon, his first work published in English, "Provisional Notes on the Postcolony," suggests that the authoritarian modality in the postcolonial state is marked by coercion, violence, and extortion as well as by collusion, compliance, and performance, when the face of power looks like your own. In discussing the grotesque and carnivalesque mobilization of male and, especially, female bodies for the postcolonial state's show of power and popular support, Mbembe draws out the following all too common images:

> In the postcolony bodies have been used to entertain the powerful in ceremonies and official parades. On such occasions some of the bodies have had the marks of famine upon them: flaky scalps, scabies, skin sores. Other bodies have attracted small crowds of flies. But that has not stopped them from breaking out into laughter or peals of joy when the presidential limousines approached. They stamped the ground with their feet, blanketing the air with dust. Wearing the party uniform with the picture of the head of state printed on it, women followed the rhythm of the music and swung their torsos first forward, then back; elsewhere they pulled in, then thrust out their bellies, their undulating movements evoking as usual the slow, prolonged penetration of the penis and its staccato retreat.[22]

Mbembe argues that the power of the state is dramatized as ecstatic sexual master of women's bodies.

African women's concern with sexuality is most often heterosexual, but that is fraught with inequalities that many women want to overcome. Mbembe's provocative work contends that women are not just vehicles of the ruler's power or of that of the postcolonial state; they are also sexual tokens or trophies of office for male bureaucrats:

> I could mention too the way bureaucrats harass students at school exits, honking their car horns behind schoolgirls walking down the street, cruising up to them, stopping and opening their doors to invite them to sit in the "seat of death." The everyday life of the postcolonial bureaucrat consists of the following: alcohol, amusements, lewd propositions and bawdy comments in which the virtue of women comes under scrutiny by allusions to the sexual organs of office secretaries and the prowess of declared favourites and young mistresses.[23]

African feminists address these excesses of the postcolonial state as directly concerned with disciplining of the female body. Feminists I worked with during my second extended stay in Zimbabwe, another former white settler colony in southern Africa, as a Fulbright lecturer at the University of Zimbabwe during 1983–1984, used both discourses of rights and discourses of socialist feminism to protest the disciplining of the female body. I arrived in Zimbabwe just days after the government had begun a massive effort to rid the capital city of prostitutes and vagrants—Operation Clean-Up. I joined with an interracial, international group of feminists in the Women's Action Group to end Operation Clean-Up and to release women arrested and held in detention during the sweep. Due only in part to our protests and publicity campaigns, the women were released and Operation Clean-Up ended. To aid this effort, in 1983 and 1984, Women's Action Group members wrote protest letters to the editors of the major newspapers and published analytical articles in influential newsmagazines. One such statement engaged the discourse of rights and indicated how basic the rights recently won by women in Zimbabwe were:

> In Zimbabwe the question of women's liberation was first raised in the struggle for independence. And social changes, especially since independence, have meant that some women, particularly in cities, have been able to acquire a measure of freedom denied to them traditionally (but granted to men)—such as the right to live where they like, rights to work, to walk unaccompanied, to choose their own associates and to go about their daily lives without interference. These freedoms and rights have all been challenged by the "clean-up" campaign.[24]

Within this discussion of the rights of women is a protest of the control, management, and discipline of the female body.

In the press, black Zimbabwean Women's Action Group members were also demanding socialist feminism and trying to understand the moment as one of a transition to socialism. Their sentiments were echoed in the biting criticism lodged by Tsitsi Dangarembga and Juliet Baah in an article written for a popular political magazine that presages the arch-feminism of Dangarembga's novel *Nervous Conditions*:[25]

> The problem is: women are oppressed in ways that do not seem to be economic, so this oppression will be the last to be destroyed. But if it combines with the new socialist jargon it can lead to worse oppression.

For example, since socialisation of the means of production is a basic aim of scientific socialism, socialist men in the transitional stages, who still regard women as mean-objects, will happily subscribe to the notion of socialisation of women—joyfully and lustily throwing to the capitalist any shreds of decency and self-discipline they might have had in this respect. So we see a married man, enjoying an evening out with his "sugar mummy," who claims that this is an aspect of traditional socialism that was stifled by the present capitalist system.[26]

The solution Dangarembga and Baah propose: revolutionary consciousness and solidarity among women, with women recognizing that they are as good as, as intelligent as, and as useful as men in the home and throughout society. The authors tell men that if they value women in society, appreciate their contributions, and are willing to join forces with them, then "We promise you, you will not regret it."[27] According to Dangarembga and Baah, the economic and political changes of socialism are necessary to women's liberation, but dignity and respect for women cannot be accomplished without focusing energies directly on changing social and cultural evaluations of women and ideas associated with what it means to be male or female. In the late 1990s, discourses on socialism are absent as Zimbabwe is embroiled in World Bank and International Monetary Fund–sponsored economic structural adjustment programs. In cutting social supports and health benefits, decreasing public financing for education, and retrenching employment, these programs too show powerful effects on women's bodies.

African women in Zimbabwe are concerned with the way in which their bodies are subject to the discipline of society and with what this discipline means to their own subjectivity. In my future research in Zimbabwe, I intend to investigate how Zimbabwean women's notion of themselves as women (the particular strengths and vulnerabilities of female bodies that they perceive and their desire to attract men and to attach themselves to men) influences their health and welfare as participants in Zimbabwean civil society. This research is especially crucial in Zimbabwe now, given its status as one of the countries in the world hardest hit by the AIDS epidemic, and in the light of or shadow of the virulent antifeminism and homophobia in the country.[28] What a long route I have taken to get to this position, with many lessons taught to me, intentionally and unintentionally, by African women. Beginning with the sense that my body could not be properly disciplined as a child, moving to discipline exacted through competing and contradictory discourses, to lessons learned from African women and from women-loving women, I regained knowledge of myself, surrendered to the interplay between the personal and the political, and now I find myself returning to Africa to understand the discipline of the black female body in Zimbabwe in the era of AIDS and political and economic constriction. I have come full circle to a politic of black feminist anthropology.

NOTES

1. My notion of discourse, presented in greater detail in Carolyn M. Shaw, *Colonial Inscriptions: Race, Sex, and Class in Kenya* (Minneapolis: University of Minnesota Press, 1995), is particularly hybrid, drawn from Michel Foucault, *Discipline and Punishment: The Birth of the Prison*, trans. Alan Sheridan (New York: Random House, 1979); idem, *The History of Sexuality*, vol. 1: *An Introduction* (New York: Random House, 1980); and idem, *Power/Knowledge: Selected Interviews and Other Writings*, ed. Colin Gordon (New York: Pantheon, 1980); Hayden White's interpretation of Foucault, "Michel Foucault," in *Structuralism and Since: From Lévi-Strauss to Derrida*, ed. John Sturrock (Oxford and New York: Oxford University Press, 1979); and an amalgam of social anthropology, including the political anthropology of Marc Swartz, Victor Turner, and Arthur Tuden, *Political Anthropology* (Chicago: Aldine Publishing, 1966). I have used the term *discourse* to convey the ideas and social practices, including language, through which differences are created and meanings and power mobilized. I try not to use *discourse* as a substitute for what the term *culture* implies, but to use discourse to capture the sense that there may be more or less temporary conjunctions of ideas and practices by which individuals and groups come to understand who they are and what powers they are subject to (and more to the point, to act on these, even if they do not consciously understand them). Realization of oneself as a subject of one's own actions and as subject to other forces lays the ground for resistance as well as compliance.

    Part societies I think of as the space just beyond the "borderlands" (see Gloria Anzaldúa, *Borderlands/La Frontera: The New Mestiza* [San Francisco: Spinsters/Aunt Lute Books, 1987]), where the center does, if only momentarily, hold. The idea is that there may be some degree of coherence in fragmented social fields.

2. See especially chapter 1, "Introduction: Social Theory and Colonialism," and chapter 7, "Race, Class, Empire, and Sexuality," in Shaw, *Colonial Inscriptions*.

3. Michelle Rosaldo, "The Uses and Abuses of Anthropology: Reflections on Feminism and Cross-Cultural Understanding," *Signs* 5, 3 (1980): 289–317; and Eleanor Leacock, *Myths of Male Dominance: Collected Articles on Women Cross-Culturally* (New York: Monthly Review Press, 1981).

4. My use of the term *discipline* follows on Foucault's discussion of biopower, identifying disciplinary discourses that shape minds and bodies (see Foucault, *History of Sexuality* and *Power/Knowledge*). In delineating disciplinary power, Foucault emphasizes power that is more dependent on bodies and what they do than on the wealth and commodities.

5. Although I disagree with Collier and Yanagisako's argument against the inclusion of biology as a prediscursive given in the construction of gender, I find that, on the whole, they mount a convincing argument for the social construction of gender. See Jane Collier and Sylvia Yanagisako, eds., *Gender and Kinship: Essays toward a Unified Analysis* (Stanford: Stanford University Press, 1987).

6. See Bettina Aptheker, *Woman's Legacy: Essays on Race, Sex, and Class in American History* (Amherst: University of Massachusetts Press, 1982); Angela Davis, *Women, Race, and*

Class (New York: Vintage, 1981); idem, *Women, Culture, Politics* (New York: Random House, 1989); and Donna Haraway, *Primate Visions: Gender, Race, and Nature in the World of Modern Science* (New York: Routledge, 1989).

7. See Zora Neale Hurston, *Their Eyes Were Watching God* (1937; reprint, New York: HarperCollins, 1990). Soon after Hurston's protagonist Janey discovers her own blossoming sexuality, she is married and transfers her labor to her husband. In an extended metaphor, Hurston likens black women to beasts of burden, mistreated and discarded when no longer of service—the black woman is the mule of the world (p. 29). Janey's quest for love and tenderness ends with her destroying her one true love and returning home to live, independently and expectantly, on her own.

8. See Foucault, *History of Sexuality*, for a study of how discourses in medicine, religion, education, psychiatry, and population management contributed to the production of "normal" forms of sexuality and at the same time delineated and produced those patterns of sexuality that lie beyond the boundary of the normal.

9. Harryette Mullen, "Gender and the Subjugated Body: Readings of Race, Subjectivity, and Differences in the Construction of Slave Narratives," Ph.D. dissertation, University of California, Santa Cruz, 1990; and idem, "'Indelicate Subjects': African-American Women's Subjugated Subjectivities," Feminist Focused Research Activity Conference, University of California, Santa Cruz, 1991.

10. Ruth Yeazell, "Podsnappery, Sexuality, and the English Novel," *Critical Inquiry* 9 (1982): 343.

11. For further discussion of the treatment of Mau Mau in newsmagazines in the United States, see chapter 6, "Mau Mau Discourses," in Shaw, *Colonial Inscriptions*.

12. See especially chapter 2, "The Production of Women: Kikuyu and Gender Politics," in Shaw, *Colonial Inscriptions*.

13. Historians indicate that the Kikuyu age grade system was important in territorial expansion and the acquisition of land. Young initiated men, warriors, working for elders could become tenant farmers on the land they helped clear. During the colonial period, the number of young men who were landless increased as colonial authorities limited movement and their access to land. The internal tension between young and old and landed and landless played a part in the Mau Mau uprisings. See Godfrey Muriuki, *A History of the Kikuyu, 1500–1900* (Nairobi, London, and New York: Oxford University Press, 1974); and Gavin Kitching, *Class and Economic Change in Kenya: The Making of an African Petite-Bourgeoisie* (New Haven and London: Yale University Press, 1980).

14. The female initiation ceremony traditionally included clitoridectomy. When I was in the field in 1971–1972, genital cutting was still being practiced although the large-scale celebrations, concurrent ceremonies for boys, and associated education by older women had all but died away. The overwhelming majority of women I interviewed in one village in Murang'a District had had clitoridectomies and wanted their daughters to undergo genital cutting. Since that time, the government of Kenya and some women's groups have made efforts to end female genital cutting. Today women are more divided about the practice, with some holding on to the idea that only with it will their daughters make good marriages and will their well-being be ensured. I discuss this in greater detail in chapter 3, "Kikuyu Women and Sexuality," in Shaw, *Colonial Inscriptions*.

15. From the late 1950s through the 1960s, the work of Africanist anthropologists of the Manchester School, those at or influenced by research from the University of Manchester in Great Britain, was sometimes referred to as processual anthropology or processual analysis. This approach sought to elucidate the effects of the involvement of African populations in wider political and economic networks, to reveal the variability and openness within African communities, and to assess structural and incidental change over time. This is the approach that I was schooled in before I began my dissertation fieldwork in Kenya. For studies of the involvement of African populations in wider political and economic networks, see Max Gluckman, *The Judicial Process among the Barotse of Northern Rhodesia* (1940; reprint, Manchester, England: Rhodes-Livingstone Institute, University of Manchester Press, 1958); A. L. Epstein, *Politics in an Urban African Community* (Manchester, England: Rhodes-Livingstone Institute, University of Manchester Press, 1958); idem, *Urbanization and Kinship: The Domestic Domain on the Copperbelt of Zambia, 1950–1956* (London and New York: Academic Press, 1981); and Marc Swartz, "Situational

Determinants in Kinship Terminology," *Southwestern Journal of Anthropology* 16, 4 (1960): 393–397. For studies that show variability and openness within African communities, see Swartz et al., *Political Anthropology;* Bruce Kapferer, ed., *Transaction and Meaning: Directions in the Anthropology of Exchange and Symbolic Behavior* (Philadelphia: Institute for the Study of Human Issues, 1976); and Victor Turner, *Schism and Continuity in an African Society: A Study of Ndembu Village Life* (Manchester, England: Rhodes-Livingstone Institute, University of Manchester, 1957). For studies that deal with structural and incidental change over time, see especially Phillip Mayer, *Townsmen or Tribesmen: Conservatism and the Process of Urbanization in a South African City* (Captetown: Institute for Social and Economic Research, Rhodes University, Oxford University Press, 1961); and Victor Turner, *Ritual Process: Structure and Anti-Structure* (Chicago: Aldine Press, 1969).

16. Rudo Gaidzanwa, *Images of Women in Zimbabwean Literature* (Harare, Zimbabwe: College Press, 1985).

17. I profited from conversations in a stimulating feminist environment in Santa Cruz. While an independent scholar living in Santa Cruz, California, bell hooks wrote *Ain't I a Woman: Black Women and Feminism* (Boston: South End Press, 1981).

18. This use of "subjugated knowledge" derives from Foucault, "Two Lectures," in *Power/Knowledge,* but also compare it with Donna Haraway, *Simians, Cyborgs, and Women: The Reinvention of Nature* (New York: Routledge, 1991), in her "argument for situated and embodied knowledges and against various forms of unlocatable and so irresponsible knowledge claims. Irresponsible means unable to be called into account. There is a premium on establishing the capacity to see from the peripheries and the depths. But here lies a serious danger of romanticizing and/or appropriating the vision of the less powerful while claiming to see from their positions. To see from below is neither easily learned nor unproblematic, even if 'we' naturally inhabit the great underground terrain of subjugated knowledges" (p. 191).

19. See Alison Jaggar, *Feminist Politics and Human Nature* (Totowa, N.J.: Roman and Allenhead, 1983), for a discussion of forms of feminism. According to Jaggar, socialist feminists infuse radical feminism, the recognition of women as an oppressed class, with aspects of Marxist analysis, foregrounding the problems of capitalist patriarchy with its corollaries of racism and imperialism. The goal of socialist feminism is to eliminate the sexual division of labor in every realm and to transform the determinative social relations.

20. Gwendolyn Mikell, ed., *African Feminism: The Politics of Survival in Sub-Saharan Africa* (Philadelphia: University of Pennsylvania Press, 1997), 5.

21. Ibid., 4. Suffice it to say that despite this too brief characterization, Mikell also recognizes several versions of "Western feminisms."

22. Achille Mbembe, "Provisional Notes on the Postcolony," *Africa* 62, 1 (1992): 20.

23. Ibid., 24.

24. This excerpt is taken from an article by Women's Action Group founding members Rudo Gaidzanwa and Petronella Marambe, "Operation Clean-Up," *Connexions: An International Women's Quarterly* 12 (1984): 18.

25. Tsitsi Dangarembga, *Nervous Conditions* (Seattle: Seal Press, 1988).

26. Tsitsi Dangarembwa and Juliet Baah, "Seizing Power," *Social Change and Development* 1, 9 (1984): 23.

27. Ibid., 22.

28. See Margrete Aarmo, "How Homosexuality Became 'UnAfrican': The Case of Zimbabwe," in *Female Desires: Transgender Practices across Cultures,* ed. Evelyn Blackwood and Saskia E. Wieringa (New York: Columbia University Press, 1999), 255–280, for an overview of the current situation. In the wake of an AIDS epidemic in which one in four adults of reproductive age is estimated to be HIV positive, religious fundamentalism and nationalism have combined to create a hostile environment for feminists, gays, and lesbians.

KARLA SLOCUM

5

NEGOTIATING IDENTITY AND BLACK FEMINIST POLITICS IN CARIBBEAN RESEARCH

BEGINNINGS IN NATIVE ANTHROPOLOGY

Native anthropology represents an approach to and perspective on anthropological inquiries in which questions of self-identity, politics, and research methods are central. Anthropologists of color and from the Third World embraced the concept beginning in the 1970s, arguing that researchers "native" to or "inside" a particular region or community had valuable but often neglected insights to lend to our understandings of how people live, think, and act. In doing so, they questioned anthropology's reliance on European-derived models for interpreting non-European people's lives. They also challenged the common assertion that for the sake of objectivity, researchers should be personally distant from those they study.[1] Proponents of native anthropology, then, sought to render the discipline more inclusive by incorporating typically unheard anthropological voices and perspectives. Their goal also was to reconfigure notions of "appropriate" researcher–informant relations. Despite what some critics and revisionists of native anthropology have charged,[2] the point of this reconfiguration was not to claim that one group of anthropologists could always understand a community better than another or that so-called native anthropologists had a particular corner on knowledge about the community with which they identified.[3] Indeed, most anthropologists and other researchers sympathetic to the idea of a native anthropology have admitted that sometimes they found themselves partially "outside" of a research community. Some also mentioned that they have had to gain acceptance for research plans through members of a community with whom they felt they shared racial identity, gender identity, nationality, and/or residence.[4]

In recent years, there has been a slight resurgence of interest in native anthropology. Critiquing and rethinking the field, authors have looked more deeply at what it means to be "native" or "inside," asking especially if one can be and when.[5] Kirin Narayan's article "How Native Is 'Native' Anthropology" represents one of the latest explorations of the concept from a postmodern position.[6] Narayan rejects native anthropology because she believes that it ignores the social locations from which we can know a society (whether we claim it as our own or not). Thus, for her, the concept operates on essentialist assumptions about identity and authenticity. To explode the native category, she uses her own status as an Indian national with a diverse family and residential background to argue that she could never be a native researcher in India.

> The daughter of a German father and American mother, [my mother] had just married my Indian father. Yet these terms— *German, American, Indian*—are broad labels deriving from modern nation-states. Should I instead say that my mother, the daughter of a Bavarian father and a WASP mother who lived in Taos, New Mexico, became involved with her fellow student at the University of Colorado: my Indian-from-India father? Yet, for

anyone familiar with India shouldn't I add that my father's father was from the Kutch desert region, his mother from the dense Kathiaware forests, and that while he might loosely be called "Gujarati" his background was further complicated by growing up in the state of Maharashtra? . . . I invoke these threads of a culturally tangled identity to demonstrate that a person may have many strands of identification available, strands that may be tugged into the open or stuffed out of sight.[7]

Narayan goes on to claim that perhaps a non–Indian national who had spent a few years living in the country would be more native than herself or would perhaps be able to grasp dimensions of local life to a far greater extent than herself. She asserts that our abilities to be distant at one moment and close at another with people we study vary with context. Achieved closeness through long-term interaction is more valid and may provide greater insights than closeness conferred by birth.

Centering her contentions within a contemporary anthropological and postmodern discourse about the shifting and multiplex nature of identities, Narayan is correct to deconstruct reified categories such as "native" and "insider," and to call for a more complex reading of how identity and social position shape our interactions. But I believe that the way she maps her identity to all of its infinite pieces leads her into a few potential problems. First, because she means to suggest that identity is constructed and multifaceted, she spends less time discussing why, for both professional and personal reasons, we may choose to render particular aspects of our identities significant in certain contexts. She refers to the way a researcher's personal position and allegiances may shape the research, but she does not give much thought to why and how that personal stance or allegiance may play out:

We are all incipiently bi- (or multi-) cultural in that we belong to worlds both personal and professional, whether in the field or at home. While people with Third World allegiances, minorities or women may experience the tensions of this dual identity the most strongly, it is a condition of everyone even of that conglomerate category termed "white men." Whether we are disempowered or empowered by prevailing power relations, we must all take responsibility for how our personal locations feed not just into our fieldwork interactions but also into our scholarly texts.[8]

This brings me to my second point. Narayan rightfully refers to a sense of professional responsibility that exists for all of us, but she ignores how a researcher's politicized identity may engender a sense of responsibility that extends beyond the professional realm. She sidesteps the possibility that many of us link ourselves to a particular community because we attach specific goals and actions to who we are, how we view ourselves, and how we are seen by others from that community. Put more succinctly, as researchers we may assume specific roles and responsibilities precisely because identity traits such as gender, race, and nationality—however socially constructed—have real implications for how we and the people we study can and do live our lives.[9] For this reason, we may purposefully "tug into the open" particular strands of our identity to make a point. The politics of research can be based on this interplay of how we view ourselves, how we position ourselves in terms of our socially constructed identities, as well as how others (in a community we have defined as "ours") receive and perceive us.

I have chosen then to reclaim the value of native anthropology's political dimension by discussing the role that my own identity politics played in shaping my master's research project. How I thought about my Black female identity when conducting a project about Black Caribbean women influenced the conception and design of that work. It did so especially in terms of my effort to create less hierarchical informant–researcher interactions between the women participating in my project and myself. Thus, I argue that the way I channeled my identity politics into the research design to create more even relations between myself and other Black women in the project is a Black feminist anthropological concern. At the same time, I reveal some of the field research awakenings that led me to appreciate the nuances in differences between myself and the Caribbean women I studied, in particular the unavoidable separation between us as North American researcher and West Indian informant. Ultimately, these awakenings led me to concur with Narayan that we must be cognizant of the extent to which the fluid and constructed nature of our identities can connect us to people in the field. However, in contrast to Narayan, I argue that developing a research strategy because of those identities is also possible and important, particularly to a project centered in Black feminist politics.

FEMINIST INSIDERS AND BLACK FEMINIST POLITICS

In the 1970s and 1980s, a feminist literature developed that, like the native anthropology material, interrogated the intersection of politics, (gender) identity, and research methodology. It also sought to carve out a wider space for the often-neglected female voice in the social sciences and to acknowledge the greater ease that women researchers might have in understanding women's experiences in society. Taking the native anthropologist stance further, feminists in this camp argued that taking a feminist research stance should mean attempting to avoid hierarchies between oneself and one's female informants, while seeking to address gender inequalities in general. One means to achieve this, they said, is to openly reveal (sometimes cultivate) one's tacit connection to the women participants in our studies.[10] Admitting and taking into account one's identity background and beliefs about the research topic could also help to decenter researcher privilege and work toward larger feminist goals.[11] Articulating a feminist standpoint theory, Sandra Harding stated:

> The best feminist analysis . . . insists that the inquirer her/himself be placed in the same critical plane as the overt subject matter, thereby recovering the entire research process for scrutiny. . . . We are often explicitly told by the researcher what her/his gender, race, class, culture is, and sometimes how she/he suspects this shaped the research project. . . . Thus, the researcher appears to us not as an invisible, anonymous voice of authority, but as a real, historical individual with concrete, specific desires and interests.[12]

Underlying these arguments is a preference for expressing and engaging a sense of responsibility to and unity with informants and potentially to their causes.[13] Also at the heart of these arguments are feminist beliefs that a woman's gendered position provides crucial insights.

Yet, feminists in the latter part of the 1980s and into the 1990s debated what a woman researcher can know (about the women she studies). In a discussion of "situated knowledge," Donna Haraway argued that women occupy various identity spaces that are related not only to gender but also to race, class, age, and nationality.[14] Multiple identity positions render it impossible for women researchers to hold complete knowledge of the world of female informants; the two groups would differ from one another at least by professional status. "What then is our role?" and "What can we aim to achieve?" were some of the questions academic feminists asked. The response was an ensuing discussion about the intersection of identity and research possibilities. It is interesting how these discussions differed from ones about native anthropology. Part of the feminist concern was linked to questions about how we can best wed our feminist stance with "appropriate" research strategies; the concern was never to wonder whether one can be different from other women and feminist at the same time. Yet recent critics of native anthropology—not seeing the political content to the concept—have not asked what the difficulties of a "true" native anthropology mean for (ethical or responsible) research practices. Instead, they have been consumed with questioning whether it is possible to be native at all.

Black feminists perhaps have been involved with all of these questions. Part of Black feminist writings includes discussion about feminism and research pedagogy, taking into account the role that gender and race identities play within informant–researcher relations. For instance, many Black feminist researchers seek to address or help undo the oppression that Black women experience as an outgrowth of their social identities.[15] Patricia Hill Collins is one of the best known social scientists to articulate a Black feminist position. She applies feminist standpoint theories to argue not only that all Black women have some shared experiences of race and gender oppression but also to contend that Black academics have a particular role to play in explicating and ameliorating these oppressions. For her, there is a critical connection between Black feminist (academic) thought and action, and there is a specific role for Black feminist "intellectuals" in the transformation of Black women's condition:

> Black women intellectuals are central to Black feminist thought
> for several reasons. First, our experiences as African-American
> women provide us with a unique standpoint on black womanhood

unavailable to other groups. . . . Second, black women intellectuals provide unique leadership for black women's empowerment
and resistance. . . . Third, black women intellectuals are central
in the production of black feminist thought because we alone can
create the group autonomy that must precede effective coalitions
with other groups. [16]

In this passage, Collins underscores a connection between a Black
feminist scholarly consciousness (about Black women's experiences)
and the call to act on it.[17] It is this call that signals a political dimension to academic work performed by Black feminists and directed toward changing and/or working with(in) Black women's
causes.

Black women anthropologists engaging in ethnography and
other forms of research about Blacks and/or women have articulated aspects of this thought as well as aspects of the thoughts expressed by native anthropologists and feminists. They have done
so most notably by expressing personal and/or political convictions
about the topics of their research. Many, often referring to their
involvement in and sensitization to civil rights issues in the United
States, write about how race consciousness motivated their research
on issues of race inequality.[18] These and others speak honestly
about their desires to channel that work into transformative action
or to correct widely held stereotypes about Black women in particular. Thus, we have witnessed Black women anthropologists attempting to marry their political and personal allegiances to groups
that are partially defined by race and/or gender with the approaches
and outcomes of their work. Our best intentions notwithstanding,
some of us have had to think through how we are different from
the Black men and Black women we study and how these differences intersect with our professional goals, leading us to a negotiation of expectations. It is this tricky negotiation that I explore
further in this chapter.

TRAVELS IN RACE, GENDER, NATIONAL IDENTITY, AND PRACTICE

One point in my life when I found myself reflecting deeply on the
meaning and politics of my identity as a Black woman occurred
when I was traveling in the Caribbean on a work assignment. In

1986, I worked for an international agency as group leader to twelve U.S. high school students who would participate in community development projects in Grenada. The goals of the project were twofold: to assist a Grenadian organization in their youth skills projects, and to provide U.S. students with a cross-cultural exchange experience. The students in my group tutored local youth in academic areas and worked alongside them in various vocational training projects. This focus on youth skills and academic performance reflected the agency's link to former Grenadian leader Maurice Bishop's socialist New Jewel Movement, in particular its commitment to educational reform.[19]

Grenada is probably best known to inhabitants of the United States as the island country in which we carried out a military invasion in 1983. The official reason for that invasion was to "rescue" U.S. students enrolled there in medical school who may have been caught in some of the country's political upheavals. However, the country's socialist path was certainly unsettling to U.S. political interests in the region and likely helped spur the sudden military takeover. Three years after the invasion—at the time of our group's stay—the legacy of the U.S. presence was evident in many ways. We saw graffiti thanking the United States for its "intervention" and heard tales of the days when the U.S. military arrived. At times, the stories suggested a bias in favor of the United States, although this sentiment certainly was not universal.

Like most Caribbean territories, Grenada has a population that consists of a majority who can claim African descent, a small East Indian minority, and an even smaller White contingent. The White presence is publicly invisible but, as in the rest of the region, has left the imprint of its domination through various postcolonial social configurations such as a popular valuing of things European and, more recently, things American. But this trend is not universal. Our group resided in a Grenadian town in which there was open hostility toward Whites, especially Americans.[20] This was significant because all but one student (an Asian American) and myself were White. It was not long before most of the group had had several unsettling encounters. Community members gave them hard stares, uttered racial epithets, and made threatening gestures toward them. On one memorable occasion, this anti–United States/White hostility was expressed by several Grenadians in a truck, who vigorously waved machetes and shouted racial epithets as they passed the students on the road. For the students, this moment was particularly jolting and shaped many of our future discussions of cross-cultural encounters and expectations about foreign travel as (White) Americans. After all these experiences, the students modified their behavior in an attempt to appear less like "typical" Americans, and as they began to work in the community, the relations between the townsfolk and themselves were not as tense.

My own initial experience, however, was quite different from that of the rest of the group. When alone, and even sometimes when with the students, I did not receive the same critical comments about being American, or about being White. When walking in other Grenadian towns, I was often mistaken for a local or a resident of another Caribbean island—that is, until I spoke and revealed my American accent. And when I walked around the town in which we lived, people were intrigued by me as a foreign Black person, wondering how I could look like them and be American at the same time (as if all Americans are White). I found Grenadians to be immediately accepting of me and curious because of this common look, rather than showing hostility toward me as an American.

Thus, the status that the students experienced versus the status that I experienced in the United States, both of which were partially circumscribed by race, were inverted in this momentary space. The Grenadian setting provided a kind of paradox to the typical daily existence to which we were accustomed. As White, wealthy Americans, the students had been accustomed to roaming relatively uninhibited in the world; their race, class, and nationality afforded them that mobility. In Grenada, however, they did not hold the privilege with which they were most familiar; they learned that wealth and Whiteness did not grant them full access wherever they chose to live. In my case, I maneuvered with greater ease and in a less obtrusive way than I did in many U.S. settings. Paradoxically, I seemed to have access to more venues than usual.

The notion of my racial identity connecting me to Caribbean Blacks came up for me again in another Caribbean travel moment. A few years after my Grenada experience, and in part because of my Grenada experience, I went to St. Vincent (an island just north of Grenada) to embark on field research for my master's thesis. As a master's student, I intended to study Vincentian women who transported and sold produce in other parts of the Caribbean. Market women's activities have been a focus of anthropological studies of the Caribbean. Most studies of market trade have emphasized the economic "rationality" of women's noncapitalist practices or the role the women played in the small-scale agricultural production and distribution system.[21] I believed that although this emphasis acknowledged the predominance of women in the field, it had glossed over the implications of women's participation in such work; I also noted that it had almost completely ignored the question of race. Thus, I sought to engage the research further by looking into the meaning of trading for Black women's lives. I wondered: What did it mean for women to participate in this activity? How did women inter-island traders, who engaged in transnational work practices and who often managed households on their own, negotiate their domestic and trading responsibilities?

The questions I developed grew primarily out of my training in development anthropology, a field in which part of my studies considered transitions to capitalism in noncapitalist or precapitalist economies of the Third World. I also pursued the subfield of women and development, and was especially interested in shifts in the sexual division of labor and in women's work loads—shifts that resulted from the separation of reproductive and productive activities under the formation of state societies and capitalism. My Vincentian study, therefore, was couched within a 1980s social science feminist trend, especially with a "women and development" focus, to investigate the exploitation of women's labor under capitalism.[22] This research, with its Marxist and development orientation, did not view race as central a variable as class and gender. Yet, race was at the forefront of my personal motivations for pursuing the topic. I was sensitized to the central and historical place of African-descended women in Caribbean market systems and was motivated by an understanding of this history.

In addition to following a feminist Marxist approach, I was persuaded by the literature on feminism and research methodologies.[23] So I began my project with the assumption that adopting a feminist research pedagogy would help link me to Vincentian women's work struggles—as I perceived them. Part of my appreciation for a feminist research approach stemmed from a course project I conducted concerning women victims of domestic violence.[24] In that project, I looked at the women's shelter experience as a form of empowerment for women who had been battered. I purposefully inserted my personal thoughts into the interviewing process to diminish my distance from the women interviewees and to avoid appearing as someone without a position on the women's experiences. Similarly, in the St. Vincent study, it was important that I equalize my relations with the women traders. Showing support for them was crucial to me not merely as a feminist but as a Black feminist studying Black women. Certainly, my personal experiences and race consciousness brought me to that place.[25] And as I said, my appreciation of the history of Black Caribbean women in informal trading activities, and in managing heavy domestic and extra-domestic work loads, also influenced the role that race would play in shaping my project as a political one.

Thus, I chose to place myself as participant observer, interviewer, and ethnographer of traders' work spheres to achieve my goal of uncovering Afro-Caribbean women's work struggles. As in my study of women victims of domestic violence, I held preconceived ideas about the topics I wanted to pursue and the approaches I wanted to take, but by applying feminist research strategies and methods, I also intended to allow the traders themselves to define their concerns and issues. I felt that such strategies, coupled with my own race-based political goals, would create a research methodology through which I could reveal my support for other Black women's social experiences. To me, this approach meant that I could experiment with less hierarchical encounters between us. Surprisingly, my notion of building solidarity between the women I studied and myself took unexpected twists and turns in the field.

UNDERSTANDING THE SOCIAL AND ECONOMIC CONTEXTS OF THE WORK OF WOMEN TRADERS

Located in the eastern Caribbean and comprising one of the Windward Islands, St. Vincent is a small country of 150 square miles and approximately 110,000 people. Like most former British West Indian colonies, the island has a legacy of plantation slavery and colonialism. These features produced an enduring European influence in a context in which African descendants have been in the majority in most of these island populations from the sixteenth century to the present. St. Vincent's economy is geared toward growing and exporting agricultural goods, particularly bananas,[26] although this focus has not prevented the development of domestic and regional trading. Throughout the latter part of the twentieth century, independent itinerant traders formed a vibrant part of the country's informal economy by purchasing produce in St. Vincent and trading it in different Caribbean markets.[27] In the late 1960s, the Caribbean Commonwealth's creation of free trade zones facilitated this activity, but in the mid-1970s, as free trade between islands diminished, several changes occurred.[28] Among these was a shift in the gender composition of inter-island traders so that by the early 1990s, more than 70 percent of Vincentian traders were women, although in earlier times men had been in the majority.[29] Although women had never been barred from inter-island trade, it seems likely that men's domination of this lucrative field had defined it as a male work sphere. But rather than inter-island trading dying out as men abandoned it, smaller-scale women traders entered in the 1980s. Monique Lagro and Donna Plotkin suggest that as the field reorganized to become a smaller-scale venture, more women took up trading partly because of the small capital outlay needed and also because of the previously established social networks among kin across the region upon which the women could draw.[30] Small numbers of men continued to trade intra-regionally in the 1980s, but those who did were concentrated in the activities that yielded higher returns, such as importing appliances and exporting livestock. Caught within a gendered work hierarchy, women, by contrast, worked in the areas that brought smaller returns and required more physical labor and time. Part of their motivation stemmed from the independence afforded by this task as well as the possibilities for expanding into greater and more lucrative trading activities. As part of their weekly routine, they purchased various crops from Vincentian producers and landowners, shipped the goods by boat to Barbados or Trinidad, and then flew to these overseas markets where they would sell their goods.

Aware of these features from my reading of the literature, I focused my research on material constraints and gender ideologies as obstacles to women traders' work, and I became interested in the ways women participated in social networks to overcome these obstacles. I argued that inadequate shipping and handling resources diminished traders' possibilities for profit making. Yet, I observed that women and men were impacted differently by these inadequate resources because virtually all of the male inter-island traders were financially better suited to withstand economic setbacks.[31] For example, many men operated fairly large businesses and channeled their goods to a wide array of markets in the Caribbean, and sometimes beyond, thus cutting their risk of being hit hard by shifts in a given market. By contrast, as a way to gain revenue, most women traders relied strictly on the closer and more accessible markets in Barbados and Trinidad. When these markets bottomed out (as they did at points in the 1980s and early 1990s), women lost money and usually gave up trading for a period of time.

My research in this area also showed that at an institutional level, gender ideologies worked against women. A good example was the composition of the Traffickers' Small Business Association (TSBA), an organization responsible for coordinating transportation of traders' goods and providing material resources. Although all traders drew on TSBA resources, not all were actively involved in making and influencing TSBA policies. Rather, an all-male contingency of large-scale traders dominated the board of directors and other formal positions within the organization. In 1990, only one woman sat on the board of directors, and none held a formal position in the TSBA. Meetings of the TSBA membership also were highly hierarchical and stratified along gender lines. Typically, the TSBA director informed traders of new policies and asked for their vote; the women members were completely silent and always voted in favor of whatever policy the director presented

In effect, although it was a traders' organization, the TSBA was not an agency *for* women traders. Alternately, most women relied on assistance from family and friends; they often paid relatives or friends living in Barbados or Trinidad to sell their products in overseas markets. Such networks were a key mechanism through which women managed their responsibilities as mothers and mates, and they enabled women to participate in this transnational activity.[32]

My concern with the traders' work constraints and their means of dealing with them stemmed from my anthropological interests in economics, gender, and development. I knew that women heading households in the region frequently worked amid a variety of economic constraints.[33] I also knew that social and informal networks were a common way that Black Caribbean women dealt with these circumstances.[34] Black women's tendencies to manage work roles inside and outside of the household by using informal exchange networks had historical ties to African slave women's experience in the Americas.[35] These historical and contemporary dynamics rendered the topic of my project a Black feminist concern precisely because they pointed to the legacy of slavery, gender ideologies, and labor exploitation among Black women. These academic, historical, and personal features led me to position myself as a Black female researcher who strove to offer support to Black Caribbean working women's struggles by documenting their working lives and exposing the problems they encountered. My goal was not to achieve solidarity by participating as a social activist or by using my work to lobby against women's problems. Rather, my intention was to support the women traders' cause by making their situation more widely known and by explicitly revealing my political and academic stance on the matter.

HONORARY WEST INDIAN, CHILD, AND STRANGER

In retrospect, I now realize that my thoughts and intentions at that time bordered on romanticizing the field experience and that, contrary to my goals, I risked minimizing important differences between myself (a North American academic) and the women I studied (working-class Caribbeans). In this dilemma I was not alone. In the last two decades, several researchers claiming a native or (partial) insider position based on race and/or gender have struggled to coordinate their pre-research politics with field realities.[36] Indeed, part of this contingency includes Black women anthropologists who have returned from the field and frankly discussed how they were unprepared for the different racial categorizations and gender ideologies in South America and the Caribbean. Local identity constructs challenged their preconceptions not merely about gender and race but also about who they were or could be vis-à-vis their informants. Many mention having to reconcile their preconceived assumptions about a link between themselves and the people they would study,[37] whereas others admit grappling with the ways they were locally constructed (unexpectedly) as racialized, gendered, and national researchers.[38]

This was the case with two Black women anthropologists working in Jamaica, Faye V. Harrison and A. Lynn Bolles. In different ways, both noted that people they encountered in the field were suspicious of their work and drew a clear distinction between the anthropologist as North American researcher and themselves as West Indian working-class people. Bolles states that in her study of working-class Jamaican women, she intended to practice ethical research and engage her sense of responsibility toward the "powerless people" she wanted to study. Yet her class, education, and national identity served as "barrier[s] to both friendship and research."[39]

Similarly, Harrison reveals that

> Oceanview folk perceived me to be almost anything other than my own self-conception, i.e., a Black social scientist with a strong identification with oppressed Black Jamaicans. While the majority of Oceanview people saw in me a middle-class "brown" woman, some presumed and insisted that the "American doctor doing research" was socially—if not genealogically—"white." . . . Interestingly, my gender may have assuaged some of the hostility and suspicion surrounding my role as researcher. On the one hand, I was an outsider asking a lot of questions; and I was an American asking questions during a time when the American presence was considered by many to be ominous. On the other hand, I was a seemingly innocent young woman, in many respects naïve about Jamaica.[40]

In my own case, as I embarked on various strategies to obtain data about the traders, my initial attempts were impeded by traders' perceptions of me. I tried to talk with women on shipping days while they were waiting to load goods onto the boats, yet at first they showed extreme disinterest in meeting with me. Most avoided me by not responding to my approaches or by blatantly telling me to talk to someone else. Eventually, as most anthropologists do, I broke through this barrier and later learned why people were hesitant to talk with me. When they first saw me asking questions at the docks, most had placed me not as a North American but as a Vincentian. Approaching them with questions caused the women traders to assume that I was a government representative sent to obtain information about traders' work. This meant that I was marked as someone to fear because I might charge them higher fees or monitor their compliance with shipping regulations.[41] In their eyes, I appeared to fit local categories of class, and probably color, that were different from the ones the traders (mostly rural, "lower-class" women) occupied. They also placed me into their categories of nationality, assuming I was Vincentian as well.[42] As in Grenada, it is likely that my outward appearance as a Black person led them to not see me as an American. Even as I became closer to some of the women over the months, they remained surprised that I could be Black and American. They sometimes went to great lengths to place me somehow as a Vincentian or West Indian, on occasion objecting when others (who did not know me) referred to me as White due to my complexion and/or social class.[43]

Throughout my journey in St. Vincent, I encountered moments of being close and distant to the traders. What guided these fluctuations were traders' perceptions of my identity and my own perceptions of and responses to their ideas. I saw myself like them and had expected that, similarly, they would see themselves like me, at least according to our race and gender commonalities. Instead, they placed me in local constructions of identity, sometimes in ways that made me "like them" and at other times in ways that made me "different." Initially, they saw me simultaneously as Vincentian because of my appearance (race) and as "above them" because of my status as a researcher. As time passed, the ways in which we were differentiated and familiar included gender as well.

I learned very quickly, for example, that we did not hold a similar consciousness about the racial dimension of gendered work. Whereas I expected to support their struggles as women working in a historically undervalued, male-led, and labor-intensive activity, they did not perceive their work obstacles in this way. To them the major obstacles were material constraints and divisiveness among traders. None of the women I encountered ever complained of gender inequality in the TSBA, nor did they speak of the low value attached to trading as a Black woman's task. Some even echoed the sentiments of the TSBA directors that it was inappropriate for women to be in the official leadership roles of the organization. Thus, we could not build a bond based on our conversations about women's work either in historical or contemporary contexts.

At the same time, my experience interacting with the traders was a very gendered one. Rather than seeing me as an adult working woman who could empathize with their lives or who could appreciate their work dilemmas, they connected to me as a surrogate daughter. As a young, single, childless woman in pursuit of education, I fit their ideal of what a daughter should be. Ironically, in many cases, I was only a few years younger than some of the traders themselves. But because I looked much younger, was in school, and was single and childless, they incorporated me into their family and working lives as one of their own female offspring. For example, all of the traders with whom I lived considered it more appropriate for me to be a companion to their daughters than to themselves. Whether I visited or lived in their homes, they expected me to socialize with their daughters rather than spend time talking about trading. As a household guest, I always slept in the rooms with their teenage daughters for "company," even in cases where a single room could have been available to me.

As with their daughters, traders told me how to style my hair and wear my clothes, and they corrected me when they felt I had performed these tasks improperly. I also participated in household chores, watched children, and prepared and served meals to their male partners. There was no moment more difficult for me than when, at a trader's request, I carried a prepared lunch to her partner at his work place. As I walked through the village carrying a basket of food to an all-male construction site, I received many comments of acceptance for this act, even though it was an uncomfortable role for me to play. But daughters, my study showed, often substituted for their mothers in various work tasks, and the traders clearly thought this was an appropriate role for me.

That I was expected to fill in for the traders by performing tasks almost seemed to be the women's way of resisting the true purpose of my stay. They acknowledged that I was there to study traders' lives, but simultaneously they displayed curiosity and discomfort about my inquisitiveness and note taking. This part of my life did not seem to fit the role they expected of me as a young female student. My independent female status also puzzled them, prompting questions—about my mother, why I was in St. Vincent without her, and why I did not still live at home with my parents in the United States. My response that I lived and traveled alone because of school won me nods of understanding and also generated simultaneous looks of disbelief at the level of my independence.[44]

Although as a "daughter," I was made familiar within the ways of St. Vincent, the traders also situated me as an outsider. One example was the surprise they expressed at what I did (e.g., my independence and note taking); another is the ease with which they told me what I could not do or handle because of my foreigner/ outsider status. Although local children were expected to find their way through villages, I, a stranger, was not presumed to have the same level of competency. The women frequently sent very young children to accompany me whenever I traveled through local communities, even though my months of residency and traveling alone in the areas demonstrated that I was quite capable of independent movement. In a similar vein, traders bought food for me that was not customary to their diet, or they would cook atypical meals. Not only were they attempting to show me local food or to honor my visit, but they were implying that local food was not suitable for me. As an American in their homes, I was in the elevated status of honorary guest, but my age, educational pursuit, and unfamiliarity with local life placed me under their protection.

The insider/outsider, daughter/student spaces I occupied were made most clear to me in my friendship with "Ellen." She was the first woman who had responded to my inquiries at the docks on my first day. Although Ellen was no longer a trader, I spent more time with her than with anyone else. From her I acquired a history of the earlier days of trading and knowledge of the multiple work spheres in which women traders operate. But as Ellen and I grew closer, I learned several valuable lessons about myself as researcher, Black woman, student, and friend.

From the start, unlike some of the traders, Ellen made frequent references to our class and nationality differences. Such references, embedded in her comments about my behavior in contrast to hers, not only revealed her expectation of our specific roles; they also indicated that she saw me as a stranger most times and as a child almost always. During my first visit to her house, she revealed her concern about our class distinctions when she profusely apologized to me for her living conditions. "You see my house? Me poor," she said, seeming to anticipate shock from me over her surroundings. My own behavior in her world seemed to surprise her because it contradicted her expectations of me: "Look!" she exclaimed to herself when I took up a seat on the ground next to her, "she's sitting down on the ground [rather than on the chair]!" Such surprise suggested that Ellen thought it beneath me, as a foreigner/American, to sit next to her on the bare ground.

What she permitted me to emulate was limited if she thought the behaviors too inappropriate—"No, you can't do it!" she scolded loudly when I tried to help her carry sacks of produce. The more I tried to participate in her activities, the more she seemed frustrated with my attempts to "be like her." As I sought to work alongside of Ellen, so as not to appear to be above her, she expressed her belief that it was inappropriate for me to work or eat like her. She frequently reprimanded me, as she would a child, insisting that I should not step outside of who I was supposed to be (foreigner/researcher/American) and reminding me that we were not the same. Only when I assumed the role of passive observer and listened to her stories or watched her work around the house was she more at ease.

By continuously foregrounding the status differences between us, Ellen and the other traders almost shattered my goals because they constantly reminded me that the most we could ever be were distant friends or perhaps close strangers. Ironically, only in my role as surrogate daughter did I learn the most about gender roles in the household and about mother–daughter relations. These social relations were critical to how traders managed the obstacles they confronted in their domestic trading and work. Because such obstacles were, after all, a major concern of my research, I ended up with the quintessential participant-observer experience. At the time, however, I did not realize the value of my experience or of the data I collected, unintentionally, because I had not expected to be involved or to support traders' working lives in this way. Thus, although I was frustrated by my daughter status, it became critical to my subsequent analysis and understanding of how Black Caribbean women negotiate personal and domestic obstacles to their work. More important to my political goals, I was able to contribute concretely by alleviating some of the domestic tasks that interfered with traders' busy schedules.

RESOLVING THE "POLITICAL NATIVE" IN ME

According to Brackette Williams, our informants "construct our value" through their own cultural translations of who we are and who we represent while among them.[45] For her, as we traverse the slippery terrain of being neither entirely "native" nor entirely "foreign," we experience a kind of shifting "betwixt and between" of who we are and who we can be as participant observers in diverse field settings. But for some of us who desire to claim insider status, the foreigner space is uncomfortable. It seems to go against everything we expect of ourselves as participant observers, especially if we attach a political purpose to that role. I felt discomfort in my daughter status because I feared that it would impede my political goals of solidarity with the traders. As a result, I resisted the local categories into which the traders placed me, not realizing that just like them, I too was trying to impose my own constructions of them, and my relation to them, based on my belief that we shared common bonds around race and gender. I learned a lot from the traders, who became my teachers, but the knowledge I acquired was not only about their trading work schedule or about social networks. Rather, they revealed to me the impossibility of dislodging the imbalance in the researcher–informant relationship. Most significantly, they taught me that in the field encounter, researcher and informant participate in a mutual construction of one another—constructions that shape the nuanced nature of the stranger–friend dynamic, and that ultimately determine under which conditions we can be close and under which we are distant.

But what does all of this mean for native and Black feminist anthropology? Today, it feels embarrassing to acknowledge the struggle I underwent to negotiate out of who I was and who I represented to the traders. I take comfort in the admissions of several other native anthropologists mentioned previously, who came before me, and I am convinced there are others yet to come. For these latter, I would admonish that for those of us who see ourselves as partial insiders, and who are concerned to accentuate and engage that partial part of our identities as anthropologists, we should be less concerned about whether and how we are outsiders. Attempting to downplay differences of class, education, or even gender does not allow us to circumvent the outsider part, if for no other reason than that our informants will not let us forget who we are.

Being simultaneously outsiders and partial insiders need not frustrate our political motivations and goals, even when we acknowledge difference and power between ourselves and those we study. Indeed, although my ideas about solidarity with Vincentian women traders stemmed from an idea of gender inequality, work, and race that did not correspond to their lived realities, my Black feminist anthropology politics remained. This was evident in the methods I chose, in the particular aspects of women's lives that I chose to document, and also in the critiques I made of the constraints under which Black Caribbean working women continue to operate.

Even while the women I studied rightfully deconstructed my idea of shared race and native possibilities, I channeled my work in a political direction that suited my professional and personal goals. Thus, an important lesson for me has been the recognition that we can reconcile our "native politics" with field realities. That is, we can interrogate the local categories of identity construction in the places where we do our research, but we need not see the categories as obstacles. Rather, as we analyze how we differ from those we study and consider the impact of such differences on our research goals, we can still identify a set of responsibilities to which we will adhere in our work and which we hold toward the people who participate in our research. If our purpose as engaged Black feminist anthropologists is a political one (e.g., to challenge power and oppression), we can draw on our knowledge both as insiders and outsiders. In this way, we can better connect the field experience with our politics.

NOTES

A portion of the research for this essay was funded by the Inter-American Foundation and the Special Projects Committee of the State University of New York, Binghamton; the writing was supported by the Carolina Minority Postdoctoral Fellowship at the University of North Carolina–Chapel Hill. I thank Irma McClaurin for her useful editorial remarks, and I am grateful to Karen Gibson and Kimberly Nettles for their insightful comments on earlier drafts.

1. Delmos Jones, "Towards a Native Anthropology," *Human Organization* 29 (1970): 251–259; John L. Gwaltney, "The Propriety of Fieldwork," *The Black Scholar* 11, 7 (1980): 32–39; idem, "On Going Home Again—Some Reflections of a Native Anthropologist," *Phylon* 37, 3 (1976): 236–242; Khalil Nakhleh, "On Being a Native Anthropologist," in *The Politics of Anthropology: From Colonialism and Sexism towards View from Below*, ed. Gerrit Huizer and Bruce Mannheim (The Hague and Paris: Mouton Publishers, 1979), 343–352.

2. See, for example, John L. Aguilar, "Insider Research: An Ethnography of a Debate," in *Anthropologists at Home in North America: Methods and Issues in the Study of One's Own Society*, ed. Donald A. Messerschmidt (Cambridge: Cambridge University Press, 1981), 15–26.

3. Faye V. Harrison, "Ethnography as Politics," in *Decolonizing Anthropology: Moving Further toward an Anthropology for Liberation*, 2nd ed., ed. Faye V. Harrison (1991; reprint, Arlington, Va.: Association of Black Anthropologists and American Anthropological Association, 1997), 88–110.

4. See Helán Page, "Dialogic Principles of Interactive Learning in the Ethnographic Relationship," *Journal of Anthropological Research* 44 (1988): 163–181; Patricia Zavella, "Feminist Insider Dilemmas: Constructing Ethnic Identity with Chicana Informants," *Frontiers: A Journal of Women Studies* 13, 3 (1993): 53–77; and John L. Gwaltney, *Drylongso: A Self-Portrait of Black America* (New York: Vintage Books, 1980), xii–xxx; Nakhleh, "On Being a Native Anthropologist."

5. E. L. Cerroni-Long, "Introduction: Insider or Native Anthropology?" in *Insider Anthropology*, ed. E. L. Cerroni-Long (Arlington, Va.: National Association for the Practice of Anthropology, 1995), 1–16; José Limon, "Representation, Ethnicity, and the Precursory Ethnography: Notes of a Native Anthropologist, in *Recapturing Anthropology*, ed. Richard Fox (Santa Fe: School of American Research Press, 1991, 115–136).

6. Kirin Narayan, "How Native Is 'Native' Anthropology," in *Situated Lives: Gender and Culture in Everyday Life*, ed. Louise Lamphere, Helena Ragone, and Patricia Zavella (New York and London: Routledge, 1997), 23–41.

7. Ibid., 26

8. Ibid,. 35.

9. The term *race* is often placed in quotation marks to denote its status as a socially constructed category. Because I believe that it has real-life implications, I do not mark it in this way.

10. See Liz Stanley and Sue Wise, *Breaking Out: Feminist Consciousness and Feminist Research* (London: Routledge, 1983); Ann Oakley, "Interviewing Women: A Contradiction in Terms," in *Doing Feminist Research*, ed. Helen Roberts (London: Routledge, 1990), 30–61; Joyce Ladner, "Introduction to Tomorrow's Tomorrow: The Black Woman," in *Feminism and Methodology*, ed. Sandra Harding (Bloomington: Indiana University Press, 1987), 74–83.

11. Sandra Harding, "Introduction: Is There a Feminist Method?" in *Feminism and Methodology*, 1–14.

12. Ibid., 9.

13. Diane L. Wolf, "Situating Feminist Dilemmas in Fieldwork," in *Feminist Dilemmas in Fieldwork*, ed. Diane L. Wolf (Boulder, Colo.: Westview Press, 1996), 1–55; Ladner, "Introduction to Tomorrow's Tomorrow."

14. Donna Haraway, "Situated Knowledges: The Science Question in Feminism and the Privilege of Partial Perspective," *Feminist Studies* 14, 3 (1988): 575–601.
15. Ladner, "Introduction to Tomorrow's Tomorrow"; Patricia Hill Collins, *Black Feminist Thought: Knowledge, Consciousness, and the Politics of Empowerment* (1990; reprint, New York and London: Routledge, Chapman and Hall, 1991).
16. Collins, *Black Feminist Thought*, 33–35.
17. In a discussion of three waves of Black women's activism in U.S. history, Ula Y. Taylor shows that nonacademic Black women (e.g., political activists and health care activists) also have developed a feminist and race consciousness that they channeled into action, addressing Black women's oppression. In this sense, she extends Collins's ideas to include a broader spectrum of Black women actors attempting to improve the condition of Black women. See Ula Y. Taylor, "Making Waves: The Theory and Practice of Black Feminism," *The Black Scholar* 28, 2 (1998): 18–27.
18. Harrison, "Ethnography as Politics"; Leith Mullings, *On Our Own Terms: Race, Class and Gender in the Lives of African American Women* (New York and London: Routledge, 1997).
19. Much of the Caribbean that was colonized by the British still follows a model of the British education system. Students who do not pass Common Entrance exams at the end of their primary school education have limited options for continuing in school. Many drop out in their adolescence.
20. Another group of students sponsored by the same U.S. agency worked in a town on the other side of the island, where they were received more favorably than the students in my group. According to the leaders of that group, the townspeople were glad to have a group of Americans living among them.
21. Victoria Durant-Gonzalez, "Higglering: Rural Women and the Internal Market System in Jamaica," in *Rural Development in the Caribbean*, ed. P. I. Gomes (New York: St. Martin's Press, 1985), 103–122; Sidney Mintz, "Men, Women and Trade," *Comparative Studies in Society and History* 13 (2): 247–269.
22. Lourdes Benería and Gita Sen, "Accumulation, Reproduction and Women's Role in Economic Development: Boserup Revisited," in *Women's Work: Development and the Division of Labor by Gender*, ed. Eleanor Leacock and Helen I. Safa (New York, Westport, and London: Bergin and Garvey Publishers, 1986), 141–157.
23. Harding, "Introduction: Is There a Feminist Method?"; Wolf, "Situating Feminist Dilemmas in Fieldwork"; Ladner, "Introduction to Tomorrow's Tomorrow"; and Haraway, "Situated Knowledges."
24. Karla Slocum, "Methodological Research on the Empowerment of Women," unpublished paper, May 1989.
25. Harrison, "Ethnography as Politics."
26. See Lawrence S. Grossman, "The Political Ecology of Banana Exports and Local Food Production in St. Vincent, Eastern Caribbean," *Annals of the Association of American Geographers* 83, 2 (1993): 347–368.
27. Monique Lagro, *Women Traders in Saint Vincent and the Grenadines*, Consultant Report (Port-of-Spain, Trinidad: United Nations Economic Commission for Latin America and the Caribbean [UNECLAC], 1988).
28. Andrew Axline, *Agricultural Policy and Collective Self-Reliance in the Caribbean* (Boulder and London: Westview Press, 1986).
29. Lagro, *Women Traders in Saint Vincent and the Grenadines*; Monique Lagro and Donna Plotkin, *The Agricultural Traders of St. Vincent and the Grenadines, Grenada, Dominica and St. Lucia*, Consultant Report (Port-of-Spain, Trinidad: UNECLAC, 1990).
30. Lagro, *Women Traders in Saint Vincent and the Grenadines*; Lagro and Plotkin, *Agricultural Traders of St. Vincent and the Grenadines, Grenada, Dominica and St. Lucia*.
31. Karla Slocum, "Managing Markets and Households: The Case of Women Inter-island Traders in St. Vincent," M.A. thesis, Binghamton University, 1991.
32. Ibid.
33. Joycelin Massiah, *Women as Heads of Households in the Caribbean: Family Structure and Feminine Status* (Paris: UNESCO); Dorian Powell, "Caribbean Women and Their Response to Familial Experiences," *Social and Economic Studies* 35, 2 (1986): 83–129; Nancie L. Solien Gonzalez, *Black Carib Household Structure: A Study in Migration and Modernization*

(Seattle: University of Washington Press, 1969); Helen I. Safa, *The Urban Poor of Puerto Rico: A Study in Development and Inequality* (New York: Holt, Rinehart and Winston, 1974).

34. Christine Barrow, "Finding the Support: A Study of Strategies for Survival," *Social and Economic Studies* 35, 2 (1986): 131–176; Judith Gussler, "Adaptive Strategies and Social Networks in St. Kitts," in *A World of Women: Anthropological Studies of Women in the Societies of the World,* ed. E. Bourguignon (New York: Praegar, 1981), 185–209.

35. Karen Olwig, "Women, 'Matrifocality,' and Systems of Exchange: An Ethnohistorical Study of the Afro-American Family in St. John, Danish West Indies," *Ethnohistory* 28, 1 (1981): 59–78; Marietta Morrissey, *Slave Women in the New World: Gender Stratification in the Caribbean* (Lawrence: University Press of Kansas, 1989).

36. Zavella, "Feminist Insider Dilemmas"; Harrison, "Ethnography as Politics"; A. Lynn Bolles, "Of Mules and Yankee Girls: Struggling with Stereotypes in the Field," *Anthropology and Humanism Quarterly* 10, 4 (1985): 114–119; Ingrid Banks, "Black Expectations: Hair, Transparency and Discomfort in the Research Field," paper presented at the annual meeting of the American Anthropological Association, 1998.

37. Angela Gilliam, "From Roxbury to Rio—and Back in a Hurry," in *African-American Reflections on Brazil's Racial Paradise*, ed. David Hellwig (Philadelphia: Temple University Press, 1992), 173–181; Bolles, "Of Mules and Yankee Girls"; Harrison, "Ethnography as Politics."

38. France Winddance Twine, *Racism in a Racial Democracy: The Maintenance of White Supremacy in Brazil* (New Brunswick, N.J.: Rutgers University Press, 1998), 9–11; Irma McClaurin, *Women of Belize: Gender and Change in Central America* (New Brunswick, N.J.: Rutgers University Press, 1996), 16–18.

39. Bolles, "Of Mules and Yankee Girls," 116.

40. Harrison, "Ethnography as Politics," 99–100.

41. Despite my dress and accent, which were not typically Vincentian, it is possible that the prevalence of emigration led people to assume either that I was a returning migrant originally from the island or that I was raised abroad but had Vincentian parents. Migration is a key feature throughout most of the Caribbean, and various economic conditions and government policies have rendered it a fixture in St. Vincent society. Those who have migrated and those who have not remain connected, materially and ideologically, through a variety of transnational practices. See Linda Basch, Nina Glick Schiller, and Christina Szanton Blanc, *Nations Unbound: Transnational Projects, Postcolonial Predicaments and Deterritorialized Nation-States* (Australia: Gordon and Breach, 1994).

42. I include color here because I have a fair complexion that, especially in the Caribbean context, can link a person to a higher social class.

43. Although no one in the United States has questioned my identity as a Black person, oftentimes in the British Caribbean people have commented on my relatively fair complexion. Some have wondered if I am biracial, or as one person put it, "if my people are Black."

44. Dorinne Kondo describes her field experiences as a Japanese American in Japan, where she negotiated a similar daughter status. The Japanese family she lived with assumed that because she was Japanese American, she would fit into their constructs of a young, single Japanese female. This led her to experience conflicts between her Japanese self and her American self. See Dorinne Kondo, "Dissolution and Reconstitution of Self: Implications for Anthropological Epistemology," *Cultural Anthropology* 1 (1986): 74–96.

45. Brackette Williams, "Skinfolk, Not Kinfolk: Comparative Reflections on the Identity of Participant-Observation in Two Field Situations," in *Feminist Dilemmas in Fieldwork*, 72–95.

6

ANGELA M. GILLIAM

A BLACK FEMINIST PERSPECTIVE ON THE SEXUAL COMMODIFICATION OF WOMEN IN THE NEW GLOBAL CULTURE

"Doesn't matter where you've been, just where you're bound." My paternal grandfather's words were used to silence my father or his sisters whenever they asked where he was from. That saying evokes more than my heritage; it represents a leitmotif of my life in its perpetual quest of permanent movement. I am at a crossroads in my intellectual pathway, and this work tells where I have been and where I am bound. In writing these tales, I summon an authority that goes beyond merely the academic—indeed, I seek a strength that is mythical and ancestral—to confront the sensitive and painful subjects that have produced Black women's historical marginalization in former colonial plantation systems. I ask several questions by juxtaposing specific conceptual strands: How does the historical eroticization of subordinated women relate to the contemporary commodification of women and children in the new forms of global culture? How do race and socioeconomic class, as cultural markers of male dominance, affect how and where women are positioned in hierarchical societies? I have come to realize that only when my own story is part of what I observe do my theoretical contributions get closer to the truth and enable me to speak for a more complete vision. It is where I am bound.

SPRINGTIME PILGRIMAGE IN PARIS, 1994: ON BEING A BLACK FEMINIST ANTHROPOLOGIST

In describing the road I took to Black feminist anthropology, I use vignettes to ground my journey. The parables meander, using a flexible approach to time and chronology to construct my intellectual pathway. This is the first chronicle.

One breezy March day in Paris, my sister anthropologist Leith Mullings and I set out on a mission. We had decided to confront the vaunted Musée de l'Homme in Paris, where Saartje "Sarah" Baartman's remains were presumably preserved and on view to the public. A strange silence engulfed us that day, as though our quest weighed down both of our spirits in shared mournful grief. Why did we feel so strongly about someone who lived two centuries ago?

Sarah Baartman was born in 1791 in what is now South Africa and died in France on January 1, 1816, at the age of twenty-five.[1] A Khoikhoi woman, she was merely the first of several indigenous women who were taken from the Cape region of South Africa to be exhibited like animals in Europe. But only Sarah Baartman's body is known to have been reduced to body parts for preservation.

As we entered the large imposing building that was the Musée de l'Homme, we asked the guard where we should go to see the Sarah Baartman remains. I don't remember what words we used in our limited French, because part of our mission was to look squarely at the jars holding her genitalia and brain.

The guard at the entrance to the museum was a young Black man.

"*Mais pourquois*? But why? Why would you want to see her body?"

"*Pardon, s'il vous plait*. Excuse us, please," Leith began. Neither one of us was sufficiently fluent in French for such a complicated discussion as the one we were preparing to attempt.

"*Vous ne comprenez pas*. You don't understand." I also tried hard to explain the purpose of our trip that day. "We are two Black American anthropologists, and our coming to see Sarah Baartman's remains is due to the connection we feel with her."

"Do you know what this exhibit is and do you know what it means to those of us who are from Africa and who live here? For years we have been trying to have such an embarrassing exhibit removed from the museum." The dark blue uniform seemed to get more crisp as the museum guard's determination increased.

"Yes, we know that after she died, her *corps délicat* (delicate parts) were cut from her body and preserved in brine for exhibit."

Leith and I were jointly trying to clarify our position. Above all, we wanted to distinguish ourselves from the prurience that had contributed to the exhibit's fame.

"She was subjected to *inhumanité et douleur* (inhumanity and pain)," Leith began.

"*Elle est notre ancestre africaine*. She is one of our African ancestors," I continued.

"You will have to write a letter to the director of the museum to get special permission, because they took that jar away and it is now hidden in the offices upstairs." The grimace on the face of the guard signaled his disdain. And that ended our mission—for the time being.

Leith and I later would share memories and questions about the enormous shadowy building, and seeing the plaster mold of Sarah Baartman's body, her skeleton, as well as the "scientific" commentaries written about the "Hottentot Venus." We also would contemplate what it all meant for us first as Black women, then as feminists, finally as anthropologists to embark on this journey. Or was it *finally* as feminists?

Was it patriarchy that made the museum guard embarrassed

for us as well as for Sarah Baartman? Why did it almost seem like a spiritual quest to go to the museum that day, as though it were our solemn duty to confront it? What kind of ideas of the times in which Sarah Baartman lived made it normal to dissect the body of a human being, make a plaster mold of it, remove the brains, and slice off the genitals for exhibit into the twentieth century? How did that pilgrimage affect my definition of Black feminist anthropology?

UNIVERSAL OR PARTICULAR: WHAT IS BLACK FEMINIST ANTHROPOLOGY?

In the early 1970s, I initially resisted the label "feminist"; it seemed so tainted by association with elite spokespersons. I also sometimes refer to myself as a "counter-anthropologist" because of the founding heritage of the field, engulfed by its connections to colonialism. But the scholarship I now do in the name of Black feminist anthropology frequently confronts the global economic crisis of those people who leave their home countries in search of work. For women who travel without patronage or cultural capital, the possibility of ending up without control over one's body is still as much of an ever-present danger as when Sarah Baartman tried to navigate a Europe to which she had forcibly been taken. Thousands of women *and* men all over the world are currently involved in a progressively harder quest for sustainable work. Internationally oriented women activist-scholars increasingly situate the racialization of the search for work within the new global economy.[2]

I have been inspired by the pioneering work of feminists in many countries whose intellectual activism is pressing the world to recognize the linkages between race and/or Third World identity and the new patterns of global migration linked to work.[3] Furthermore, I have taken this new intersection as a way to deepen our understanding of the rise in the international sex trade.[4] This has permitted me to establish continuity with the work about race, language, and power in Brazil that I began in 1970.[5] Today, without a doubt, I agree with those who argue that within a worldwide reinvestment in patriarchal capitalism, women and children are the most vulnerable to the social and economic transformation currently taking place in the world—a fact particularly relevant for women of color in industrial societies such as the United States.

But how did I get here? In a way, it starts out with an unusual blessing: the capacity to imitate, which I applied to the learning of foreign languages—especially Spanish and Portuguese. In a renowned chapter on language, Frantz Fanon reveals how immediately verifiable academic competence in European languages on the part of African-descended peoples can be of particular advantage when confronting established elite scholars.[6] This fact was uppermost in my mind as I realized that my ability to reproduce the Portuguese language at near-native Brazilian level was a significant factor in the social construction of my identity as a scholar within Brazil. This linguistic capacity meant being able to do my own language work in the field: I could read, write, and speak Portuguese, and do my own translations. Additionally, I would be considered "White" if I spoke English and refused to speak Portuguese properly, which would reinforce my identity as a foreigner. I was Black to the degree that I seemed (linguistically or phenotypically) Brazilian—yet even this varied from region to region.

The quandary of my place within Brazilian culture seemed to me to be captured succinctly by Guerreiro Ramos's classic study of the "pathology of the Brazilian White." In a trenchant critique of what he identified as the pseudoscience of the scholarship of northern Brazilian writers such as Arthur Ramos or Gilberto Freyre, Guerreiro Ramos took to task those darker "Whites" from the northern part of Brazil who used their research on Black people to separate themselves from that identity:

> Upon taking the Black as a subject, elements of the minority "White" sector become more white, approximating themselves to their esthetic archetype—which is the European. It is for this reason that the anthropological and sociological literature about the Black has found its cultivators principally among the intellectuals of the "Northern" or "Northeastern" states [regions that were formerly the center of the colonial plantation economy].[7]

As I gradually came to understand this dynamic, it propelled me toward a situation of purposefully adopting a "Brazilian" (Black) identity on the one hand, thereby rejecting "honorary White status," and on the other, deliberately using my facility with Portuguese to form my resistance to racist events that happened to me. I took Guerreiro Ramos's challenge one step further and posed the question to myself of whether studying Blacks in one country perforce "whitens" Blacks from another? An abiding concern of activism and praxis became this: if I did scholarship about Brazil, was I whitening myself? And what would I have to do to make sure that my research served the people who gave me information about their lives?

This awareness came about when I volunteered as a Portuguese-English interpreter/translator for Abdias do Nascimento during the late 1960s and early 1970s, when he was in exile in New York.[8] It is in this context that I found my first full exchange of ideas about Brazil's myth of racial democracy. At the 1977 Second World Festival of Black and African Arts and Cultures in Nigeria, Nascimento confronted several Brazilian scholars who persisted in perpetuating the myth of racial democracy. His subsequent critique of this encounter can only be construed as a formal challenge to the cadre of primarily White Brazilian social scientists who "represent" the Afro-Brazilian experience abroad.[9]

The most important question Nascimento's book raised was the unresolved contradiction throughout the Americas: Which came first, the Brazilian culture or the African influence? For Nascimento, the "Racial Democracy Narrative" sat heavily on the shoulders of the Black woman, whose social role was inextricably linked to both forced labor and sexual assault.[10]

It is ironic that it would be two male scholars who would contribute to my reaching toward the development of a Black feminist anthropological approach as I studied Brazilian culture. But it is the radio interview I did in 1983 with a Black feminist anthropologist from Brazil, the late Lélia Gonzalez, that brought it all home. At that time, she expressed the view that historically, Brazilian capitalism had perpetually imprisoned the Black woman into service work.[11] I maintain that today global capitalism similarly entraps many of the world's women. These circumstances mean that the work Black feminist anthropologists do is complicated by an implied imperative to develop intellectual work for multiple audiences. As a result, she (and such a person usually is a woman) is committed to produce work that enables people in her community to understand how and why they live in conditions continuously marked by poverty. Another goal of the Black feminist anthropologist is to unmask, critique, and work for the transformation of structural inequalities, no matter where they exist. But within this directive, place or who constitutes "her community" are not givens or fixed entities but constantly changing variables.

Black feminists also must wear an intellectual lens that contributes to the necessary reinvention of scholarship. For Black feminists across the globe, this means more and more a simultaneous construction that links racism and patriarchy, and analyzes how these two phenomena are historically part and parcel of capitalism. Such a linkage, I would argue, lends itself to the validation of "standpoint theory" in that it summons the possibility of recognizing the diverse, yet parallel conditions under which so many Black women live. It becomes the task of Black feminists to articulate such standpoints, because as Patricia Hill Collins reminds us, "An oppressed group's experiences may put its members in a position to see things differently, but their lack of control over the ideological apparatuses of society makes expressing a self-defined standpoint more difficult."[12]

For a number of reasons, standpoint theory recently has fallen out of favor. In this respect, Luiza Bairros also offers a cogent interpretation of standpoint theory, but one that reveals its limitations for understanding the complexity of Black women's lives: "Thus, a Black working class woman is not triply oppressed or more oppressed than a white woman in the same social class, but she experiences an oppression starting from a specific place, that affords a different standpoint about what it is to be a woman in a racist, sexist, and unequal society."[13]

Standpoint theory is a complex category of intellectual inquiry. Because women are subordinated, they all share the same optic or experiences. But for many Black feminists, such an analysis omits socioeconomic class and generally precludes a more global understanding of ensuing divisions. This generates a complicated tension between those who embrace a concept like "women's ways of knowing" and those who resist the notion that women are a class distinct from men. I align myself with Collins and reinforce Norma

Alarcón's critique of bourgeois feminism in her original 1990 essay.[14]

Because of the geographical diversity of their ethnographic experiences, Black feminist anthropologists recognize that oppression frequently crosses borders and conventional boundaries. Thus, they realize that domestic and international labor crises are often experienced by Black women in different ways. A broad analysis by necessity links the global economy to the international narrative about women.

In my estimation, the work that Black feminist anthropologists do is focused toward bridging a complex gap between male dominance in the community-wide struggle against racism and White female dominance in the battle against sexism. Thereza Santos adds another dimension to this question: So what of the Black woman who seeks to integrate and conjoin all three dynamics? For Santos, within the struggle among workers and on the Brazilian Left, addressing the specific problems of Black women is doubly complicated by the fact that it is primarily elite White males who frequently represent the workers' voices.[15]

It is my desire to bridge the three dynamics of race, class, and gender, to which Santos alludes, by describing the route I took first as activist, and later as feminist scholar, on my journey to develop an understanding of the current problems faced by working-class women today—in particular, those who live in Brazil. My trajectory toward this theoretical location has involved a gradual navigation into complicated borderlands where reciprocity and exchange in the "field" have forced me to be ever vigilant of potential honorifics that might limit my understanding of the real lives of people.

Learning foreign languages became a passport into situations with people whom I would not have met otherwise or whose lives would not have enriched mine. This linguistic cultural capital is something that I have diligently passed on to my daughter.[16] Through language fluency, although fraught with possibilities of the unpredictable and the unexpected, I (and my daughter, alone or together) have frequently slipped freely through the bars of the cultural cage framed by a U.S. national identity. In this respect, the road to Brazil was long and my interest in feminism not direct. As part of the foray, first I had to confront my own country, its past, and its historical construction of the Black woman.

BLACK FEMINIST THOUGHT: A REASON FOR BEING

> It will probably be asked, Why not retain and incorporate the blacks into the state and thus save the expence of supplying the importation of white settlers, the vacancies they will leave? Deep rooted prejudices entertained by the whites. . . . These . . . objections . . . are political . . . physical and moral. The first difference which strikes us is that of colour. Whether the black of the negro . . . proceeds from the colour of the blood, the colour of the bile, or from that of some other secretion, the difference is fixed in nature, and is as real as if its seat and cause were better known to us. . . . Is it not the foundation of a greater or less share of beauty in the two races? . . . Add to these, flowing hair [of whites], a more elegant symmetry of form, [blacks'] own judgment in favour of the whites, declared by their preference of them, as uniformly as is the preference of the Oranootan [sic] for the black women over those of his own species. . . . I advance it therefore . . . that the blacks . . . are inferior to the whites in the endowments both of body and mind. . . . Among the Romans emancipation required but one effort. The slave, when made free, might mix with, without staining, the blood of his master. But with us a second is necessary, unknown to history. When freed, he is to be removed beyond the reach of mixture.[17]

The above commentary, expressed with conviction by a founding father of the country of my birth, the United States, is where I began my intellectual pathway toward a Black feminist anthropology. Thomas Jefferson is considered by many to be the most intellectually grounded of the founding patrons of the United States, and his answer to Query 14—one of twenty-three such inquiries put to him—is where he expressed a broad range of views about Black people in general.[18]

Yet it is Jefferson's animalized depiction of Black women that is stamped forever in my mind. That vivid description is by and large unacknowledged by historians and therefore unchallenged in the founding myths. I cannot recall the details of how I first experienced reading these reflections on law and race by Thomas Jefferson, but I think it was at a moment when I had decided to "escape racism" in the United States and briefly sought to emigrate to Brazil in 1963. Today, almost four decades after my permanent return to the United States, it still feels as though I carry Jefferson's accusations of the bestiality of Black women within my Spirit soul—forever etched. This lingering weight makes me pause to consider if Jefferson's influential ideas of the Enlightenment period might have affected Sarah Baartman's existence in Europe?

In an incisive critique of anthropology and the Western tradition, Joseph Pandian identifies the Enlightenment era and its relationship to slavery as a central component in the construction of "the Other." And the "Black Other" occupied a very special place in Enlightenment thought: "The creation of the Black other as a distinctive being, biologically and intellectually inferior to the Western white us, was linked with the institution of slavery. . . . The Black, in the context of slavery, came to represent the epitome of racial differentness, the supreme contrast by which Western man could compare and define himself."[19]

Pandian, however, stops short of evaluating the broader implications of his argument. For example, how might his critique be modified and brought into even sharper relief were he to address the category of gender?

The same questions and critiques about omissions could be raised about my early work. My initial interest in anthropology was similar to Pandian's—I wanted to confront parallel uncomfortable and complex conjunctions: definitions of civilization and development, concepts of racial identity as they were juxtaposed with notions of "the primitive." I also wished to examine how such realities were affected by culture and state power in situations of geopolitical domination.[20] It was through experience—while teaching one day in the South Pacific at the University of Papua New Guinea—that I realized all of these questions were leading to an integrated gender-based analysis.

"EM NAU": DEBATING CIVILIZATION AND CONCEPTS OF DEVELOPMENT IN PAPUA NEW GUINEA, 1979

Small groups of students and faculty were sitting in the cafeteria enjoying the late afternoon sun that day at the University of Papua New Guinea, which everybody called UPNG. The five men students at the table next to mine were involved in an animated discussion that got more interesting by the minute. "I'm asking you mate. Tell me how, if PNG had agriculture, thousands of years ago according to recorded archeological evidence—and before Europeans did— why we didn't 'discover' them, instead of vice versa?"[21] As if pleased to have pronounced the central question about cultural evolution, the student who raised this issue sat back and sighed, "*Em nau.*" That's it then, right there. *Em nau* was a wonderfully concise phrase in Tok Pisin, the creole lingua franca of PNG, but its pithy all-purpose meanings are not so easily translated into other languages. It always felt like the "Amen" Black American folk say for added emphasis at the end of a particularly meaningful idea.

I eagerly awaited the answer from one of the students, for nothing was guaranteed to get the UPNG student population more agitated than a verbalized evaluation about the process of human development through time. In fact, I had accepted the offer to teach in this South Pacific nation, three years after independence in 1975, precisely to learn how Papua New Guineans were confronting "postcolonial" problems like this. It was here at UPNG that I met Bettylou Valentine, another Black American anthropologist.[22]

Little did I know that I would actually be called on to participate directly in issues related to intellectual decolonization. This theoretical intervention developed in unexpected ways, such as my suggestions to a Tok Pisin professor that the language needed to be decolonized. He didn't understand what I meant until I asked him to think of the implications in the difference between *marit long lotu* (married in a Christian church) and *marit nating* (married in a traditional Papua New Guinean ceremony). *Nating* had its roots in the word "nothing," and when it was used as an adjective, it devalued any word it followed.

It was a shame that I was not going to be able to eavesdrop on the students' discussion some more. In reality, at that moment I was preparing to go home. I also was waiting for the last round of the debate to appear on the Free Speech Bulletin Board on the library wall near the entrance. I never learned how the posted daily missives, signaling the debate theme of the day, were started in the morning, for no matter how early one arrived to campus, a controversy would have already been posted on the library wall.

That day, the furor concerned an edition of Australian *Playboy* magazine and the woman who was the nude centerfold. She was a young woman from Bougainville, the Papua New Guinean Solomon Islands. Solomon Islands people are famed for being exquisitely beautiful with their velvet Black skin tones and slightly lighter dark brown hair, which women and men both traditionally wear in fluffy haloes. Numerous commentaries on the bulletin board had been added throughout the day:

> "The breasts are a natural part of the body and a part of mother-hood."
> "Nudity has always been a part of traditional PNG culture."

(After reading about how African women had been pressured into believing "modern" women only used infant formula, I always appreciated the fact that it was against the law for pharmacies in PNG to sell baby bottles, nipples, or formula without a doctor's prescription.)

> "It is the missionaries who have made nudity evil."
> "Why shouldn't PNG women be proud of our bodies?"
> "Our women's bodies are for natural functions and should be protected from the vulgarity of Western magazines."

Some of these expressions were reminders that the student body was 90 percent male.

I left the cafeteria and headed toward the library. And there it was—the quotable and pointed comment that effectively closed the debate on the Free Speech Bulletin Board that day:

> "Wearing high heels is not civilization!"

CONFRONTING GLOBAL STEREOTYPES OF BLACK WOMEN

How then do Black women engage a society comprised of those who historically have assumed the right to not only control her body but to represent her? It was this lesson that emerged clearly from the debate in PNG. This experience, coupled with my own as a Black woman in America, began to make me aware that views about Black women around the world stemmed from a heritage of inequality—one that was much in evidence in early ethnographies. It was a prized gift that brought this fact to my attention directly.

A mysterious book given to me by fellow anthropologist Debby D'Amico-Johnson, *The Secret Museum of Anthropology*, is just such an example; it uses mostly nude photographs of women of color and de facto defines non-European bodies as the purview of anthropology. In this book, which was published privately by the American Anthropological Society and without author in 1935, one sees the exhibitionistic dimensions of an ethnography that almost borders on the pornographic. The work is comprised mainly of pictures copied from the German-language original, *Das Weib bei Den naturvolkern* (Women of the natural peoples). The original book by F. F. von Reitzenstein was more detailed and maintained that some features of Black women's bodies (the hips) represented the way Europeans' bodies had looked centuries before.[23] Presumably referring to the ample hips of Paleolithic figurines such as the Venus of Willendorf (Austria), Reitzenstein's work and *The Secret Museum* enforce the notion of Africans as "contemporary ancestors"[24]— people who are today like the presumed Europeans of millennia long past. This heritage of "ancestorship" constructs Blacks as "primitives" and has a profound effect on how many non-European peoples of the world are viewed by Europeans. This idea of the modern "primitive" certainly affected my students in PNG—both men and women. The pervasiveness of a universalized image of "backwardness" reproduces the limitations to people's existence and sharply reduces their panoply of life choices.

When such beliefs are overlaid with gender, there are palpable differences in the social, economic, and political choices one can make and the quality of life issue. What this translates into is the fact that for women in many parts of the Western Hemisphere, there is frequently a direct correlation between their phenotype— the way they look—and the types of employment available to them, most of which are in the low-paid, service sector. My travels were gradually allowing me to see heretofore-unknown connections.

As a result of this, and because of a response by one of my PNG students, I continued to write about the Pacific for a decade after I actually left the region: "We were primitive until the missionaries

came, and now we are on our way to being civilized." On the day
that comment was made, the student who said it and I searched
the UPNG library and bookstore in vain for pro-Independence critiques of colonialist views written by PNG writers. Failing to find a
PNG historian or social scientist to counter the missionary and
modern anthropological "primitive" images, I realized that I would
not be able to "return" to research about Brazil until I had worked
with Pacific scholars to produce a book that, were we back in that
moment, I could assign to that student to read.[25] As powerful as
this experience was, my understanding of the direct impact of international economic formations on the historical struggles of
women to assert their intellectual and cultural citizenship had begun to ferment in Africa, a full two years before I landed in the
South Pacific.

GOING TO THE MOUNTAINTOP: CAPE VERDE ISLANDS, WEST AFRICA, AUGUST 1976

"Can you come to our village town up in the mountains to talk to
our group?" This was the message that had been sent to me in the
capital city of Praia by Dona Dulce. *Dona* was a way of addressing
someone who commanded respect; it was more intimate than
Senhora (Mrs.) but implied esteem. It had taken a day of walking
up the dry and sandy road to reach the mountain town of Santa
Catarina on the island of São Thiago in Cape Verde. I had been
asked to talk to a group of young women and their mothers about
women's role in the newly independent country. What could I possibly say about that? These women had been involved in a successful struggle to eliminate Portuguese colonialism in Africa.

Later in Dona Dulce's animated conversation, it was clear that
she had thought a great deal about women's rights. I could only
offer small observations gained through a modest amount of study
and travel. Her cozy house was a small wood cottage, home to several happy children, who all returned once it got dark outdoors.
My own five-year-old daughter, Onik'a, had immediately wanted
to join the town's children in play once we arrived, but they spoke
mostly Crioulo, the creole language that Cape Verdeans speak. By
now, after almost a year in Portugal, Onik'a even spoke to me in

Portuguese, and we both looked like the Cape Verdean people we saw around us.

The doors to Dona Dulce's greeting room were open so that the full moon could help to provide some light. Someone had brought candles, which lent a festive air to the occasion and the indoor darkness. The lights had gone out—because of the drought that year, electricity was at a premium. Dona Dulce called the meeting to order and spoke in a mixture of Portuguese and Crioulo.

"Angela, the women of this town are honored to have you here with us, especially at this proud moment in the history of Cabo Verde. *Nô taconchê nó historia.* We understand our history. Opportunities come and go. Our society is changing, and we women have a chance to participate in that change. And our daughters need education, or they will miss this opportunity that has presented itself to us women." Dona Dulce continued speaking with enthusiasm.

"Do you see that little brick house out back?" The moonlight gave an eerie glow to the skeleton outline of the unfinished brick house in the process of construction.

"That house is being built by my husband, a good man. Like so many of the husbands and fathers of the women in this room, he works in Holland. He gets a vacation every two years, and comes home to meet the baby he made the last time. And to make a new one. We don't want that for our daughters. If they learn how to control their births, then they can participate in this glorious moment here in Cabo Verde. We know that there is a way to count the days of the month so that you control how many babies you have. Please teach us how to count and control the month."

Dona Dulce then sat down in the midst of a still room. She turned her face in my direction, and I could feel dozens of eyes burning in the dark, waiting expectantly for my lesson. I sat there in shock.

"*Pois* . . . Well . . . " It took a while to gather my wits and think about what I was going to say—it was so different from the overblown speech I had prepared.

"You have to know your own individual cycle." This is what they had asked me to come all the way up the mountain to talk about? And I took the birth control technology in the United States so much for granted that "counting days" was a part of my distant past. ". . . and then you count backward for fourteen days . . . " Oh dear God, this is so important. ". . . that is the point where you are most fertile." What if I had it wrong?

A fresh-faced young woman carefully placed the candles near where I was sitting so that they could see my face better. I repeated my counting formula, as though the repetition would guarantee the accuracy of my presentation.

That night lingers in my memory as the occasion on which I learned the most about the real-life issues in which so many of the world's women are entangled. I had been teaching American studies for eight months at the University of Coimbra in central Portugal and had participated in many conversations about cultural transformation in the former Portuguese colonies. It is one thing to talk about social change and quite another to see how complex and unexpected it can be in real life.

Cape Verde was a small island country with an extremely well-informed populace—it was from a Cape Verdean truck driver, whose vehicle doubled as a taxi, that I learned about Ben Chavis and the Wilmington Ten in the United States. And yet Cape Verde is like so many other countries whose citizens send home the money from abroad that helps to sustain national economies. What happens when some of those citizens are women? What kind of work do they get in their own country? I mark that night, as women struggled to learn how to gain control over their bodies and reproduction, as the beginning of my consciousness as a Black feminist.

"BLACK WOMEN FOR WORK": ON THE LINGERING EFFECTS OF THE LEGACY OF SLAVERY

It was during a trip to Brazil in the 1960s that I first heard the proverb that would ultimately shape the direction of my intellectual production as an anthropologist interested in Brazilian themes: *"A White woman for marriage, a mulatto woman for fornication, a Black woman for work."* In my twenties at the time, the phrase helped me comprehend the full meaning of the social context behind my experiences in Brazil. It seemed apparent that the unspoken subtext to the saying was that the optimal situation for a Brazilian man would be to have a Black woman to cook and clean, a mixed-race mistress whose stereotyped embodiment of the seductress included some African descent, and a White woman to present to society as the bearer of his "legitimate" children. The proverb accurately depicts the relationship between social class and the various types of "conjugal union," to use Verena Stolcke's felicitous phrase.[26]

I had first read this rhyme in the work of Gilberto Freyre, whose classic, *The Masters and the Slaves*, seems to be possessed by it.[27] In my view, the assumptions put into place by Freyrean analysis reflected "the great sperm theory of national formation."[28] More recently, I had decided to pursue one of Freyre's footnotes, which made reference to a nineteenth-century German scholar's citation of the above-cited folk proverb—possibly the first time it was in print. The value of reading Heinrich Handelmann is that his work unmasks what social relations were like in Brazil well before emancipation from slavery in 1888. In 1856, Handelmann wrote what appears to be a three-part comparative study of Brazil, the United States, and Haiti in which he evaluates each country as a possible site for German immigration. The section on Brazil was published separately in 1860 and only translated into Portuguese some seventy years later. I found it telling that Handelmann reproduced the very same ideas about European settlement postslavery that Jefferson had hypothesized about earlier in the century: "the salvation of Brazil rests in the spontaneous immigration of free European farmers, for whom the essential conditions are the extinction of the traffic in African slaves and the establishment of a solid system of distribution for [European] settlement."[29] It was largely this folk proverb, and what I felt to be its significance in the development of Brazilian culture and other former colonial-plantation systems (including the United States), that forced me to reevaluate my decision to emigrate to Brazil. With the naïveté of youth, I had assumed it would be possible to escape the racism of the United States by living in Brazil.

My disappointment over the implications for my personal life of that Brazilian proverb about Black women was recorded in my very first published article. "From Roxbury to Rio—And Back in a Hurry" was written for a small, short-lived poetry journal targeted to a broad cross section of the U.S. Black community. This article was subsequently revised to appeal to a broader academic audience and published first in the *Pan-African Journal*, from which it was ultimately reprinted in *Présence Africaine*.[30] Years later, when David Hellwig asked me if he could use the original article to exemplify a change in the Black American understanding of race relations in Brazil, I told him that he could do so only if he allowed me a footnote on the first page explicating my transformation through time toward a more internationalist critique.[31]

The African struggles for independence from colonial rule had begun to inspire an engagement by U.S. Blacks with the African continent on the one hand and to challenge Eurocentrism on the other, and many U.S. activists were beginning to embrace an "international" as well as a national identity. Increasingly, as more Blacks abandoned the quixotic search for "kings and queens," and other cultural vestiges of nobility in the precolonial African past, a newly energized "diaspora" found dignity in the collective efforts—both past and present—of Blacks to have a say in the disposition and price of our labor.

My intellectual engagement with Brazil around the question of race and labor hopefully now reflects this shared political pathway from narrow, individualist concerns to broader, pluralistic ones, and from a nationalist to an internationalist perspective. Ironically, it is my incipient analysis in "From Roxbury to Rio" that is cited today and critiqued as representing those who "read the Brazilian scene from the North American perspective and experience using the latter as a model,"[32] while my subsequent, more nuanced work is sometimes overlooked by these same scholars.

It has always been my desire, however, to theoretically intersect cultural anthropology and political economy with the struggle of Black women anywhere in the world to confront the presumption that they are good only for domestic work. Is there a difference between the United States and Brazil in the battle for rights among domestic workers? Was the civil rights struggle in the United States simply a battle for equal access to the nation's resources or a struggle for wider (global) social transformation? For many U.S. Black women, leaving domestic work seemed to be a unique achievement of the Civil Rights movement. Thus, 1970 represented the first time in the twentieth century that less than half of Black women workers in the United States were employed in public service jobs or private domestic worker employment.[33]

For U.S. women, leaving domestic work was part of a struggle for equal access to all job categories. Most Brazilian domestics have elected instead to push for respect and recognition as workers within the broader labor movement. This is an important distinction that rests in part on the powerful potential of the large number of domestics in Brazil. In Brazil, then, the major battle for the domestic worker of today is the right to FGTS—the guaranteed severance fund—that all recognized workers receive as a condition of employment.[34] Leadership in this area began with the pioneering efforts of Laudelina Campos de Mello, a domestic worker from São Paulo State who began organizing domestic workers in 1936.[35] Dona Laudelina's work to achieve formal recognition by organized labor continues through the efforts of women such as Anna Semião de Lima, the former president of the Brazilian National Federation of Domestic Workers. This yeowoman effort is forcing society to redefine a job description that still reeks of the slave past.

> The category of domestic worker in Brazil emanates from slave labor and the processes that impeded work options after the false abolition. For the first half of this century what predominated was non-remunerated female domestic work. It was common to obtain the labor power of young girls who migrated from the countryside to family homesteads, working in exchange for lodging, food, clothing—a little "help." Today, at the turn of the millennium, that practice is still very common for domestic workers. . . . In spite of our job category being composed of five million workers, 70% of whom are Black women, we are still not recognized nor seen in Brazil or the rest of the world as part of the working class that contributes to production.[36]

Recently, I was proud to provide the Portuguese-English translation for Anna Semião on the occasion of her presentations to local labor activists during the week of the 1999 World Trade Organization meeting in Seattle.

In addition to the burden of being viewed as domestic workhorse, today's young poor women in Brazil endure social pressures that make them succumb to a sexualized representation of themselves, one very entrenched in the culture as the above-cited proverb reveals. This sexualization is frequently racialized in Brazilian culture, and it incorporates elements of socio-economic class as well. One unsavory aspect of this "proverb" about Black women in Brazil was the presumption of impunity undergirding and legitimizing a "predatory patriarchy"—in which elite males from the dominant social class and ethnic group had free rein to encroach upon—and appropriate the bodies of—subordinated women. Elsewhere, I have maintained that Black women's lives often encompass a complex dual reality in Brazil: they are objectified and depicted as seductive *mulatas* in their youth and defeminized to represent the Black woman nurturer-nanny-maid as they age.[37] These multiple intersections and juxtapositions are complicated and demand a definition of Black feminist anthropology that is at once global and particular, individual and shared, and able to cross what are construed as plural ethnic borders.

The valorization of the struggles of people whose hands do the world's actual labor and the contestation of capitalism's "slow-paced and harmony-based" concepts of social change have been key components of Marxist theory. Yet when such a class analysis is applied, it sometimes underestimates or otherwise misinterprets the complexity of Black women's experiences.

CIRCUITOUS TRAILS: ON DISCUSSING BRAZILIAN BLACK WOMEN WITH THE SOVIETS WHILE IN INDIA, 1978

They had all finished their presentations and had asked that we please write our questions down on paper for clarity and pass them to the front. The themes of ethnicity and ethnic relations were the precise subjects the Soviet delegation had covered. Of all the presentations, I was most interested in the one by E. L. Nitoburg, an Americanist and specialist in Black American affairs, and who, as I recall, had delivered a compelling paper postulating the political effects of integrationist versus separatist movements in the United States.

I had, however, come to the Soviet session at the Tenth International Union of Anthropological and Ethnological Sciences to confront one of the most well known Soviet anthropologists about his interpretation of interethnic "marriage" in Brazil. Yu. V. Bromley had used an argument that reflected male bias in his description of the conditions under which race mixture took place in Brazil and the way the process of this mixture directed tendencies of social change in the Western Hemisphere. As the then head of the Soviet Institute of Ethnography, Bromley had pondered what he called "ethnic processes" in Latin America in general and in Brazil in particular:

> The role of the breakdown of endogamy in the appearance of new ethnic units is . . . provided by ethnic and racial mixing in Latin America, which played a tremendous role in the shaping of a majority of modern nations. Thus in Brazil, as a consequence of the conclusion of interracial marriages, the percentage of persons of mixed origin [primarily mulattoes] increased from 20% to 60% of the total number of inhabitants in somewhat less than 100 years (from 1819 to 1910).[38]

I had read this analysis in Bromley's book on Soviet ethnography and had found it incomplete because it did not deal with the reality of the social conditions (rape within slavery) under which race mixture took place and the class basis of the concept of "marriage." I decided to write a question at the conference and pass it to the front. I remember what I wrote just as surely if this happened yesterday: "If the primary pattern of 'ethnic processes' took place where the man was of one ethnic group and of the dominant social class, while the woman was always a member of a subjugated group, why should that be described positively? Isn't that in fact a concrete definition of exploitation and oppression?"

I diligently counted the questions that went up to the front of the table where the delegation sat. There were fourteen pieces of paper. Different members of the Soviet delegation answered each question—thirteen times. My question was never addressed. I decided on another strategy. I went up to Nitoburg afterward to commend him on an interesting interpretation of the Black American experience.

"Do you speak English? I was hoping we could talk about your presentation."

"Sorry, no English." He seemed truly sorry, and his face reflected frustration.

But it was clear he wanted to communicate. "*¿Habla español?*" he asked. Wonderful! We could communicate in Spanish. I decided to bring up the issue of the Soviet session. It was in the course of our subsequent discussions in Spanish that I came to call him Eduardo.

"*¿Por favor, por qué no contestaron mi pregunta*? Why didn't your group answer my question?"

"*No se preocupe.* Don't worry. I can arrange a private interview with Bromley." He made this seem like a simple task to complete.

"*¿Cuando*? When?"

"The Soviet delegation is staying at the Akhbar Hotel. Is it possible to do it there?"

That was where I was also staying. I couldn't believe my good fortune, because it meant that I would not have to travel in New Delhi alone at night. And true to his word, Nitoburg arranged the meeting with Bromley two days later. With Nitoburg's assistance, this meeting was to be a bilingual conversation, from Spanish to Russian and back, with some English added as a special reward.

The booth where we met on the designated evening had space for about six people. At least five people had accompanied Bromley, whose shock of white hair gave him an imposing demeanor. It was clear that Bromley's role as head of the Soviet Institute of Ethnography rendered him an important person. By observing the other scholars, I discerned a definite hierarchy, and wasn't sure how to address him. With Nitoburg's assistance, I decided to introduce myself first, gently.

"Señor Bromley, thank you for agreeing to meet with me. The work of scholars from around the world has always been important to my development. I have been grateful for having learned other languages and being able to read the ideas from many parts of the world. Unfortunately I do not know Russian, but I have read your work in English. And with the help of Mr. Nitoburg, we can have this important conversation."

"Yes, this is an important conversation. And forgive me for not answering your question, but we didn't have the time to do justice to it." He seemed very gracious. I assumed the other scholars—all men—were there not so much to join in as to observe.

"I am interested in what Soviet scholars refer to as ethnic processes—the multifaceted contacts between different peoples. How can you describe as 'intermarriage' the social relations between elite men and dominated women in the Western Hemisphere?" Though I wanted to get an answer to that particular question, I was hoping to surreptitiously introduce one related to the situation in the Soviet Union as well.

Bromley assumed a patient air. "You see, you are confusing ethnic processes in the socialist world, which are a normal part of cultural contact between peoples of the world, with the exploitative relations under capitalism."

I decided to move this issue closer to home—and back to the concept of what constitutes development and the pathway "forward." "But what makes cultural contact—let's say, language contact—in the different Soviet republics less oppressive than culture contact in the West?"

"There is no question that the different cultures and languages of the Soviet Union have enriched Russian culture. Look at me. I used to be uninterested in the music from our Asian republics, but it has become so much a part of Russian culture that I have actually acquired a taste for it." Bromley seemed oblivious to the dominant role he was ascribing to Russian as opposed to Asian cultures.

I decided to tiptoe toward the concepts of "advanced" versus "backward" peoples.

"Are you saying then that people in the republics learn Russian, but only Russians who live in a specific republic are required to learn other national languages?" I mentally tried to apply what he was saying to the situation in the United States.

Bromley nodded affirmatively. I couldn't leave this discussion and return to the original reason for the interview.

"But that means that you must have some notion of the 'next stage' in Soviet culture?" I sat back while Nitoburg translated from Spanish into Russian.

All of a sudden, the entire group said "A-a-ah" in unison. Bromley smiled and said, "That is the most hotly debated topic in the Soviet Union today." The discussion with Bromley was suddenly over after an all too brief hour of conversation. Little did any of us realize that the "hotly debated topic" would explode ten years later.

Over the next two days, I took advantage of the fact of Nitoburg's interest in Black Americans, and he answered my questions about Soviet Jewish life. We debated the meanings of each of our lives in our respective countries and briefly crossed that most formidable of boundaries—the cold war. Nonetheless, I left the conference realizing that the legacy of slavery was still very much a contested domain for scholars all over the world and that Gilberto Freyre's theory of plantation social relations—in which he postulated that elite men appropriating the bodies of dominated women contributed to the establishment of a racially democratic society—circulated in unexpected corners of the world.

THE CARNIVALIZATION OF POVERTY: CONTEMPORARY SEXUAL COMMODIFICATION OF BRAZILIAN WOMEN

Bromley and the Soviet Union are no longer with us, but that ethnographer's commitment to ethnic integration clearly elided the role of power and hierarchy in Brazilian race and gender relations. In the past two decades, the enhanced globalization of the economy has complicated interracial gender relations across borders. Many poor Brazilian women and children have become increasingly identified as elements in a growing sex trade. For much of this current trade, the motive force of its expansion has been the market-centered drive from wealthy countries. In the Brazilian case, however, the traditional erotic attachment to the Afro-Brazilian woman has been shaped by Brazilian national culture. The tradition of romanticizing and "not talking" about predatory patriarchy within an intensified global economy is now accompanied by the privatization of public services—those very services that poor women have used to aid their families for decades.

The subordinated agency of the Afro-Brazilian woman has been sustained within a history of "whitening" as national norm and a generalized Afrophobia[39] at the level of international elites.[40] The eroticizing of structural inequality has historically been an unacknowledged factor in the hierarchical relationship between men and women in Western cultures.[41] The ways in which a society is organized to distribute the goods and services reflect this structure. Some get more than their share of the rewards of a culture; others garner a disproportionate amount of punishment.

Just as frequent is the titillating marketing of Brazilian women by the Brazilian state government agencies for the purpose of enhancing tourism. Brazil is frequently depicted internationally as a place where women are easily available.

> Official and private agencies in the Northeast were responsible for the sale of numerous "travel packages" and for the utilization of images of regional women as tourist products in pamphlets, videos, magazines and other forms of advertising, distributed in the principal targeted countries. . . . The merchandising of black culture as a symbol of Bahia, the stereotypes constructed around the sexuality of black women and men, all contributed to feed a growing market—that of sexual tourism—and with specific products such as the *jambo* colored brunette, for example.[42]

Central to the appeal of such women is their characterization as "exotic" or different, and their subordination rests within the unequal economic and social exchange between visitors and the places to which they travel as tourists. The concept of the exotic also sediments the "erotic" attachment to women from demographic groups that do not have ready access to state power.

According to Delores Root, a trope of exoticism "is the fascination with the erotic possibilities of the colony."[43] This "eroticization of racial power" derives, she argues, from the colonists ability to exert economic and military control over the colony in a way that links the exotic images of women with colonial fantasies of power. Thus, the carnivalization of poverty and Brazil's dependence on the tourism industry have pushed many poor women into situations where they seek escape from their minimal access to the nation's resources via sex tourism, a form of commodification that exposes the inexperienced to unstable living conditions both within Brazil and abroad.

Another factor fueling young women's desire for interaction with foreign men is the influence of Eurocentric standards of beauty and normalcy—which for poor, Black women remains an elusive, unachievable goal. Yet the lure of the unattainable is powerful:

> For some . . . the desirability of a *loiro de olhos azuis* [blond man with blue eyes], leaving the country does not mean entering the sex trade, but rather following a movie narrative to a happy ending. With this backdrop, a new form of trafficking [in] *negros* emerges. . . . In fact, the victims deliberately seek out their tall, blond, blue-eyed buyers . . . [who] appear to be smiling angels. . . . Thus, it is in this exuberant Brazilian culture, with its exotic beauty,

that the meeting of the northeastern, Black, girl-women [sic] with the "Viking Prince" takes place.[44]

In contrast, for many foreign men, the image of Brazil as a site of "permanent party" uses, reproduces, reissues, and reshapes the carnival image. In spite of the fact that the nation has one of the largest gaps between wealth and poverty, virtually all of the country's port cities are full of (frequently older) men from wealthier countries looking for poor young women.

Vania Kahrsch, a Brazilian feminist working with prostituted Brazilian women in Germany, traces the emergence of this sexual marketing of Brazil to the period of the military dictatorship.

> Twenty years ago, there were very few foreign tourists found in the Northeast region of Brazil. Only during the dictatorship (1964–1985) was this region transformed into the El Dorado of mass tourism. The military needed foreign currency and a new image. The country of terror and torture should transform itself on the outside into the paradise of the tropics. The big campaign for "everybody's tourism" in the Northeast counts on two cliches: beautiful beaches with palms, and exotic, hot-blooded, beautiful *mulatas* in provocative tangas.[45]

Moreover, it was during this period, in August 1975 at the height of militarism, that the first Brazilian edition of *Playboy* in the Portuguese language appeared.

Marketing materials from the United States also explicitly mention the "darkness" of the Brazilian woman, suggesting an incontrovertible link between them and "polygamous customs" from Africa. In the face of Brazil's exoticized genetic mix, thought to be all the more lascivious because of the polygamous Blacks brought in chains from Africa,[46] the idea of the European man as helpless before such "wanton libido" is reinforced. To borrow Leith Mullings's framework, this mammy/*mãe preta* versus Jezebel/*mulata* bifurcation is yet another version of the madonna/whore binarism so prevalent in Western society.[47]

ONE NIGHT IN ANDARAÍ, RIO DE JANEIRO—DECEMBER 1998

"Mom! Wake up! They've got guns." My daughter's terror was apparent although she was whispering loudly in my ear. I came to with a start, forgetting for a moment that we were in Rio de Janeiro. We were riding in a typical taxicab in Rio, and it was about two o'clock in the morning. We were also in the Andaraí neighborhood, which borders the middle-class zone of Tijuca. Here, individual or single-family dwellings are increasingly rare now, and tall buildings dominate. My daughter and I were traveling in the taxi with a Brazilian friend and his thirteen-year-old daughter. Indeed, we were really accompanying this teenager as she returned home from a party celebrating one of her friend's fifteenth birthday.

I looked out the back window, and my heart beat wildly and seemed to leap into my throat. A strange vehicle—which I later learned was a *Patamo*—that resembled a military tank had pulled us over. Two men in blue uniform, each holding a machine gun in the identical slanted position across the chest, leaped out of the car in military formation, one to the left and the other to the right. They positioned themselves at the rear of our cab. Another man emerged from an opening in the roof of the tank and had positioned his weapon as well. A fourth man was heading toward the driver's side of our taxi. The uniforms identified them as the *policía militar*. All were White.

"*Calma*, Angela. Let me handle this. Don't you say a word."

P. was trying to exude a sense of control, but he had sensed my fright. I could only detect the outlines of his face.

I dutifully obeyed, even though I briefly considered speaking in English and pulling out the "honorary" White status that citizenship in the world's most militarily powerful nation afforded U.S. Blacks overseas.[48] All of us, including the taxi driver, were Black, although Onik'a and I were somewhat lighter skinned. When the driver lowered his window, the military policeman peered in and looked at the three women in the back and started to ask questions.

"Where are you coming from?"

P. spoke in a voice that exuded confidence. "We are returning from a family gathering."

"Where are you going?" The military policeman now had the men's documents in his hand, and he looked down to read them with his flashlight directed toward the cards.

"We are going to Copacabana, where they live." The *policía militar* hesitated for a moment, shuffled through the cards and papers for at least five minutes. He then returned the documents and signaled that we were free to go. Later, I thought how ironic that my daughter had arrived in Rio as a human rights legal intern with the Center for Marginalized Peoples, to study precisely the kind of violence that accompanies events like the very one we had found ourselves in that night.

Who were we to the military police? Was it the racist presumption that Black people are prone to criminality that warranted our being stopped? In other words, was this a case of what in the United States is referred to as "racial profiling"? Would the taxi driver have been stopped if his passengers had been White? If class were a more important marker than "color" or race, then the clothing we wore that night should have affected the police behavior toward our group.

Indeed some scholars in both the United States and Brazil maintain that the primary distinction in race relations in Brazil versus the United States rests in the existence of a "multipolar" racial identity in the former nation-state and a "bipolar" one in the latter. Hence the way Brazilian society presumably responds to people of different phenotypes is ambiguous, far from uniform, and therefore more Latin American or Brazilian.[49] "Multipolar" analysis avers that in effect, there are no rigid lines of racial affiliation in Brazil; rather, there is a continuum of identity that is situational and can be transformed and altered depending on a number of factors.

On the other hand, the United States is historically characterized by social values in which interpretations of racial differences are ensconced within a dichotomous or bipolar discourse. One is either Black or White, with no gray space in between. My life's work has been dedicated to challenging the presumed distinctions between U.S. and Brazilian variants of race relations; for poor Black women there is little ambiguity.

You might maintain, based on this, that due to these racial "ambiguities," in Brazil racial labels are "elective." But subsequent relating of this tale to Brazilians reveals that similar experiences with the police are shared by Black women and men all over the country. These circumstances problematize the distinctions between Brazil's "multipolar" and the United States's "bipolar" racial systems.[50]

As some Brazilian Blacks seek ways to reinvent their individual and collective identities, sometimes they have collided with controversies about race and race relations. To refuse the euphemisms *pardo* (dark) or *moreno* (brunette) can be construed as a militant political position. But as the proliferation of magazines such as *Raça Brasil* demonstrates, Brazilian Blacks increasingly adopt the classification of *negro/a* as a point of self-identification. This is especially prevalent among women whose phenotypes could position them as *mulatas* but who reject such an identity either for political reasons or for the historical opprobrium it carried within the colonial plantation traditions.

My pathway to and around these issues as a feminist has not been without its conflicts, not the least because of identity issues throughout my career. In my view, that night in Andaraí was a life-threatening event resembling the problems of navigating public space that Black people have in a "bipolar" society like the United States. As I learned more about Brazilian culture and shared the goals and social roles of Black Brazilian women, the boundary between Self and Other often disappeared. And I continued efforts to always ensure that my intellectual production would not incorporate the processes of "Other-ization."

This is especially germane to my current work, which links a contemporary interest in the struggles of domestic workers to the difficulties around the international sex trade. Such connections represent a complex cultural conjunction. On the one hand, the domestic worker sometimes "starts as a maid, but ends in the trade," which happens when many women workers, for example, leave their home village or country for domestic work in another society. On the other hand, the question of labor in private versus public space is part of the complexity. Thus, in many former colonial plantation systems of the Western Hemisphere, Black women are fighting to transform attitudes and job descriptions that began in slavery.

In the United States, for example, housekeepers at one southern university—a group composed primarily of Black women—fought long for recognition as workers worthy of unionization. Complicating their objective was the fact that public-sector employees are not permitted to unionize in any of the states of the Confederacy—those states that fought to retain slavery in the nineteenth century.[51] Thus, the University of North Carolina housekeepers were restricted to forming a labor association, Local 153, rather than a full-fledged union. In this respect, their plight can be compared with that of domestic workers in Brazil, whose efforts to be recognized as part of organized labor encounter similar challenges.

As I embrace the struggles of the domestic workers in Brazil, I pay homage to my own foremothers, who cooked, cleaned, or served for a living, and I ground my intellectual production to those movements for dignity and survival that surround Black women's lives globally. Linking my intellectual production to the historic domestic production of Black women inevitably raises questions of who has the right to represent whom? This issue is one that is relevant in both Brazil and the United States, where Black working-class intellectuals are separated from the academic elites who are positioned as conduits and, hence, representatives to the wider society. This is the delicate "Standpoint Dance" that decries the "it takes one to know one" ideology, yet recognizes authority to understand life as it is lived.

Despite their differences, both public intellectuals and academic scholars agree that contemporary privatization of the search for meaningful labor across frontiers is intimately connected to the current stage in the advancement of capitalism and the concomitant loss of women's rights worldwide. This is especially true for the Third World, where signs of a return to colonialism gain strength.

That Black women experience a life of servitude within the capitalist world has historically affected our lives through time and around the world. The estrangement that Black women feel from their own bodies masks a category of intellectual inquiry that deserves further study. This alienation goes back centuries and sometimes affects the work we are permitted to perform.

When Sarah Baartman was kidnapped for exhibition in Europe in the early nineteenth century, her body was placed at the unsavory intersection of slavery, an Enlightenment classificatory system, and quasi-pornographic notions of medicine. The Black woman's body was both an instrument of prurient fascination and a historical symbol of service-oriented labor.

Sarah Baartman would not have garnered more attention than any European woman if the image held by colonial society of Africa-descended people had been more humanized. The doctor who dissected her body in 1816 compared her to an ape,[52] summoning the concepts that Thomas Jefferson had expressed a few years earlier in Query 14. The pervasiveness of the *mulata* image and the longevity of "Black domestic" as a job category are sufficient evidence that Black women today are imprisoned in an enduring and mythic cage that is centuries old. In the face of such cultural and historical evidence, how could I not see myself as a Black feminist? I could not avoid using my understanding of different languages and cultures to confront somehow the enduring power and effect of such images. Most importantly, this confrontation underscores the way I have taught, lectured, and even raised a womanchild in this country.

Could it have been otherwise? When all is said and done, in making visible historically situated complexities, many Black feminist anthropologists, myself included, have found that our objective— to uncover, critique, and transform global and structural inequities— is affirmed. *Em nau.*

NOTES

I am indebted to the perennial intellectual support given by my daughter, Onik'a Gilliam-Korver; to Angela Merkur, Marianne Hoepli, and Sonja Panzenbock, who assisted me with pertinent data and translations from German; and friends, colleagues, and sisters Carletta Wilson, Debby D'Amico-Johnson, Karen Stuhldruher, and Jenn Bowman, whose confidence in my pathway empowered my journey. All translations of Portuguese to English are my own unless otherwise noted; assistance with the spelling in Portuguese was provided by Irene Hirschberg and Hebe Guimarães Leme.

1. The film *The Life and Times of Sarah Baartman*, directed by Zola Maseko and featuring the analysis of Khoikhoi historian Yvette Abrahams, was aired on South African Broadcasting Corporation (SABC) television in Capetown in 1998 and is available in the United States from First Run Films. It is an excellent historical critique of the "science" that legitimated Sarah Baartman's entrapment in nineteenth-century Europe. History has given her the unfortunate sobriquet of the "Hottentot Venus," which in part reflects the pejorative epithet that anthropology once imposed on the Khoisan peoples of southern Africa. The contemporary Khoikhoi people see the struggle to repatriate Baartman's remains as part of their demand that the South African nation recognize their identity as an indigenous people within South Africa. Former President Nelson Mandela is reported to have written a letter to French officials requesting return of Sarah Baartman's body. Today, the call for the return of her remains in dignity is part of an international campaign. At the fourth World Archaeology Congress (WAC) at the University of Capetown, January 10–14, 1999, the delegates put forth a resolution supporting President Mandela and the South African people on this question. This was especially cogent, given the significance WAC attaches to the repatriation of indigenous remains. I attended this international meeting as a result of receiving an Al Gore–Thabo Mbeki Binational Com-

mission Grant in 1998. My paper, "Reclaiming Honor, Resurrecting Struggle: Black Women, Patronage, and the Global Heritage of Afrophobia," made reference to Baartman and hence put me in touch with some of the Khoikhoi people who attended the conference.

2. Making the link between local and global economic issues is of growing importance to Black feminists. Three that incorporate many of the issues in this chapter are A. Lynn Bolles, *Sister Jamaica: A Study of Women, Work, and Households in Kingston* (Lanham, Md., and London: University Press of America, 1996); Gloria T. Emeagwali, ed., *Women Pay the Price: Structural Adjustment in Africa and the Caribbean* (Trenton, N.J.: Africa World Press, 1995); and Faye V. Harrison, "Anthropology as an Agent of Transformation: Introductory Comments and Queries," in *Decolonizing Anthropology: Moving Further toward an Anthropology of Liberation*, 2d ed., ed. Faye V. Harrison (1991; reprint, Arlington, Va.: Association of Black Anthropologists and American Anthropological Association, 1997), 1–15.

3. Thai feminists, especially those affiliated with the Foundation for Women in Bangkok, have used women's meetings at the United Nations as a way of redefining the international sex trade as a problem of migration, human rights, and the quest for work. See especially Siriporn Skrobanek, Nattaya Boonpakdi, and Chutima Janthakeero, *The Traffic in Women: Human Realities of the International Sex Trade* (London and New York: Zed Books Ltd., 1997).

4. My essay "The Brazilian *Mulata*: Images in the Global Economy," *Race and Class* 40, 1 (1998): 57–69, connects historical patriarchal dynamics in Brazil with current pressures in the global economy.

5. In 1970, I published "From Roxbury to Rio—And Back in a Hurry," *Journal of Black Poetry* 1 (13): 8–12. This essay was expanded for an academic audience in "Black and White in Latin America," *Pan-African Journal* 5, 3 (fall 1972): 321–330, and later republished in *Presénce Africaine* 92 (1974): 161–173. I continued working with the language themes as I moved toward a more internationalist perspective: "Sociolinguistic Configurations of African Language in the Americas: Some Educational Directives," in *Black English: A Seminar*, ed. Deborah Harrison and Tom Trabasso (Hillsdale, N.J.: Lawrence Erlbaum Associates, 1976), 95–103; "Language and 'Development' in Papua New Guinea," *Dialectical Anthropology* 8 (1984): 303–318; "Tell Tale Language: Race, Class and Inequality in Two Latin American Towns," in *Anthropology for the Nineties*, ed. Johnnetta B. Cole (New York: The Free Press, 1988), 522–531. "Tell Tale Language" began its life as a paper titled "Clase, raza y etnicidad en Brasil y México" for the session "Raza, etnicidad, clase y marxismo: El punto de vista del nativo" (Race, ethnicity, class and Marxism: The native's point of view) and was delivered at the 73rd annual meeting of the American Anthropological Association in Mexico City in 1974. It was later published under the same title in *Nueva Antropología* (Escuela Nacional de Antropología y Historia) (Mexico) A no. II, 5 (July 1976): 91–103.

6. Frantz Fanon, *Black Skin, White Masks* (New York: Grove Press, 1967).

7. Alberto Guerreiro Ramos, *Introdução crítica à sociologia brasileira* (Rio de Janeiro: Editorial Andes, 1957), 181.

8. During the late 1960s and early 1970s, I shared Portuguese-English translation/interpretation tasks with other New York–based colleagues for Abdias do Nascimento. This period not only coincided with his exile in the United States during the Brazilian National Security State but was critical as an era in which he began to paint depictions of the Yoruba cosmogony, an element of important African religious expression in Brazil.

9. Abdias do Nascimento, *"Racial Democracy" in Brazil: Myth or Reality?* (Ibadan, Nigeria: Sketch Publishing Company, 1977), 90. Nascimento has had an extraordinary and prolific career articulating the problems faced by Blacks in Brazil. Founder of the Experimental Black Theater in the 1940s and elected first a member of Congress in the 1980s and then senator from Rio de Janeiro State in the 1990s, he has used drama, expressive arts, and elective office to give voice to concerns about racism. His most recent appointments were in Rio de Janeiro state government, as the founding secretary for defense and promotion of Afro-Brazilian population (1991–1994) and the secretary of human rights and citizenship (1999–2000).

10. Abdias do Nascimento, *Mixture or Massacre? Essays in the Genocide of a Black People*, trans.

Elisa Larkin Nascimento (Puerto Rican Studies and Research Center, State University of New York at Buffalo: Afrodiaspora, 1979); idem, *O Quilombismo* (Petrópolis, Brazil: Vozes, 1980). The original meaning of the word *quilombo* was "runaway slave community" or "maroon settlement." By applying the word to mean a contemporary theoretical response to racism, he charges it with new power.

11. This commentary is from a dialogue with the late Lelia Gonzalez, at the end of November 1983, for "Everywoman's Space," a radio program that I produced for WBAI in New York. My collaboration with Gonzalez, begun in Pittsburgh during the Latin American Studies Association meeting in April 1979, centered around her presentation, "Culture, Ethnicity and Labor: Linguistic and Political Effects of the Exploitation of Women," in my session—Linguistic and Cultural Manifestations of Sexism, Racism and Chauvinism in Brazil. The association with Gonzalez continued into 1985, when she joined Lindiwe Mabuza (South Africa), Mamphela Ramphele (South Africa), Susana Ounei (New Caledonia), Rose Catchings (United States), and me in a meeting that compared the experiences of Black women worldwide and that was funded by Catchings through her office at the United Methodist Church. The latter teamwork occurred in Nairobi, Kenya, during the 1985 World Conference to Review and Appraise the Achievements of the United Nations Decade for Women. Lelia Gonzalez's written achievements include the following: "The Unified Black Movement: A New Stage in Black Political Mobilization," in *Race, Class and Power in Brazil*, ed. Pierre-Michel Fontaine (University of California, Los Angeles: Center for Afro-American Studies, 1985), 120–134; and "Mulher Negra" (Black woman), *Afrodiaspora* (Ipeafro, Rio de Janeiro) 3, 6–7 (73): 94–104. When Gonzalez died in 1994, she was the director of the department of sociology and politics at Pontifícia Universidade Católica in Rio de Janeiro.

12. Patricia Hill Collins, *Black Feminist Thought: Knowledge, Consciousness, and the Politics of Empowerment* (New York: Routledge, 1991), 26.

13. Luiza Bairros, "Nossos feminismos revisitados" (Our feminisms revisited), *Estudos Feministas* 3, 2 (1995): 461. This article was included in the journal's first special edition on Black women.

14. Norma Alarcón, "The Theoretical Subject(s) of 'This Bridge Called My Back' and Anglo-American Feminisms," in *Making Face, Making Soul/Haciendo Caras; Creative and Critical Perspectives by Women of Color*, ed. Gloria Anzaldúa (San Francisco: Aunt Lute Foundation Books, 1990), 356–369. See also Angela Gilliam, "Women's Equality and National Liberation," in *Third World Women and the Politics of Empowerment*, ed. Chandra T. Mohanty, Ann Russo, and Lourdes Torres (Bloomington, Ind.: Indiana University Press, 1991), 215–237.

15. U.S. feminists succinctly captured the problematic dynamic for Black women around the world with the book title *All the Women Are White, All the Blacks Are Men, but Some of Us Are Brave*, ed. Gloria Hull, P. B. Scott, and Barbara Smith (New York: Feminist Press, 1982). Santos has added to this analysis in a dramatic way. In a telephone interview from Brazil on January 11, 2000, she gave a compelling example of the consequences of ignoring the importance of racism when conceptualizing issues of class. As the only Black Brazilian woman forced into exile during 1964–1984, the period of the Brazilian national security state, Santos believes that her loss of support in this crucial moment of Brazilian history (she left in 1972 and did not return until 1978) was directly due to the Left's minimization of the interlocking relationship between race and gender. For an expanded discussion of these and parallel issues, see especially Thereza Santos, "My Conscience, My Struggle," in *Racial Politics in Contemporary Brazil*, ed. Michael Hanchard (Durham, N.C.: Duke University Press, 1999).

16. Angela Gilliam and Onik'a Gilliam, "Negociando a subjetividade de mulata no Brasil," *Estudos Feministas* 3, 2 (1995): 525–543 (the journal's first special edition on Black women). This article was translated and updated as "Odyssey: Negotiating the Subjectivity of *Mulata* Identity in Brazil," *Latin American Perspectives* 26, 106 (May 1999): 60–84; idem, "Raça Brasil: Por quem, para quem?" (*Brazil Race* [magazine]: By whom, for whom?) *Cadernos Pagú* (Campinas, São Paulo), nos. 6–7 (1996): 307–310.

17. Thomas Jefferson, "Query 14," in "The Administration of Justice and the Discription [sic] of the Laws," *Notes on the State of Virginia*, first hot-pressed edition (Philadelphia: R. T. Rawle; Printer John Thompson, 1801), 249–292.

18. Thomas Jefferson is believed to have written only one major book, *Notes on the State of Virginia*, a collection of twenty-three essays or "queries" that apparently began as a series of questions put to him by one or more interviewers on different occasions. Query 14 is the chapter in which Jefferson pontificates about slavery and the law, and makes special effort to compare and contrast Africans and Europeans.

19. Jacob Pandian, *Anthropology and the Western Tradition: Toward an Authentic Anthropology* (Prospect Heights, Ill.: Waveland Press, 1985), 80.

20. Angela Gilliam, "On the Problem of Historicist Categories in Theories of Human Development," in *Conflict in the Archaeology of Living Traditions*, ed. Robert Layton, One World Archaeology series (London: Unwin Hyman, 1989), 68–81; and idem, "Militarism and Accumulation as Cargo Cult," in *Decolonizing Anthropology*, 170–191.

21. Cf. Jo Mangi, "The Role of Archaeology in Nation Building," in *Conflict in the Archaeology of Living Traditions*, 217–227. Mangi's references provide a number of sources that debate this question.

22. Both Betty Valentine and her husband, Charles Valentine, worked on anthropological questions surrounding concepts of development in the Pacific. See especially *Going through Changes: Villagers, Settlers and Development in Papua New Guinea*, ed. C. A. Valentine and B. L. Valentine (Port Moresby: Institute of Papua New Guinea Studies, 1979).

23. F. F. von Reitzenstein, *Das Weib bei Den naturvolkern* (Berlin: Neufeld Henius, 1923), 35.

24. Paul Mercier, *Histoire de l'anthropologie* (Paris: Presses Universitaires de France, 1966).

25. Lenore Foerstel and Angela Gilliam, eds., *Confronting the Margaret Mead Legacy: Scholarship, Empire and the South Pacific* (Philadelphia: Temple University Press, 1992). A special source of pride to the editors of this volume was the participation of historically significant Pacific Island scholars. The epistemological challenge to anthropologists—to consider that thinkers from kin-based cultures could provide theoretical models to scholars from other societies—was ignored by most U.S.-based scholars. See also Angela Gilliam, "Symbolic Subordination and the Representation of Power in *Margaret Mead and Samoa*," *Visual Anthropology Review* 9, 1 (1993): 105–115.

26. Verena Stolcke, *Marriage, Class and Colour in Nineteenth-Century Cuba: A Study of Racial Attitudes and Sexual Values in a Slave Society* (London: Cambridge University Press, 1974), 43.

27. Gilberto Freyre, *The Masters and the Slaves: A Study in the Development of Brazilian Civilization* (translation of *Casa grande e senzala*) (New York: Alfred A. Knopf, 1946). Much has been written about Freyre's work, but it is Medeiros's detailed critique of Freyre's book that elucidates how the sexual violence against indigenous and Black women came to be seen as the very source of democracy. Maria Alice de Aguiar Medeiros, *O elogio da Dominação: Relendo "Casa grande e senzala"* (In praise of domination: Rereading "The masters and the slaves") (Rio de Janeiro: Achiame, 1984).

28. I first used this phrase in "Women's Equality and National Liberation," in *Third World Women and the Politics of Feminism*, 226.

29. Heinrich Handelmann, *Geschichte der Amerikanischen Kolonisation und Unabhangegkeit die Staaten der Weissen und schwarzen Race: Vereinigte Staaten, Hayti, Brasilien.* Volume 3 was translated as *História do Brasil* by Lucia F. Lahmeyer for the Instituto Histórico e Geográphico Brasileiro (Rio de Janeiro: Imprensa Nacional, 1931), vii.

30. See Gilliam, "From Roxbury to Rio," as first published in *Journal of Black Poetry* and later expanded for an academic audience as "Black and White in Latin America" in *Pan-African Journal* (1972) and *Presénce Africaine* (1974).

31. Angela Gilliam, "From Roxbury to Rio—And Back in a Hurry," in *African-American Reflections on Brazil's Racial Paradise*, ed. David J. Hellwig (Philadelphia: Temple University Press, 1992), 173. This book was reviewed by Antonio Sergio Alfredo Guimarães in "*Brasil–Estados Unidos: Um diálogo que forja nossa identidade racial*" (Brazil–United States: A dialog that forges our racial identity), *Estudos Afro-Asiáticos* 26 (September 1994): 141–147.

32. Rita L. Segato, "The Color-Blind Subject of Myth; or, Where to Find Africa in the Nation," *Annual Review of Anthropology* 27 (1998): 132. See also Peter Fry, "Politics, Nationality, and the Meaning of 'Race' in Brazil," *Daedalus: Journal of the American Academy of Arts and Sciences* (special issue, Brazil: Burden of the Past, Promise of the Future) (spring 2000): 83–118.

33. D. L. Newman, "Black Women Workers in the Twentieth Century," *Sage* 3, 1 (1986): 13.

Cited in translation in Angela Gilliam, "O ataque contra a ação afirmativa nos Estados Unidos—Um ensaio para o Brasil," in *Multiculturalismo e racismo: Uma comparaçao Brasil–Estados Unidos* (Multiculturalism and racism: A Brazil–United States comparison), ed. Jesse de Souza (Brasília: Paralelo 15, 1997), 39–61. The chapters in this volume were originally papers presented at a July 1995 conference titled Multiculturalism and Racism: The Role of Affirmative Action in Contemporary Democratic States, organized by the Secretariat of Citizenship Rights of the Ministry of Justice in Brasília.

34. Felipe Werneck, "Domésticas exigem votação de projeto" (Domestics demand vote on project), *O Estado de São Paulo (Economia)*, September 23, 1999, B6. This article interviews Anna Semião, president of the National Federation of Domestic Workers, who maintains that the struggle to have the FGTS applied to domestic workers has been stalled in the legislature for ten years.

35. Dona Laudelina continues to inspire others by her example. She bequeathed her home to domestic workers' organizations so that her work should continue after her death. She is the subject of a mammoth master's thesis by Afro-Brazilian scholar Elisabete Aparecida Pinto, whose multivolume work is titled "Etnicidade, gênero e educaçao: Dona Laudelina Campos Mello (1904–1991)" (Ethnicity, gender and education), (vol. 1, School of Education, State University at Campinas, 1993). Mary Castro is one feminist anthropologist whose academic work and support of domestics are appreciated by organizational leadership in the Bahia state domestic workers association. See especially Elsa M. Chaney and Mary Castro, eds., *"Muchachas" No More: Household Workers in Latin America and the Caribbean* (Philadelphia: Temple University Press, 1989).

36. Anna Semião, "O processo da imigração no Brasil" (The process of immigration in Brazil), presentation at the "Women Workers and Immigration in the Global Economy" conference, Seattle, Washington, December 4, 1999. By using the phrase "false abolition" Semião was reinforcing her analysis that slavery did not end in 1888 for people of African descent who found themselves living under minimal conditions for survival. The conference at which Semião delivered this paper was organized by the Workers' Voices Coalition as part of a series of local activities developed around the World Trade Organization meeting in Seattle in 1999. On this occasion, the Northwest Labor and Employment Law Office (LELO) mobilized a coalition of fifteen local grassroots organizations to unite around the invitation of nine Third World labor rights activists, including Anna Semião. Semião also participated in the AFL-CIO activities on November 30. I interpreted /translated for Semião at this and other related events.

37. See Gilliam and Gilliam, "Negociando a subjetividade de mulata no Brasil."

38. Yu. V. Bromley, *Soviet Ethnography: Main Trends* (Moscow: *Social Sciences Today* Editorial Board, USSR Academy of Sciences, 1977), 28.

39. I am grateful to Black American historian Gerald Horne for the cogent term *Afrophobia*. He maintains that the contemporary assault on U.S. social programs such as welfare is in part due to their negative association with Black women. The assault on such programs reproduces an age-old negative association with Africa, its peoples, and the like. Gerald Horne, *Reversing Discrimination: The Case for Affirmative Action* (New York: International Publishers, 1992), 1.

40. I am convinced that this form of Afrophobia has been promulgated around the world, in large part, through the influence and power of the media.

41. Marianne Hester, *Lewd Women and Wicked Witches: A Study of the Dynamics of Male Domination* (London and New York: Routledge, 1992), 198.

42. Jonas Dias Filho, "Palavras, coisas, imagens e textos: A discursividade em torno da figura da mulata como produto do turismo baiano" (Words, things, images and texts: The discursivity surrounding the figure of the *mulata* as a product of Bahian tourism), unpublished paper, 1996. The color *jambo* comes from the Brazilian fruit of the same name. It is best described as caramel-like or burnt tan.

43. Deborah Root, *Cannibal Culture: Art, Appropriation and the Commodification of Difference* (Boulder, Colo.: Westview Press, 1996), 40.

44. C. Prestello and C. Dias, *Night Girls: Once upon a Time There Was an Enchanted Prince* (Olinda, Brazil: Coletivo Mulher, n.d.).

45. Vania Kahrsch, "Sextourismus in Brasilien," in *Zweiwochen dienst* [pamphlet] (1994), 10–12.

46. C. Fussman, "Rio Loco," *GQ,* February 1995, 196.
47. Leith Mullings, "Images, Ideology, and Women of Color," in *Women of Color in U.S. Society,* ed. Bonnie Dill and Maxine Baca-Zinn (Philadelphia: Temple University Press, 1994), 269.
48. Gilliam and Gilliam, "Negociando a subjetividade de mulata no Brasil"; idem, "Raça Brasil: Por quem, para quem?"
49. The debate about race relations analysis in Brazil assumed new importance with the appearance and critique of Michael Hanchard's *Orpheus and Power: The Movimento Negro of Rio de Janeiro and São Paulo, Brazil, 1945–1988* (Princeton: Princeton University Press, 1994). Of particular interest is how this book confronts the "multipolar" versus "bipolar" categories of intellectual inquiry. For more of the debate on this question, see especially Peter Fry, "O que a Cinderela negra tem a dizer sobre a 'política racial' no Brasil" (What the Black Cinderella has to say about racial politics in Brazil), *Revista Universidad de São Paulo* 28 (1995–1996); Michael Hanchard, "'Americanos,' 'Brasileiros,' e a cor da especifidade humana: Uma resposta a Peter Fry" ('Americans,' 'Brazilians,' and the color of human specificity: An answer to Peter Fry), *Revista USP* 31 (1996): 164–175; Angela Gilliam, "Globalização, identidade, e os ataques à igualdade nos Estados Unidos: Esboço de uma perspectiva para o Brasil" (Globalization, identity, and the attacks on equality in the United States: Outline of a perspective for Brazil), *Revista Crítica de Ciências Sociais* (Portugal) 48 (June 1997): 67–101 (this article is also forthcoming in *Identities*); Livio Sansone, "As relações raciais em Casa Grande e Senzala revisitadas a luz do processo de internacionalização e globalização" (Race relations in *The Masters and the Slaves* revisited in light of the process of internationalization and globalization), in *Raça, ciência e sociedade*, ed. Marcos Chor Maio and Ricardo Ventura Santos (Rio de Janeiro: Editor Fio Cruz, 1996), 215. Segato followed up her initial critique (see Segato, "The Color-Blind Subject of Myth") with a spirited defense of the multipolar position in a romantic vision of the Brazilian domestic worker, titled "A babá brasileira: A dupla rejeição de raça e gênero" (The Brazilian nanny: The double rejection of race and gender), in Simpósio Internacional: Gênero e Relações Interétnicas entre a Juventude das Cidades Contemporâneas (International symposium: Gender and interethnic relations among youth in contemporary cities), University of Campinas, São Paulo, Brazil, December 1–3, 1998. (My paper in this Rockefeller project was titled "Only the Rich Have Children, The Poor Have Troubles: Globalization of the Economy and the Disappearance of Childhood.") Helen I. Safa is a recent entry into the discussion about race relations in Latin America in general and the multipolar–bipolar debate in particular. See especially her "Introduction," *Latin American Perspectives* (special issue, Race and National Identity in the Americas) 25, 3 (May 1998): 3–20.
50. Thereza Santos maintains that similar events happen to Brazilian Blacks such as herself. In addition, junior scholars in Brazil and beyond are bringing new insights into race relations analyses and challenging the dominant narratives. See especially Joel Zito Almeida Araujo, *A Negação do Brasil—O negro na telenovela brasileira* (The denial of Brazil—The Black person in the Brazilian soap opera) (São Paulo: Editora Senac, 2000); Jose Carlos Gomes da Silva, "Rap na cidade de São Paulo: Música, etnicidade e experiência urbana," Ph.D. dissertation, State University of Campinas, 1998 (I was a member of the doctoral committee; Luiza Bairros, "Pecados no 'paraíso racial': O negro na força de trabalho da Bahia, 1950–1980" (Sins in the "racial paradise": The Black in the Bahian labor force, 1950–1980), in *Escravidão e invenção da liberdade: Estudos sobre o Negro no Brasil* (Slavery and the invention of freedom: Studies on the Black in Brazil), ed. João José Reis (São Paulo: Editora Brasiliense, 1988); Flávio dos Santos Gomes, *Histórias de quilombolas: Mocambos e comunidades de senzalas no Rio de Janeiro—Século XIX* (Stories of the runaway slaves: Hideout shacks and slave quarter communities in Rio de Janeiro—19th century) (Rio de Janeiro: Arquivo Nacional, 1995); Dijaci David de Oliveira, Ricardo Barbosa Lima, and Sales Augusto dos Santos, "A cor do medo: O medo da cor" (The color of fear: The fear of color), in *A cor do medo* dijaci, ed. David de Oliveira, Elen Cristina Geraldes, Ricardo Barbosa Lima, and Sales Augusto dos Santos (Brasília: University of Brasilia Press, 1998); Nilma Lino Gomes, *A mulher negra que vi de perto: O processo de construção da identidade racial de professoras negras* (The Black woman who I saw up close: Black female teachers and the construction of racial identity) (Belo Horizonte: Maza

Ediçoes, 1995); Mariestela Barbosa Silveira e Silva, "Racial Relations in Brazil and the United States: Black Women's Literary Production as Counterhegemonic Tools against 'White Supremacist Capitalist Patriarchy,'" M.A. thesis, Washington State University, 1999; France Winddance Twine, *Racism in a Racial Democracy: The Maintenance of White Supremacy in Brazil* (New Brunswick, N.J.: Rutgers University Press, 1997).

51. Savi Horne, personal communication, January 9, 2000.
52. Maseko, *The Life and Times of Sarah Baartman;* see n. 1.

7

CHERYL MWARIA

BIOMEDICAL ETHICS, GENDER, AND ETHNICITY
Implications for Black Feminist Anthropology

The field of biomedical ethics (bioethics) is a subdiscipline of moral philosophy. In the 1970s and 1980s, it expanded with the development of medical technology and debated such issues as reproductive rights, care and treatment of the chronically ill and the disabled, mandatory screening for HIV, medical research on human subjects, and euthanasia. Anthropologists steered clear of these debates, leaving them to philosophers, theologians, lawyers, and physicians, whose opinions dominated the popular and professional literature. There was little public discussion about resource allocation or the implications of ethical decisions, especially in the United States, for women, minorities, or the poor.

This reflected the conceptual foundation of biomedical ethics, whose origins in law and philosophy emphasize individual rights and autonomy. This emphasis seems far removed from an anthropological perspective with its traditional emphasis on cultural relativity, a perspective that considers the ethical aspects of health care as givens and neglects ways in which they may relate to moral questions and ambiguities. Nevertheless, as Patricia King asserts, the social and ethical issues pertaining to biomedical research in any society harboring racist and sexist assumptions about the inferiority of given categorical members of that society invariably burden rather than benefit those deemed inferior.[1] Nowhere is this clearer than when considering the position of African American women and their sisters of color throughout the Third World with regard to medical research involving human experimentation in which imperialist, Eurocentric, and patriarchal goals have been inflicted on women of color with little or no regard to ethics.

These women have frequently been the unacknowledged heroines of medical research as well as its victims. Their experiences have led to a dilemma wherein a history of racist and sexist abuse at the hands of medical experimenters has made them justifiably reluctant to participate in clinical trials. Yet that same racism and sexism have often excluded them from clinical trials that could yield data tailored to their benefit.

Today, bioethical questions about medical research on human subjects, particularly on women of color, have moved to the center of discourses on bioethics. Yet there remains much room for a greater analysis of the critical role women of color have played both as subjects in medical research and as critics of medical research. Even more importantly, a feminist perspective borne of the experiences of these women has raised new questions and concerns challenging the current focus on abstract concepts of autonomy and the assumed objectivity of medicine as a scientific discipline. Thus, I contend that the concepts of power and authority, both cultural and social, whether invested in individuals, ideas, or institutions, lie at the heart of the intersection of feminist anthropology, bioethics, gender, and ethnicity.

I believe that as concerned researchers, we have a responsibility to examine the role that anthropology, particularly Black feminist anthropology, can play in expanding our understanding of this role and in framing public policy pertaining to bioethics.

BIOETHICS AND CIVIL RIGHTS

The modern medical profession, as it has emerged in the United States, arose as an insular and privileged profession whose practitioners were accountable only to themselves. This rise to sovereignty of American physicians was neither accidental nor inevitable. Rather, as Paul Starr has so cogently argued, it can be traced to the historical appropriation and growth of both cultural and social authority by the profession and "the conversion of that authority into the control of markets, organizations, and governmental policy."[2] Authority in both its classic and anthropological sense is the ability to influence without resorting to the use of force or negative sanctions. Authority itself may emanate not only from a person but also from an inanimate thing such as a text, treatise, or institution. The influence of authority is a reflection of the legitimacy granted by a culture or society upon the judgment of the authoritative figure; such judgments of meaning and value are deemed valid and true and therefore carry considerable weight. Starr calls this form of authority, involving the construction of reality through definitions of fact and value, *cultural authority*, to distinguish it from Weber's concept of *social authority*, which involves the control of action through the giving of commands.[3] Just as legitimacy is one pillar of authority, dependence is the other. Although authority involves obedience or compliance based on legitimacy, it also contains coercive power of force or negative sanctions, which are held in abeyance. These reserve powers, as Starr opines, "make subordinates dependent upon such authorities for their life, liberty, and livelihood; they create a strong basis for compliance, apart from any belief that subordinates may hold about the authorities' claim to obedience."[4]

Physicians, as professionals at the top of our hierarchical medical system, embody both cultural and social authority. The term *professional* here is consistent with the attributes outlined by Talcott Parsons: physician is an occupation that regulates itself through required training and collegial discipline; that claims competency through expertise in technical, specialized knowledge; and is service rather than profit oriented.[5] The cultural authority of physicians lies in the high regard in which science and its practitioners are held in the United States, and in the belief in the professional competence of doctors to interpret the signs of illness and the symptoms of disease and to provide an antidote for them. Illness and disease provoke discomfort and fear, thereby creating emotional dependency in patients. This dependency further strengthens the authority of physicians in the eyes of their patients. Moreover, the state empowers physicians as gatekeepers to resources and statuses desired by patients—certificates of birth, death, disability, certificates rendering them eligible or ineligible for employment, welfare, education, military service, and so forth. Such bureaucratic arrangements clearly foster dependency and compliance, quite separate from their power derived as moral authorities. Finally, physicians also embody social authority in that they are at the top of a hierarchy that places them in position to command those beneath them in the hierarchy, including other professionals, for whom they serve as gatekeepers as well. For these reasons it is easy to understand, as did Henry K. Beecher, that "if suitably approached, patients will accede, on the basis of trust to about any request their physician may make."[6] It is not only physicians who hold positions of authority vis-à-vis their research subjects. The same can be said of anthropologists, who historically have studied peoples who both politically and economically have comprised populations subject to the power of the investigators' own states. The question is, how did these insular positions of authority come to be challenged, and to what extent has that challenge been successful?

Although there is no consensus on the birth of bioethics, particularly with respect to the ethics of research, it is clear that by the early 1970s, the formerly insular world of medicine had changed considerably, at least in the United States. Historically, concern with research ethics extends back at least to the 1830s, when John William Willcock asserted in *The Laws Relating to the Medical Profession* that informed consent was necessary in medical experiments. Willcock opined: "When an experiment is performed with the consent of the party subjected to it after he has been informed that it is an experiment, the practitioner is answerable nei-

ther in damages nor on an original proceeding. But if the practitioner performs his experiment without giving such information
and obtaining consent he is liable to compensate in damages and
injury."[7] Willcock was primarily concerned with the financial responsibilities of physicians toward their subjects in a court of law
as opposed to ethical principles themselves, but he established an
important precedent.

By the late nineteenth century, the germ theory of disease led
to the development of bacteriology, pharmacology, and immunol-
ogy, each of which created demands for human experimentation,
as did the development of new diagnostic technologies, including
the stethoscope, the x-ray, and the stomach tube. These new technologies, according to Paul Starr, enhanced professional autonomy,
further distancing the physician from the patient while "expanding the role of physicians as gatekeepers to positions and benefits
in the society. . . . From the patients' standpoint, these detached
technologies added a highly persuasive rhetoric to the authority
of medicine." Yet, "the collegial exercise of authority strengthened
the claim to objective judgment."[8]

The authority of medicine, and physicians as its primary practitioners, consolidated from the end of the nineteenth century and
on through the first few decades of the twentieth, with few voices
raised in opposition to the increasing use of humans in experiments. Indeed, the use of human subjects was deemed not only
justifiable but necessary for the advancement of medical science.
The majority of these subjects came from the ranks of minorities,
the poor, orphaned children, the mentally and physically disabled,
and those deemed terminally ill. The leading voices of opposition
at the time were antivivisectionists, whose arguments were viewed
as a threat to scientific progress.[9] Although undoubtedly there were
many researchers who adhered to an informal code of ethics by
obtaining consent, informed or not, and by trying to put their patients' best interests first, or even by refraining from nontherapeutic
research, the authority that physicians held made them the final
arbiter of medical ethics.

Historically, experiments using human subjects from groups
devalued by society have caused little if any outcry. Historian James
Jones argued in *Bad Blood: The Tuskegee Syphilis Experiment* that even

as late as the 1930s, there was "no system of normative ethics of human experimentation that compelled medical researchers to temper their scientific curiosity with respect for patients rights."[10] Many have argued that the ethical surveillance of medical research began with the establishment of the Nuremberg Code, as a reaction to Nazi atrocities, and continued with the Declaration of Helsinki.[11] Stephen Lock asserts that "although both episodes are important landmarks, the first had little effect on medical practice, while even the second was the culmination of a much longer period of concern and might scarcely have come about at all if it had not been for vigorous and persistent proselytizing by a handful of concerned individuals."[12]

Two of the most significant of these concerned individuals were Maurice Pappworth of London and Henry Beecher of Harvard. Both men documented the pervasive ethical abuse of patients as research subjects. In his 1958 monograph, *Experimentation in Man*, Beecher argued, "The breaches of ethical conduct which have come to [my] personal attention are [the result of] ignorance or thoughtlessness. They were not willful or unscrupulous in origin. It is hoped that the material included here will help those who would do so to protect themselves from the errors of inexperience."[13] Beecher wrote his monograph before the birth of bioethics, and as his student Jay Katz has written, "He wanted to teach, not to indict."[14] By 1966, however, Beecher's concern about medical ethics had grown. In his hallmark article, "Ethics and Clinical Research," published that year, he raised "troubling charges" that had grown out of "troubling practices," which he documented by exposing that twelve out "of 100 consecutive human studies published in 1964 in an excellent journal" had been "unethical."[15] Beecher linked the remarkable growth of federally funded biomedical research with the growing emphasis on research in medical schools and institutions. Noting that serious attention to the problem was urgent, Beecher asserted: "Taking into account the sound and increasing emphasis of recent years that experimentation in man must precede general application of new procedures in therapy, plus the great sums of money available, there is reason to fear that these requirements and these resources may be greater than the supply of responsible investigators."[16]

Beecher's primary concern was the problem of informed consent. He noted the contradiction between what he called "the bland assumption that meaningful or informed consent is readily available for the asking"—an assumption upon which "all so-called codes are based"—and the reality that "this is very often not the case." More importantly, Beecher was aware of the authoritative position of physicians in the eyes of their patients and the subsequent vulnerability of patients to exploitation at the hands of their physicians. He wrote, as previously noted, that "if suitably approached, patients will accede, on the basis of trust, to about any request their physician may make," even submitting to inconvenience and discomfort. Yet "the usual patient will never agree to jeopardize seriously his health or his life for the sake of 'science.'"[17] There were then as now significant problems with the concept of informed consent. For one thing, many human subjects were themselves incapable of giving informed consent. This was the case, for example, with the mentally incompetent and children. Another significant problem lay in the nature of the research itself. Much of it was not therapeutic in that it was not expected to benefit either the subjects themselves or mankind. Rather, it was basic science, the benefits of which, if any, could be quite distant for all but the researcher. The question then is: Does society have the right to subject citizens to experiments that could lead to injury or death for such ends? The most important problem with informed consent, and the subtlest, is that in race-based and hierarchical societies, the authority of researchers tends to be coercive. Hierarchies create dependence. It is not surprising that those who seek help for relief from illness tend toward compliance.

Despite the alarms raised by whistleblowers in the 1960s, no real challenge to the authority of physicians came until the impact of the Civil Rights movement began to be felt. The civil rights struggle of African Americans provided a model for dozens of other social movements, including the disability rights movement and the patients' rights movement. It also provided an impetus for the feminist movement, just as the struggle for abolition had in the nineteenth century.[18] What then did it mean to invoke civil rights? It meant to restructure the power relations between physician and patient.

By 1972, the trustees of the American Hospital Association had adopted a Patients' Bill of Rights, which included not only the right to informed consent but the right to considerate and respectful care. A fundamental intellectual shift had occurred that reflected a deepening distrust of medicine and medical practitioners. At the forefront of this shift was the feminist movement. Feminists began to challenge the entrenched paternalism of medicine as practiced in the United States, by which I mean the unquestioned authority of the physician, which excluded patients from meaningful decision-making about their own care. Feminists also began to question research priorities, for example, those that emphasized "cure" over prevention.

COMPLICATING ISSUES OF ETHNICITY AND FEMINISM

Can we speak of an African American or a Black perspective in medical ethics? Likewise, can we speak of a feminist perspective or a Black feminist, anthropological one? Most bioethicists, who are, not incidentally, White, male, middle-class professionals and academics, would find the notion of an ethnic or gendered perspective problematic. Biomedical ethics, they would argue, is a subdiscipline of ethics, which is a philosophical discipline. Ethics can be defined as the philosophical study of morality. The concept of ethics is commonly divided into *normative ethics*, wherein the philosopher attempts to establish what is morally right and what is morally wrong with regard to human action, and *meta ethics* (analytic ethics), which is concerned with the analysis of both moral concepts, for example, the concept of duty or the concept of rights, and moral reasoning.[19]

Anthropologists have generally avoided these two approaches as being antithetical to cultural relativism. For instance, Raymond Firth has argued, "The anthropologist is not discussing the existence of ethical notions on the philosophical plane. But what he does show, in line with studies of Durkheim, Westermarck, Hobhouse, Ginsberg and others, is the existence of standards of right and wrong, and sensitive judgements in their terms, in all human societies. These standards vary greatly in differentiation and in social range. They are in obvious relation to the structure of the societies where they are found."[20] Descriptive ethics, then, is the attempt to "describe and explain those moral views which in fact *are accepted*."[21] Most anthropologists who have ventured into ethics have focused on descriptive ethics. The distinction lies in discussions of what is (descriptive ethics) and what ought to be, that is, it provides and advances a reasoned justification of an overall theory of moral obligation. Further, in applied normative ethics, the focus is on the resolution of real moral problems. This too is an area generally avoided by anthropologists until relatively recently. Current debates in medical ethics have been grounded in Anglo-American philosophical traditions emphasizing Kant's deontological individualism and, albeit to a lesser degree, utilitarian consequentialism. The former focuses on autonomy and individual rights, whereas the latter, although respecting the individual, focuses on the outcomes of specific actions for all concerned.

The Nuremberg Code, which encompasses these traditions, would become the standard by which research involving human subjects would be measured. The code required that the following basic principles be observed to satisfy moral, ethical, and legal concepts. First, voluntary consent of the human subject was essential. Second, experiments should yield fruitful results for the good of society; the experimental subject should be protected against even the remote possibility of injury, disability, or death; experiments should be conducted by scientifically qualified personnel; and an experiment should be terminated if injury is believed to be the likely outcome.[22] The Nuremberg Code stands as a significant achievement that has influenced many medical ethical codes that have followed; it has also been criticized as "politically naïve and unduly restrictive with respect to research involving children and other populations of patients."[23] Further critiques of prevailing principles of medical ethics focus on the lack of empirical evidence from a cross-cultural perspective. As Grant Gillet argues, "Until recently there has been a paucity of writing from other cultural traditions and a neglect of critical or post-modern views in a discussion of ethical issues. This has led to the liberal ideal of a society of free, economically independent, and competing individuals being accepted as the conceptual framework for medical ethics."[24] Anthropology can offer a constructive commitment to recognizing cultural differences and raise the level of awareness in the powerful way in which socialization, within a specific culture, influences behavioral expectations. Even more to the point, Black feminist anthropology recognizes that gender and ethnicity are part of the construction of power and authority relations in our culture and that we must be alert to the possibility of gendered and ethnic hierarchies in other cultures as well.

To return to my original query, the assertion that there can be an ethnic or gendered perspective in medical ethics has been seen as problematic precisely because it suggests that specific intellectual positions can be identified with a particular ethnic group or gender and with members of that group alone. Clearly such claims are false. However, insofar as the anthropologist understands that ethnicity and gender inform the relationships within heterogeneous societies, we as social scientists can and must investigate the different ways in which ethnicity and gender inform social relations within different heterogeneous contexts.

African Americans and people of color globally, particularly women, have historically lacked protection against medical abuse. What we are now seeing is the exploitation of women of color in various countries by pharmaceutical corporations with a global reach. As soon as biomedical ethics raised the bar for medical experimentation, even on Black women in this country, we began to see exportation of clinical trials to the Third World, where women of color became the preferred subjects. Some of these experiments, such as those designed to develop drugs to prevent or inhibit the transmission of the HIV virus from mother to offspring, seem to meet the criteria that experiments involving human subjects be designed to benefit those subjects. A closer look, however, reveals ethical lapses that would not be allowed in the United States in that African women who tested HIV positive were not told that the virus could be passed through breast milk and that therefore they should refrain from breastfeeding. Apologists for the studies have argued that the complex regimen necessary to reduce mother-to-child transmission rates in the United States is simply not feasible in the Third World, primarily because it is expensive.[25] Such arguments serve to reinforce the status quo of hierarchical privilege of Western countries. At the same time, presumed beneficence masks the more compelling motive of huge profits to be earned through the development of AIDS drugs. It should be clear why the experiences of minority women should and must play a pivotal role in informing and framing bioethical public policy debates. Far too often their voices have been omitted under the guise of objectivity and universality with respect to moral concepts and moral reasoning. Feminist scholars and activists, particularly those of color, have insisted that recognition of these racist and sexist patterns must become a part of bioethical analysis.[26] Moreover, this analysis must then be reflected in public policy.

A HISTORICAL OVERVIEW OF WOMEN OF COLOR AS SUBJECTS IN MEDICAL RESEARCH

The history of medical research that uses women's bodies dates back to the rise of biological determinism and scientific racism of the nineteenth century. Biological determinism, supported by scientific racism, represented an intellectual shift that was bent on proving that Blacks were inherently different from Whites, even on the level of species, as exemplified by the theory of polygenesis. This shift was intimately associated with a defense of slavery and a rationalization for the degradation and dehumanization of Blacks. Moreover, although racists often confined their label of inferiority to a single group, racism and sexism often go hand in hand, as was true in the nineteenth century, when women and Blacks were viewed as intellectually and morally the equivalent of White male children.[27]

While the treatment of slaves at the hands of medical men varied, by the nineteenth century there was a widespread belief among physicians in the South that Whites and Blacks differed medically—both physiologically and intellectually. Medicine as practiced in the South during the nineteenth century could scarcely be called scientific. Yet there were valid observations made by physicians and laymen of the time. Most notably, these observations documented different rates of morbidity and mortality between slaves and Whites with respect to infectious disease, especially "fevers," such as malaria. Slaves also had higher rates of nutritionally based diseases such as rickets. Little was known about disease etiology at the time. Consequently, it was generally assumed that there was something intrinsically different about Blacks and, moreover, that Blacks were racially inferior. Arguments that placed Whites above Blacks in a medical and physical hierarchy were purely polemical, thinly disguised, or overt rationales for slavery and the exploitation of black labor in medically dangerous work and living conditions. Blacks who resisted these conditions were reputed to suffer from diseases peculiar to them such as "drapetomania"—a disease causing slaves to run away—and "dysaethesia," better known as "rascality" or the resistance to work.[28]

Aside from the purely polemical rationales for slavery, medical research benefited from captive slave populations. The sick, especially those seeking help in hospitals, clinics, or even at home, could be used as "cases" to teach medical students basic treatment of disease, to illustrate unusual diseases, to test new pharmacological treatments, or to develop new surgical techniques. Blacks, both slave and free, often ended up as these "cases" or, even more frequently, as cadavers used in medical school dissections. According to folklorist Gladys-Marie Fry, between 1880 and 1920, the practice of robbing the graves of black folk for bodies to be used in experimentation and dissection was so common that the image of the "night doctor" became firmly established in African American oral tradition.[29]

Slavery as an institution afforded physicians a unique opportunity to experiment, which "they dared not do with whites."[30] Consent was not a problem, because slaves by law were property and therefore could not legally consent to anything. Slave owners, on the other hand, stood to profit from the rental or sale of slaves for experimental purposes. Furthermore, experiments that resulted in pain, disfigurement, or death were not likely to raise a public outcry. It was against this background that two of the best known and medically significant series of surgical experiments were performed on slave women. One was the series of thirty operations on slave women that was performed over four years by Dr. Marion Sims. Sims used these women to perfect his technique for repairing vesico-vaginal fistulas, a condition in which urine or feces leaks through the vaginal opening. It is not clear whether these women already had the condition when Sims acquired them. However, the technique he developed was considered a major medical breakthrough, and Sims received lasting acclaim for it.

Less is known about the slave women, except the names of three of them—Lucey, Anarcha, and Betsey—and the fact that they were heroines who survived the barbarity of these repeated surgeries without anesthesia. Sims arranged the following agreement with the owner of Anarcha and Betsey. "If you will give me Anarcha and Betsey for experiment, I agree to perform no experiment or operation on them to endanger their lives, and will not charge a cent for keeping them, but you must pay their taxes and clothe them. I will keep them at my own expense."[31] According to historian Susan Lederer, "Unlike Sims, who maintained his subjects only during his experiments, some physicians preferred to purchase slaves who were afflicted with medical conditions they hoped to study."[32]

Nor was Sims the first physician to attempt a surgical cure for vesico-vaginal fistula through the use of slave women. Dr. John Peter Mettauer performed the operation fifteen years earlier with less consistent results, and without the use of anesthesia, which was unknown at the time. Mettauer operated on more than twenty-five women, most of whom were believed to be slaves, although few details were provided about them. His only recorded failure in twenty-eight cases was that of a twenty-year-old slave whose initial condition was brought about by "a tedious and poorly managed labor."[33] After suffering through at least ten unsuccessful surgeries, this woman was ultimately blamed for the poor outcome by Mettauer, who wrote, "I believe this case, nevertheless, could have been cured in process of time, more especially if sexual intercourse could have been prevented, which intercourse, I have no doubt, defeated several of the operations."[34] Clearly, as Savitt argues, this is a statement that "no nineteenth century white woman would have permitted her physician to print."[35]

Another surgical technique perfected on slave women was the cesarean section. Louisiana physicians led by Dr. François Marie Prevost performed fifteen of these operations, all on slave women, between 1822 and 1861. To their credit, eleven mothers and eight children were saved by a procedure that at least had the merit of benefiting slave women themselves, whose poor nutrition led to an abundance of pelvic deformities.[36] Yet again, it seems clear that physicians were more likely to practice on slave women than on Whites. Although there is much documented evidence of the use of slaves, especially women, as subjects of medical experimentation, it by no means represents an exhaustive list of these practices. Many physicians and lay practitioners of medicine experimented on slaves without recording their results. Some documented experiments pre-saged those of the Nazi doctors, such as those designed to see if Blacks could withstand more pain or depletion than Whites.[37] Again, as was the case with the Nazi experiments, few medical men making use of the results of these experiments raised any moral or ethical concerns about the matter in which the data were obtained.

The abolition of slavery did not end medical experimentation on Blacks, or for that matter on women, children, the mentally dis-abled, or the poor. If anything, the search for subjects was expanded. However, opponents to vivisection and other whistle-blowers forced physicians and researchers to use some restraint, if for no other reasons than fear of litigation and loss of reputation. Still, poor Blacks remained fair game, as illustrated by the infamous Tuskegee syphilis experiment conducted by the U.S. Public Health Service.

This forty-year experiment, which ultimately had no medical or scientific merit, involved some 399 men with syphilis and an additional 201 who were free of the disease. Each of the men was poor and black. They were not told that they had syphilis, a dis-ease contracted through sexual intercourse or through birth if one's mother had the disease. Thus, they were unaware that they could easily spread it to their loved ones. These men, therefore, were not the only victims. Their wives, children, and lovers were equally vic-timized in that they were exposed to the disease without any ap-parent thought on the part of the Public Health Service physicians. Ostensibly conducted to study the effects of tertiary-stage syphilis, the experiment continued and treatment was withheld from the subjects even after an effective cure for syphilis was discovered and even after physicians involved had acknowledged that the study had no merit. The horror of Tuskegee has left a legacy of fear and mistrust in the black community, as documented by historian James Jones.[38] However, it took the Civil Rights movement and exposure of the Tuskegee experiment to produce a shift in the cultural cli-mate that would successfully challenge the authority of physicians and would usher in bioethics as we know it.

The birth of the bioethics movement in the United States raised the bar on medical experiments performed on human subjects in this country, but it did not prevent such experiments, often funded by government sources and global pharmaceutical companies, from being conducted elsewhere, particularly on women in the Third World. In 1985, a report issued by the International Social Science Council and UNESCO acknowledged the risk of exploitation facing Third World people, who increasingly serve as test populations for biomedical products or who serve as secondary markets in which developed countries dump products deemed illegal or undesirable in their own countries.[39] Some of the most pervasive abuses come from reproductive technologies that target women, particularly those who are poor, migrant, refugee, or of minority status. These many well-documented abuses include the testing of the birth control pill on women in Puerto Rico, the testing of injectable contraceptives on women in Egypt, and the pushing of IUDs on women in Kenya. Women in the Third World have been given stronger doses of contraceptive hormones under the hypothesis that their undernourished bodies would secrete the hormones faster.[40]

Two glaring examples of unethical clinical trials can be seen in the testing and promotion of the Dalkon shield, an intrauterine device manufactured by A. H. Robbins Corporation, and Norplant, which was researched and developed by the Population Council and marketed in the United States by Wyeth-Ayerst of Philadelphia. The Dalkon shield was distributed widely in Third World countries, where it was promoted as the ideal contraceptive because once inserted, it could not be removed without a physician. A. H. Robins was forced to take the device off the U.S. market due to infections and other medical complications caused by the shield. The company later sold 697,000 unmarketed shields to USAID for distribution in the Third World through the International Planned Parenthood Federation, the Pathfinder Fund, the Population Council, and Family Planning International Assistance.[41] Feminists have noted the historical association of each of these groups with the eugenics movement of old.[42]

Norplant is a contraceptive device comprised of six silicon capsules filled with the synthetic hormone lenonorgesterol, a form of progestin. The capsules are surgically implanted in the upper arm under local anesthesia. The contraceptive is designed to prevent pregnancy for up to five years by both suppressing ovulation and thickening the cervical mucus, thereby preventing the sperm from reaching the egg. Considered a technological breakthrough when first developed, Norplant was tested on poor black women in the United States, but most of the testing was conducted on women in Brazil, Indonesia, Egypt, and Bangladesh. Informed consent was generally absent, but even when consent was sought, it was accompanied by more subtle forms of coercion such as monetary incentives for insertion and dissuasion from reporting health problems.

Almost immediately problems appeared in the clinical trials. Norplant was associated with excessive bleeding, headaches, depression, nervousness, change in appetite, weight gain, hair loss, nausea, dizziness, acne, breast tenderness, swelling of the ovaries, and ovarian cysts. It has also been known to lead to pain and infection. Inserts that are not removed after five years can lead to ectopic pregnancy, while the long-term effects on a fetus are not yet known. Moreover, certain medical conditions make the use of Norplant inadvisable, including high blood pressure, diabetes, kidney disease, sickle-cell anemia, and heart disease, all of which disproportionately affect black women. As if that weren't enough, the studies themselves were poorly designed; often the women receiving the contraceptive received no adequate follow-up, and especially in the Third World, the women had no access to physicians trained to remove the devices. As feminist scholar Dorothy Roberts reports,

> The case of testing in Bangladesh raises serious doubts about both the ethics and the reliability of the Norplant research. An investigation conducted by UBINIG, a Bangladesh monitoring group, discovered alarming problems with the Norplant clinical trial conducted in Bangladesh between 1985 and 1987 on 600 urban slum women. The organization found that procedures followed by the Bangladesh Fertility Research Program, the national family planning and biomedical research organization, were marred by gross violations of medical ethics, inadequate methodology, and disregard for the health of the female subjects.[43]

Feminist activist Janice Raymond writes of similar ethical lapses, methodological errors, and medical complications found in Norplant's Brazilian test site:

> At the time that the testing of Norplant was initiated on Brazilian women, the military dictatorship was still in power, and there was effectively no public input into the decision. The government presented the test as a "fait accompli" that would involve seven clinics and a total of two thousand women. The tests performed were called "preintroductory tests." Dr. Ana Regina Gomes Dos Rios, senior official in the Brazilian Ministry of Health, which later investigated the outcome of the Norplant testing, clarified a key difference between tests that are actual trials and so-called preintroductory tests. . . . They are tests that use marketing techniques rather than clinical or epidemiological ones.[44]

In other words, the tests did not provide a detailed analysis of the reaction of each woman but rather concentrated on strategies designed to enhance acceptance of the drug. Complications such as heavy bleeding, menstrual irregularities, alterations of the central nervous system, and dramatic changes in body weight were simply covered over as "cause for removal" or "woman requested removal."[45]

While women of color are being used to test contraceptives, many White middle- and upper-class women are being coerced into testing powerful fertility drugs and technologies, often when they are not themselves infertile and apparently with just as little thought on the part of experimenters as to the long-term consequences of these experiments on their subjects.

Currently, there is an additional and equally significant problem with medical research and clinical trials: women and minorities are typically not included in legitimate studies. Given the history of women, particularly those of color, at the hands of medical experimenters, it is understandable that they might be reluctant to participate in clinical trials. Another and perhaps far more common reason for the dearth of African American women in legitimate clinical trials is that they have simply been excluded. Craig Svensson's investigation of the exclusion of African Americans from clinical drug trials found that over a three-year period, only ten out of fifty studies of new drug trials published in *Clinical Pharmacology and Therapeutics* included any racial data. In the study of antihypertensive drugs, an area in which differential racial responses to drug treatments have been well documented, only roughly half of the researchers gave racial data. The under-representation of African Americans in clinical trials suggests, according to Svensson, "that insufficient data exist to accurately assess the safety and efficacy of many new drugs in Blacks."[46] This exclusion can be as unethical and damaging as coercive participation in poorly designed studies has been. Why? Simply because disease patterns are frequently different according to sex and ethnicity. In other words, just as gene frequencies and behavioral patterns differ from one population to another, so do the diseases governed by them. It follows then that the most effective drugs and methods of treatment will differ accordingly. As Sara Goering has argued, "failing to acknowledge the differences is also a form of racism, one that is alive and well today, and that is thus perhaps more important than the distant fear."[47] Physician Lori Pierce, a professor of radiation oncology at Wayne State Medical School, has noted that "the low participation rate among blacks in clinical trials is particularly troubling because studies show that cancer patients enrolled in these studies generally have 'better outcomes' than other patients."[48]

RADICAL IMPLICATIONS FOR BIOETHICS: THE CONTRIBUTIONS OF BLACK FEMINIST ANTHROPOLOGY

The contribution of anthropology itself is clear, as Christine Ward Gailey has observed: "Anthropology can value the local, the subordinated, the creation of meaning among those who are not powerful in the reductive sense of wealth or political control or even social prestige. Perhaps it is this tendency that contributed to the formative influence that anthropologists in the early 1970s had on the development of what have become international or transnational feminisms."[49] Where, however, does this leave Black feminist anthropology? Both Black and White feminists share the basic assumption that gender is a critical dimension of human societies and cultures. Likewise we share a concern about differential social power and authority. Nevertheless, as feminist scholar and anthropologist A. Lynn Bolles so eloquently reminds us, the voices of Black feminist anthropologists have often been ignored or unacknowledged even by their fellow feminists.[50] We are distinguished by the vantage point taken in inquiry. We are often well placed to gather empirical data and to develop theory with which to inform critical discourse, because we tend to "live our anthropology." Consider, for example, the life of anthropologist and folklorist Zora Neale Hurston. According to Gwendolyn Mikell, "Hurston approached her work with the assumption that the best researcher has a commonality with the people being studied."[51] Furthermore, Mikell argues,

> Hurston had grown up in Florida with the almost "primordial" attachments to the nuances of black life in the church and the community. She understood and laughed at the intricacies of color differences, having become familiar with them from the controversies created by the marriage of her mother and her father. She delighted in the spiritual sons, the biblical stories, and the institutions of the black community. In short she had the ability to be "in culture while looking at culture."[52]

Another example of how we as Black feminist anthropologists live our anthropology can be seen in the experiences of anthropologist and activist Leith Mullings. Mullings, who as a medical anthropologist has written extensively about the health of minority women and the impact of lack of access to health care, reveals:

> It was essential that my children be born in the summer, preferably early summer. In 1976 Columbia did not have paid leave for pregnancy, and disability coverage could not be extended to pregnancy. My husband was a left activist who made very little money, and my salary from Columbia was the primary source of income for our household, which included two children from his former marriage. Furthermore, Columbia's medical plan did not provide coverage for childbirth. Therefore I could not afford to be without my $12,000 salary from Columbia.[53]

I, too, have "lived my anthropology," particularly when pregnant with my daughter while conducting fieldwork in Kenya on childbirth and childrearing. My informants were Kamba women, most of whom had had far more experience than I had with childbirth and childrearing. Yet they were kind and patient in answering my innumerable questions. Moreover, much to my delight, in what could be seen as a sense of "womanist" or feminist solidarity, they counseled my husband on the importance of satisfying my requests, no matter how irrational they might seem. As my pregnancy advanced, my African mother-in-law worried that I might go into labor alone as did many of my informants, given the then remote hamlets to which I traveled. She prepared a "delivery" kit for me similar to the one she herself had carried when pregnant. It consisted of a sterile razor to cut the umbilical cord; Dettol, an antiseptic; sterile cotton thread to tie the ends of the umbilicus; clean white cotton cloth to wrap the baby and to clean myself; and a fresh change of clothes. She also patiently taught me how to use these things, all the while assuring me it probably would not be necessary. Nor did my lessons stop after the birth of my daughter.

One day I took her to the local market wrapped to my breast in the fashion of the local women, but I had neglected to bring an umbrella to shield her. She began to cry as the sun beat down on us, while I was lost in conversation with a friend. The voices of market women began to call out, "Doesn't that child have a mother?" When I failed to attend to my baby, they suddenly swooped down on me and my companion shouting, "So, I'm hot and hungry and you ignore me!" "So, I cry and you cannot hear!" This was followed by strong pinches on our arms and legs. Neither my girlfriend nor I forgot the lessons—pay attention to a crying child, protect your child from danger and discomfort, put your children's needs ahead of your own. It was an invaluable lesson in collective responsibility for and love of children that these women had. The kindness and support women showed me extended through the death of my husband, when their example provided me with the strength and courage to continue. While literally never leaving me by myself and caring for my day-to-day needs, they also refused to allow me to wallow in self-pity. "Why are you crying Mwende?[54] Are you the first to lose your husband? Will you be the last? Are not we all to die one day?" Although painful at first, this too proved an invaluable lesson in life.

My point here is that we as Black feminist anthropologists generally share bonds of race, gender, and sometimes class with our informants, and these factors shape our experiences as well as those of our informants. Our lives are frequently intertwined on many levels. Because of these "ties that bind,"[55] we cannot and should not adopt the voice, so typical of classic male-dominated anthropology, of the distant and dispassionate observer. We are not only observers; we are also subject to being observed. The image of our informants is likely to be the image of ourselves. Under these circumstances, passionate discourse is definitely in order. It explains why feminist ideology is advocacy ideology, and I would argue, it is more so for female anthropologists of color, whose mothers, sisters, and friends are often economically positioned in ways that make them vulnerable to psychological, physical, and institutional oppression.

This is not to say that we are all the same or that we speak with one voice.[56] What it does suggest is that as anthropologists of color, we should raise a different, more critical set of questions than those currently being raised in bioethical debates, and we must do so through the lenses of race, class, and gender. Whose interests (e.g., those of a gender, class, or ethnic group) are likely to be served? Under what historical conditions do these ethical debates arise? Some of these questions are being raised in other areas by critical medical anthropology.[57] Given the medicalization of difference in public policy, particularly in the United States although not limited to it, and given the increasing globalization of pharmaceutical companies, medical technology, and patterns of medical research, such questions are vital to understanding what is at stake for women of color. As Black feminist activist Evelyn C. White of the National Black Women's Health Project asserts:

> Black women have had enough of the statistics that tell us that the life expectancy for whites is 75.3 years compared with the 69.4 for blacks; that the infant mortality rate for blacks is 20 deaths per 1,000, about twice the rate suffered among whites; that 52 percent of the women with AIDS are black; that more than 50 percent of black women live in a state of emotional distress; and that black women stand a one in 104 chance of being murdered compared with a one in 369 chance for white women.—We have to address and change the dismal predictions about our lives because we've got glorious contributions to make to society. We've got songs to sing, pictures to paint, poems to recite, children to teach, books to write, pies to bake, hair to braid, flowers to grow, businesses to run and people to love. There's a whole lot of living in us yet.[58]

As Black feminist anthropologists, we are also accountable to a wide range of folks—our professional colleagues, the general public, policymakers, our informants, and ourselves. Such accountability frequently requires political engagement. We must join our feminist

sisters in the Third World in their protests against unethical medical experiments and in their challenge to reproductive fundamentalism, while insisting on access to quality health care. This is
particularly true when discussing issues pertaining to bioethics that
frame public policy. Indeed the very acts of writing and speaking
become political. It is precisely here through the linkage of theory
and practice that we can make our most significant contributions
as Black feminist anthropologists.

NOTES

1. Patricia King, "The Dangers of Difference: The Legacy of the Tuskegee Syphilis Study," *Hastings Center Report* 22, 6 (1992): 35–38.
2. Paul Starr, *The Social Transformation of American Medicine* (New York: Basic Books, 1982), 9.
3. Ibid., 13.
4. Ibid., 9.
5. See Talcott Parsons, *The Social System* (New York: The Free Press, 1968), 433–439.
6. Henry K. Beecher, "Ethics and Clinical Research," *New England Journal of Medicine* 274, 24 (June 16, 1966): 1355.
7. John William Willcock, *The Laws Relating to the Medical Profession* (London: J. and W. T. Clarke, 1830), cited in Stephen Lock, "Research Ethics—A Brief Historical Review to 1965," *Journal of Internal Medicine* 238 (1995): 514.
8. Starr, *The Social Transformation of American Medicine*, 137.
9. Vivisection means literally cutting into a living organism. The term was used in the late nineteenth century to denote any experimental manipulation. Antivivisectionists objected to experimentation on live animals and on humans (human vivisection) when such procedures were nontherapeutic. See Susan Lederer, *Subjected to Science* (Baltimore: Johns Hopkins University Press, 1995), for a discussion of the relationship between the antivivisectionist movement and experimental research on humans.
10. James H. Jones, *Bad Blood: The Tuskegee Syphilis Experiment* (New York: The Free Press, 1993), 97.
11. The Declaration of Helsinki, which appeared first in 1964 and was revised in 1975, 1983, and 1989, is one of several codes and commentaries on research ethics designed to articulate norms for behavior and to protect the moral interests of human subjects.
12. Lock, "Research Ethics," 238.
13. Henry K. Beecher, *Experimentation in Man* (Springfield, Ill.: Charles C. Thomas, 1958), 4.
14. Jay Katz, "'Ethics and Clinical Research' Revisited: A Tribute to Henry K. Beecher," *Hastings Center Report* 23, 5 (1993): 32.
15. Beecher, "Ethics and Clinical Research," 1354.
16. Ibid., 1355.
17. Ibid.
18. The role of black women as both abolitionists and feminists and the links they forged between these movements have frequently been overlooked. Nevertheless, black women, particularly in the nineteenth century, embraced both issues precisely because as victims of the oppression of patriarchy and slavery, they understood the link between the two. See, for example, C. Peter Ripley, ed., with Roy E. Finkenbine (associate ed.), Michael Hembree (assistant ed.), and Donald Yacovone (assistant ed.), *The Black Abolitionist Papers*, vol. 4, *The United States, 1847–1858* (Chapel Hill: University of North Carolina Press, 1991), for a discussion of the roles of Mary Ann Shad Cary, Sojourner Truth, Harriet A. Jacobs, Barbara Ann Steward, and Frances Ellen Watkins Harper to name but a few.
19. The definitions of ethics and the approaches to the study of ethics in philosophy presented here are based on those given by Thomas A. Mappes and Jane S. Zembaty, *Biomedical Ethics* (New York: McGraw Hill, 1981), 2.

20. Raymond Firth, *Elements of Social Organization* (Boston: Beacon Press, 1970), 213.
21. Mappes and Zembaty, *Biomedical Ethics*, 2.
22. "Permissible Medical Experiments," in *Trials of War Criminals before the Nuremberg Military Tribunals under Control Council Law No. 10: Nuremberg, October 1946–April 1949*, vol. 2 (Washington, D.C.: U.S. Government Printing Office, n.d.), 181–182.
23. Harold Y. Vanderpool, "Introduction and Overview: Ethics, Historical Case Studies, and the Research Enterprise," in *The Ethics of Research Involving Human Subjects: Facing the 21st Century* (Frederick, Md.: University Publishing Group, 1996), 8. In a footnote (n. 34, p. 22), Vanderpool elaborates on several critiques of the Nuremberg Code.
24. Grant R. Gillet, "Medical Ethics in a Multicultural Context," *Journal of Internal Medicine* 238 (1995): 531.
25. Joseph Saba and Arthur Ammann, "A Cultural Divide on AIDS Research," *New York Times*, September 20, 1997, Op-Ed, A15.
26. Entrenched and systemic patterns of racism and sexism in modern medicine frequently go undocumented. Kevin A. Schulman et al.'s brilliantly designed study proves an exception. K. A. Schulman, J. A. Berlin, W. Harless, J. F. Kerner, S. Sistrunk, B. J. Gersh, R. Dube, C. K. Taleghani, J. E. Burke, S. Williams, J. M. Eisenberg, and J. J. Escarce, "The Effect of Race and Sex on Physicians' Recommendations for Cardiac Catheterization," *New England Journal of Medicine* 340 (February 25, 1999): 618–626.
27. Stephen Jay Gould, *The Mismeasure of Man* (New York: W.W. Norton, 1996), 112.
28. Samuel Cartwright, "Report on the Diseases and Physical Peculiarities of the Negro Race," *Medical and Surgical Journal* (New Orleans) (1831): 692–713.
29. Gladys-Marie Fry, *Night Riders in Black Folk History* (Knoxville: University of Tennesee Press, 1975), 172.
30. Kenneth F. Kiple and Virginia Himmelsteib King, *Another Dimension to the Black Diaspora: Diet, Disease and Racism* (Cambridge: Cambridge University Press, 1981), 173.
31. J. Marion Sims, *The Story of My Life* (New York: D. Appleton, 1894), 236.
32. Susan E. Lederer, *Subjected to Science: Human Experimentation in America before the Second World War* (Baltimore: Johns Hopkins University Press, 1995), 116.
33. John Peter Mettauer, "Vesico-Vaginal Fistula," *BMSJ* 22 (1840): 154–155; idem, "On Vesico Vaginal Fistula," *AJMS* n.s. 14 (1847): 117–121, as cited in Todd L. Savitt, *Medicine and Slavery: The Diseases and Health Care of Blacks in Antebellum Virginia* (Urbana: University of Illinois Press, 1978), 297.
34. Mettauer, "On Vesico Vaginal Fistula," 121.
35. Savitt, *Medicine and Slavery*, 297–298.
36. Kipple and King, *Another Dimension to the Black Diaspora*, 174.
37. Ibid.
38. Jones, *Bad Blood*, 220–241.
39. Janice G. Raymond, *Women as Wombs: Reproductive Technologies and the Battle over Women's Freedom* (San Francisco: Harper San Francisco, 1993), 14.
40. Ibid., 15.
41. Ibid.
42. See Dorothy Roberts's brilliant analysis, "The Dark Side of Birth Control," in *Killing the Black Body: Race, Reproduction and the Meaning of Liberty* (New York: Vintage Books, 1997), 56–103; Betsy Hartmann, *Reproductive Rights and Wrongs: The Global Politics of Population Control and Contraceptive Choice* (New York: Harper and Row, 1987), 100–123; and Thomas M. Shapiro, *Population Control Politics* (Philadelphia: Temple University Press, 1985).
43. Roberts, *Killing the Black Body*, 125.
44. Raymond, *Women as Wombs*, 15–16.
45. Ibid.
46. C. K. Svensson, "Representation of American Blacks in Clinical Trials of New Drugs," *Journal of the American Medical Association* 261, 2 (1989): 265.
47. Sara Goering, "Women and Underserved Populations: Access to Clinical Trials." in *It Just Ain't Fair: The Ethics of Health Care for African Americans*, ed. Annette Dula and Sara Goering (Westport, Conn.: Praeger, 1994), 189.
48. Carol Stevens, "Research: Distrust runs deep; medical community seeks solutions," *Detroit News Washington Bureau*, http://detnews.com/menu/stories/27970.htm.

49. Christine Ward Gailey, "Feminist Methods," in *Handbook of Methods in Anthropology*, ed. Russell Bernard (Altamira, Calif.: Sage, 1998), 203.
50. A. Lynn Bolles, "Decolonizing Feminist Anthropology," paper presented at the Association for Feminist Anthropology Invited Session, From an Anthropology of Women to the Gendering of Anthropology, Annual Meeting of the American Anthropological Association, Washington, D.C., November 15–19, 1995. See also idem, "Women Ancestors: A History of Black Feminist Anthropology," paper presented at the Association of Black Anthropologists and Association for Feminist Anthropology Invited Session, Black Feminist Anthropology, Annual Meeting of the American Anthropological Association, Washington, D.C., November 21, 1997.
51. Gwendolyn Mikell, "Feminism and Black Culture in the Ethnography of Zora Neale Hurston," in *African-American Pioneers in Anthropology*, ed. Ira E. Harrison and Faye V. Harrison (Urbana: University of Illinois Press, 1999), 59.
52. Ibid., 54.
53. Leith Mullings, *On Our Own Terms: Race, Class, and Gender in the Lives of African American Women* (New York: Routledge, 1997), xviii–xix.
54. Mwende was the name given to me by my Kamba informants.
55. Johnnetta B. Cole, "Commonalities and Differences," in *All American Women: Lines That Divide, Ties That Bind* (New York: The Free Press, 1986), 1–30.
56. Ibid.
57. Hans Baer, Merrill Singer, and Ida Susser, *Medical Anthropology and the World System: A Critical Perspective* (Westport, Conn.: Bergin and Garvey, 1997), 230.
58. Evelyn C. White, ed., *The Black Women's Health Book: Speaking for Ourselves* (Seattle: Seal Press, 1994), xv.

8

PAULLA A. EBRON

CONTINGENT STORIES OF ANTHROPOLOGY, RACE, AND FEMINISM

A memory was by definition not a thing, it was . . . a memory. A memory now of a memory a bit earlier of a memory before that of a memory way back when . . .

—Julian Barnes, *England, England*, 1998

BEGINNINGS

Deliberations, meditations: On the subject of anthropology and on the intersection of feminism, black feminism.

Suggested frame: "autoethnography," interpreted here as an exploration of the intersection of autobiography and anthropological practice.

Critical question: What are the terms under which one can proceed to address these subjects?

Through an intimate consideration of both form and content, I explore the topics of anthropology, feminism, black feminism, and autoethnography. It is my position that an autoethnographic approach must track back and forth between a personal sense of the way things were, the *memory* of events, on the one hand, and on the other, the institutional markers, texts, and features of public culture that provide guideposts and social referents of that experience. Autoethnography raises questions surrounding personal memory and its relationship to social history. The intersections between the self and social history and the cultural artifact of institutional structures serve as the scaffolding for mapping a social history of anthropology and feminism.

A memory: At age thirteen I discovered Zora Neale Hurston's autobiography, *Dust Tracks on a Road*.[1] This book introduced me to anthropology and the importance of African American culture kept alive in folkways and stories. These stories were exotic to my Northern imagination—magical in their apparent Otherness. They created a world outside of the terrors of junior high school. I would visit the central library and order Hurston's books from Special Collections, for she had not yet become the popular icon we have known of late. Her writing raised new questions: What was the relationship of black women to creative writing? Who had permission to authorize and convey the experiences of the black community? For many, I know that the answer was simple: It was the men of the Harlem Renaissance, who presented themselves, and were represented by scholars, as the legitimate voice for the race. Although I now have adopted a more critical stance toward Hurston's views, it is this memory, an embodied moment, that pointed me toward anthropology as a discipline. Hurston's work created a space for me to imagine black women as critical voices amid a world that dismissed black women's vision of community.

Yet Hurston, for all her guiding insight, could never have imagined the social, political, economic, and intellectual developments that allow us to speak of a black feminist anthropology today. My memory of her story cannot erase the texts, politics, and subjectivities of sixty years. Rather, my reflections upon the intellectual and social debates that have informed the context in which my own ideas developed provide a "partial truth" of this social history.[2]

Yet the reflexive mode of presentation I use obliges a self-conscious effort that I also be attentive to details that get mobilized to recount the trajectory of my ideas: What is the process of my presentation, of selection, and the ordering of the "facts"? How are temporality and location integral to the story I convey?[3]

These concerns are present even as I introduce the general direction of the essay. Indeed, my commitment to interpreting the relationship of feminism(s) to anthropology is my contribution to the broad analysis of how ideas about feminism and race, and scholarship are always unfolding in relationship to larger historical processes and social events. Indeed, it is useful to note the shifting terms under which black feminism as a category can now be naturalized. The early efforts of cultural critics Barbara Smith, Hazel Carby, bell hooks, and Patricia Hill Collins, along with the countermove by others toward the use of the alternative term *womanist*, helped the notion of black feminism circulate in wide-ranging debates. In no way, however, should these uses of the term *black feminism* be collapsed into a single meaning or invocation. I trace this formation of black women's subjectivity in multiple ways that parallel this history of changes in our understanding of the social location of women, categories at once viewed only as relations among women and men, to a more recent shift toward the use of the term *gender*. This later use finds the concept of gender to be an important analytic category. It allows one to see the intersection of gender with other power-laden social relations.

As an anthropologist, my research is sparked by an interest in representation (that is, the making of Otherness) and performance (or the enactment of self) as they relate to the social history of the African Diaspora. This interest also draws me toward issues that surround the politics of contemporary Africa. Thus, I chose The Gambia as the site for my research because of its significance for African Americans.[4] Like many, I was strongly influenced by Alex Haley's *Roots* journey in the seventies, which traced his history to a Gambian village.[5] But I have also resisted the hegemony of African American representations of the African continent.[6] As a result, a few of the research questions that have guided me are: How do we make sense of African political economies? How is The Gambia—one of the smallest countries—to survive economically without an agricultural or industrial base? How is culture turned into a commodity?

In my work I analyze representations of Africa from varied sources both in and beyond Africa. What do scholars, political leaders, African Americans, and Gambian cultural performers mean by African culture? After all, although Africa is the place of memory for those in the African Diaspora, it is also more than that—it is a place with its own varied histories and debates.

More recently, these concerns have taken me to explore the memory of Africa in the southeastern region of the United States. How have we imagined African influences in the most "African" of sites in North America? Here again, I am interested in the role of Africa in African American discourses of identity formation. But I also cannot forget the political position of sub-Saharan Africa in international debates over geopolitical relations. These interests were formed early in my intellectual trajectory through a particular political moment in which I learned the importance of an internationalist perspective that moves back and forth between particular sites of meaning, but with a sense of wide-ranging, transnational contests over power and meaning.

The privileging of race in the U.S. political arena, or the urging of one to choose a single identity over another—as if these social selves could be shed of the histories that created them—seems, in hindsight, reductive at the very least. We have now grown accustomed to the notion of multiple and shifting selves;[7] identities are now viewed as relational and situation-sensitive. As I chart my relationship to a political and social history in which feminism and race form central moments, both personally and institutionally, I use this history to illustrate the varied course of notions of blackness and feminism I have had to navigate. Feminism and black political movements figure critically in the kinds of questions that have emerged during this process and that now inform my professional practice as an anthropologist.

EMERGENT FORMS

This reflexive account owes much to recent challenges by a number of constituencies that became critical of the objectifying gaze of social scientists.[8] Critics objected to a scholarship that presented itself as a transparent window of explanation that somehow magically, and apparently effortlessly, hid the conditions of knowledge production.[9] In particular, I argue, feminist anthropology, postcolonial studies, and minority discourses have been in the forefront of such critiques. They especially have been instrumental in stimulating an exploration of various literary forms that critique the objectivist stance and ethnographic authority. Without access to mainstream audiences, these discourses developed more self-consciously reflexive ways of articulating their perspectives: through autobiography, fiction, plays, poetry, and wives tales. They created counternarratives to stand alongside the accounts found in conventional anthropology. Now these forms, at one time considered of marginal status, are currently subsumed (and legitimated) under the rubric of reflexive anthropology. Minority discourses, along with feminism and postcolonial studies, are but a few of the perspectives that are influential to my framing context; their importance signifies a particular era in the history of anthropology, during a time when the discipline formed new intersections with public discourses and events that have helped to simultaneously constitute theories of "the social" and subjectivities.

GEOPOLITICAL IMAGINATIONS

Any genealogy of subaltern-oriented theories and research projects (such as this one) is compelled to take into account shifts in world political events, and, in particular, the impact of anticolonial struggles after World War II. This is the context in which many North American anthropologists found themselves rethinking the discipline in the mid-1960s.[10] For anthropologists of the Atlantic rim, early moments in Pan-Africanism and the impact of anticolonial struggles informed a diasporic sense of connections among disadvantaged peoples. This was a moment of internationalism in which solidarity was imagined in relation to communities and nations. Its specificity becomes even clearer if we juxtapose it against contemporary concerns with global networking and the erasure of communal and national boundaries.[11] Indeed, global connections in this earlier moment drew a map of connections that imagined a critique of neocolonial relations. The postwar anticolonial struggles of the Third World were about building nations. Similarly, the social movements of the 1960s, both in the United States and in other parts of the world, depended on imaginings of nations and nation-like communal units.[12] It is in this context that progressive scholars and activists turned to counter-hegemonic nation building as a context for thinking about and participating in the elimination of inequality and oppression. Nationalism invigorated a counter-movement and provided a logic for political struggle.

During my first experience of college in the 1970s, like so many students at the time, I searched for a more meaningful set of options than what seem to present itself at the small, overwhelmingly white, liberal arts college I attended. As members of the generation just after the Civil Rights and Vietnam era, my cohorts and I were inspired by the example of those slightly older than ourselves to work for social and political transformation. My path was involvement in black cultural politics.

Black cultural political groups drew inspiration from a range of sources, but a notable inclusion in most was the selective appropriation of Pan-African cultural artifacts. From Nigeria we borrowed Yoruban religious practice; from Ghana, initiation ceremonies; from Tanzania, a political vision based on scientific socialism. These elements were fused into a cultural stew that became for many African Americans "a bit of Africa" in the New World.[13] The interest in Africa, although having long roots among Africans of the Diaspora, was in this moment inspired by the move of many African nations toward independence from colonialism.[14] This fact served to facilitate a more politically engaged appreciation of Africa's significance to the identity of African Americans.

A memory: One of the striking aspects that framed my involvement in political work during this early phase of my life was the expected place of black women in organizations focused on community development. These organizations, like their white counterparts, placed women in the position of being expected to make coffee while, of course, the men talked over important ideas. I recall protesting one day, along with other women, this bourgeois notion of women's roles. We pointed out the apparent disjuncture between worlds that marked a domestic/political divide; this forced a heated debate. Although I was much younger than the other women, I understood the significance of the moment: coming to terms over our location within these social groups offered another moment of consciousness of what it meant to be black and a woman; ours was a dual identity recognized in private but erased in public debates, where the single category of importance was race. This collective action proved that the women were no longer willing to buy the prevailing justification commonly offered up by even these progressive black men: "when the Community becomes liberated, then we can deal with women's issues."

As I became more involved with political issues, I joined the activities of groups concerned with advancing African American self-determination. Again the influence of nationalisms from the Third World was ever present in that the rhetoric of many newly liberated countries stressed political and economic sovereignty. For African Americans, our move toward self-determination took various forms, including the development of independent black schools, seen as viable alternatives to the failures we associated with public schools; political theater groups that provided ways for us to use art as social commentary and thus provided a critique that might enable transformation; and adult literacy programs, inspired by Paulo Freire's work on literacy with Brazilian peasants.[15] These were projects that powerfully shaped my sense of politics and culture.

This was also a moment when progressive U.S. domestic politics drew strength from a number of internationalist movements to formulate a plurality of visions of social change. In the United States and Europe, Third World elite students joined forces in a cosmopolitan anticolonial enterprise whereby the national fates of various colonies and ex-colonies were viewed as intertwined; some of these students, who were "citizens of the world," became important nationalist leaders.[16] U.S. movements imagined themselves, too, within this nationalist cosmopolitanism. Inspired by Third World intellectuals, many U.S. black activists understood themselves to be part of a more cosmopolitan moment.

A memory: We walked the streets of a northeastern urban community as if we were in tropical Africa, yet it was in the cold of November: women in sandals and wearing long skirts and tops—bubbas and lappas—in "African" cotton fabric designed to mimic batiked cloth. Still, these "African" clothes would mark our distinctiveness as neither Black Muslim nor ordinary resident of the neighborhood. We were in the service of a political vision: "Who are we?" we asked rhetorically. And we answered ourselves, "African people." "What must we do? Make change." And the room, again filled with cosmopolitan cultural analysis, sat divided—men on one side and women on the other.

Inspired by these internationalist commitments, I enrolled in a program in Pan-African studies. Here, the desire for connections beyond the borders of the nation helped frame my intellectual agenda. I began to learn both about Africa and about the African Diaspora. Even in these emergent years of African and African American studies programs, a sometimes-productive tension existed between African intellectuals from the continent, who stressed historical difference, and scholars of the Diaspora, who, more often than not, generated static, albeit celebratory notions of Africa. The debate rippled outward as black intellectuals from the Caribbean raised the importance of a class analysis, interrupting the privileging of race as the primary political division in U.S. discussions. These tensions pointed to the lack of an easy affinity between peoples of the Diaspora and those throughout Africa, particularly once one acknowledged Africa as a place in historic time and not simply a symbol used to further African American political desires. On the one hand, as students, we began to appreciate the fact that Africa was a diverse continent, made up of several countries and not a singular place. Colonialism affected regions differently, and class and cultural differences did matter. On the other hand, we experienced the excitement of having intellectual and political conversations across these divides.

Pan-African studies gave me new ideas about the meaning of scholarship. Notions of the Diaspora were created in the dialogue among African, African American, and Caribbean scholars and usefully de-territorialized views of culture, allowing scholars to recognize connections between Africa and those dispersed in diaspora. This idea of diasporic connection continues to inform contemporary scholarship. The creative amalgam of scholars across the lines of tension formed an imagined constituency for dialogue and debate about the culture and history of Africa and its Diaspora. This constituency stretched the academy, allowing scholarship to flower outside historic Western genealogies. Indeed, although I have become critical of many of the original concepts and frameworks we used in this early period, I continue to write into this space of multiple intersections, which invigorates me as a scholar despite the internal critical tensions, and I remain committed to merging political and intellectual questions.

Despite the radical astuteness of the political groups with which I worked at this time, none acknowledged feminism as an important social movement; nor was feminism mentioned in my academic classes. Instead, I first came to feminism through my own independent reading, a practice not uncommon among social activists who frequently formed their own eclectic reading groups to discuss certain issues. Perhaps because I first learned feminism through books, I have always been particularly appreciative of its critical force. That is, I have been captivated by feminism's ability to analyze and critique other forms of social mobilization. I also came to feminism at a time when women of color, both in the United States and around the world, were critically impacting feminist theories as well as feminist political actions. In the Third World, feminists were questioning the politics of postcolonial nationalisms.[17] In the United States, the influential women-of-color anthology *This Bridge Called My Back* was stirring up discussion of the inadequacy of white women's priorities as well as those of men of color for challenging the intersection of gender and race hierarchies.[18] Also important in this conversation was the collection *All the Women Are White, All the Blacks Are Men, but Some of Us Are Brave*.[19] In this context, I came to share a critical understanding of the kinds of nationalism that informed black cultural politics and Pan-African studies, as well as so many other social movements of those times.

Nationalism, as Benedict Anderson points out, creates a horizontal community of "brothers."[20] During the late 1960s and early 1970s, excitement at building a progressive community elided questions about who was excluded. When spokespeople for the community were put forward, they invariably were men who had the power and authority to command. It took women some time to figure out how to intervene. Although African American women were critical participants in black nationalist struggles, they were often relegated to the place of support staff with the promise that questions of gender equality would be addressed in time. With the advent of feminism, however, a powerful critique by Third World women of the limits of the nationalist political vision gradually trickled into the United States. In Africa, women who were part of national struggles in Namibia, Algeria, Mozambique, and Guinea Bissau raised questions about gender equity under postcolonial and socialist nationalisms. Women of color in North America and Europe as well began to describe their own positions within progressive social movements as problematic. Feminism intervened in African American struggles by asserting questions of gender over race; it also interrogated the place of other inequalities, such as those based on class and sexuality, within progressive contexts. All in all, feminist critique forged a new kind of scholarship composed of new ideas and frameworks, and a new constituency.

By the time I enrolled in graduate school in anthropology, feminist scholarship was an exciting, historically layered, and diverse intellectual movement. Guided by my commitments and research interests, I found myself particularly compelled by several strands in feminist scholarship: first, the sympathetic but critical analysis of oppositional nationalisms; second, the insistence on the simultaneity of multiple structures of power and difference in forging identities, both in everyday life and in social movements; and third, the importance of cultural differences in gender understandings and practices, but with tensions and disagreements characterizing the interaction of even similarly disadvantaged groups. Let me elaborate.

Given my background, I was especially excited by feminist analysis of the disjuncture between oppositional nationalism and feminism. I found myself examining the use of "Africa" in African American cultural politics, inspired by an essay by historian E. Frances White in which she analyzed the role Africa played in African American nationalist discourses and showed how imagined "African customs" were used to advocate subordinate, supportive positions for African American women.[21] So-called African ideals were assembled from a continent-wide sweep of cultural attributes, many of which, indeed, were mythic. Stressing "complementarity" between women and men, such ideals solidly reaffirmed the importance of male leadership for African American communities. White also introduced the concepts of "discourse" and "counter discourse" to interrogate the combination of progressive and conservative rhetorics that enlivened black nationalism. Her analysis allowed me to see the persuasive logics as well as the limits of oppositional discourses that develop their own regimes of truth.

These challenges posed by attention to gender by White and those critical of nationalism's exclusions and of difference were not merely confined to a re-examination of relations between men and women in the context of nationalist politics but extended beyond. Criticism was also levied against the kind of feminism that took gender as a singular, structuring principle of inequality but ignored the class and racial differences that critically shape women's relationship to each other.[22] An influential essay by Bonnie Thornton Dill incisively examined differences among women that positioned them as unequal partners in feminist struggles.[23] She highlighted the importance of race and class in the basic construction of gender differences and argued that we can only understand women's concerns if we pay attention to the multiple structures of inequality. According to Dill, these are differentially formed within certain historical contexts and impinge upon women in a myriad of ways; her analysis proved that the "feminist" concerns of black maids and their white employers were not parallel.

Cultural differences among women emerged as significant in a panoply of feminist critical discourses. By the late 1980s, feminist anthropologists had gathered a wealth of cross-cultural ethnographic data on women's roles and status. Contributions such as *Gender and Anthropolgy*, a compilation of feminist research results, curricula, and pedagogy edited by Sandra Morgen, marked a turning point in anthropology. This work made it obvious that anthropologists could no longer responsibly argue about culture and society without paying attention to gender as both a system of ideas and a system of inequalities that divided communities even as it sought to unite them. Similarly, the collection *Uncertain Terms: Negotiating Gender in American Culture*, edited by Faye Ginsburg and Anna Tsing, explored the dimensions of differences among women in U.S. contexts.[24] What each of these seminal works attested to was that at the boundaries between communities, gender forms are a particularly important arena for coercion, conflict, and negotiation.

It is this concern with gender negotiation that has informed my own research into how disadvantaged groups often relate to each other—whether in solidarity or tension—through concerns about gender. For example, I have argued (together with Anna Tsing) that African American and Chinese American gender issues communicate awkwardly, forming dense misunderstandings.[25] Such "border zones," as Chicana feminists have shown, may be particularly creative and laden sites for the negotiation of gender.[26] It was precisely these feminist concerns—with critical understandings of nationalism, multiple bases of identity and difference, and complex cultural borders—that informed my research in The Gambia. My goal in this process was to locate and appreciate cultural tensions and interruptions rather than to assimilate them into a singular understanding of cultural communities or political causes. Yet, as is invariably the case, the contingencies of fieldwork brought me to new insights as well.

AN APPRENTICESHIP IN DIFFERENCE

Despite my immersion in feminist theory, I did not anticipate the degree to which gender would become important as I gathered data during my field research. I assumed I might draw upon the "honorary male privilege" that many Western women researchers have reported as contributing to their high status in non-Western settings. Indeed, in a preliminary, short visit to The Gambia, I had taken a male role; I had apprenticed with a Mandinka *jali* (praise-singer) to learn to play the *kora* (harp).[27]

Kora playing is restricted to Mandinka men, although women jali sing and play a metal bar called the *neo* or tap the side of the kora to keep rhythm. Like a male apprentice, I studied with a teacher six to eight hours every day. During this time, we sat in the company of his friends: men who generally went about their business and occasionally interrupted to comment on my practice. At the end of my initial visit, I traveled to my teacher's village and played for the village head and residents, who all graciously accepted the foreigner's feeble attempts to play the kora.

On a second visit to The Gambia, as a "proper" researcher, in a collaborative relation with the national Oral History and Antiquities Division of the Ministry of Youth, Sports and Culture, I wanted to abide by local understandings of the place of women. During this visit, it seemed inappropriate for me to spend hours in the company of men as I had done previously, following them to their performance events while rejecting the proper training of women. Indeed, this second visit led me to understand the centrality of gender in creating the kinds of access to knowledge that constituted the social, material, economic, and political difference between men and women. This became particularly evident as I listened to repeated stories about a previous woman researcher who had assumed male privilege to learn an instrument. I found it disconcerting to hear her described as pushy, aggressive, obnoxious, and inappropriate. It was said she would do anything to obtain her goal. To complicate matters, my work took place during a moment when foreign women were seen as having come to The Gambia to look for sexual partners.[28] People constantly spoke to me of women travelers from the North who, according to Gambian standards, had no sense of propriety and social decorum. With this input, I decided rather quickly that I could not present myself as a "male" apprentice. In actuality, to maintain my respect within the Gambian context, I chose to be a "proper" woman.

These discoveries about the politics of gender changed my research agenda. Instead of learning about jali training from the "inside," by learning how to play the kora through apprenticeship, I decided to work on jali interactions with others. I relinquished the prospects of the "intimate" portraits I had first imagined and instead focused on the rhetoric through which *jaliya* operated. Jali are professional performers whose job it is to make others perform. They must move their patrons to action—and in return, the patrons must perform as patrons. Similarly, in relation to the tourist trade, jali see their job as moving their audiences into an appreciation of African history and culture. But their audiences also must perform properly. The inter-caste and inter-group rhetoric of jaliya is thus a key aspect of its imagined effectiveness. Words are powerful vehicles that can both give and take away. The jali's message can either create or ruin a patron's reputation. In taking up this study, then, I found I did not have to relinquish my interest in the construction of social categories and processes; rather, I approached them from a new angle that proved, I am persuaded, more informative.

A memory: An African American woman traveled to The Gambia for a brief time. During her visit to the home of an important man, accompanied by her sponsor who was considerably younger, she entered into a debate with us about polygamy. This newly arrived visitor wondered why women were not allowed to pursue whomever they wished exactly as men did. I sat frozen in my seat, unable to do more than side with the older gentleman in my silence. He seemed taken aback by her forthright ability to comment on a place in which she had lived for three days. In retrospect, I wonder: Where was my feminism then? Could I have at least offered a mediating opinion? At the time, I was struck by the woman's efforts to talk about what every woman, according to her, should be able to pursue—"her own hopes, dreams, and aspirations." Even African American women are capable of espousing the unproblematic notion that "sisterhood is global." But at that moment in The Gambia, such a universalizing concept of feminism confronted its limits. And persuaded by this line of thought, the visitor moved beyond the expected rules of the family and challenged the codes of behavior that were more restrictive for women than men.

As I listened to the stories that surrounded her, her mythical reputation far surpassed her actions. Yet, I was enlisted by her sponsor to "speak with her." As he explained, his reputation was on the line: "What if something bad were to happen to her?" But rather than "speak with her," I tried to understand the issues from the points of view of both people involved. After all, from a societal perspective, she was a woman traveling around without the protection of a man; as such, she appeared to be someone without moral scruples. Yet from her point of view, she desired to learn as much about Africa as she could in the short time she had to visit The Gambia. To accomplish this meant moving about and meeting lots of people. Although I did not take up the role of interlocutor, the incident confirmed for me that my own practices during my stay needed to conform to the conventions. And I believe it was more than an issue of cowardliness and simply reproducing power differences between men and women. It was an issue informed by historical relationships between the West and Africa—which, at the very least, led me to proceed with caution, while being carefully attuned to geopolitical power and the realization that gender and national status created layers of complexities in any position one might take.

These moments of debates over the social and global status of men, women, caste and class, and professional performers and their interlocutors raise the importance of performance as more than an enactment; how might it be viewed, rather, as an analytic category? Performance, of late, is a topic that has captured the anthropological imagination, for it challenges the idea that there are foundational moments that fix identities in an immutable state. Judith Butler's deconstruction of the sex/gender system offers a critical intervention in dominant understandings of gender through her exploration of notions of male and female as givens.[29] Indeed, Butler argues that gender is performed, learned, and enacted in relationship to a social expectation. Similarly, Patricia Williams, among others, offers a critique of essentialized notions of race by showing the discursive construction of race and gender in social/legal arenas.[30] These critiques provided the foundation for me to analyze performance in two contexts: the official contexts of the jali artists with whom I worked, and the performance of status and identity in social interactions. Such key insights of feminist scholarship extend the earlier moment in the seventies, characterized as the study of the anthropology of women,[31] that analyzed the relationships between men and women but without necessarily challenging the biological basis of what is meant by male and female—that is, what these social locations might mean in themselves as performances.

My project required me to be self-conscious about my own performances of gender and status even as I was being retrained by the jali with whom I interacted. I was never able to take gender and status for granted, and I observed how gender and status were presumed givens for the jali. Many of the "intimate" insider accounts of jaliya told by male musicologists naturalize the travel and mobility of men.[32] Portraying their jali informants only as talented performers, they erase the making of insider and outsider—that is, those with access to specialized jali knowledge and those who, instead, must be moved to appropriate action. Yet this is the central premise of jaliya.

The conditions of my research also pressed me to appreciate the blurred border between formal performance and the performance of everyday life. Reminded daily of the lines that divide men and women, jali and patron, elite and commoner, young and old, and Gambian and foreigner, I did not imagine a "safe" homogeneous community in which the performance of difference became irrelevant. Instead, I saw how jali as professional performers taught their interlocutors how to perform gender, status, ethnicity, and national difference. These lessons occurred not only in formal performances and ceremonies but also in the interactions of everyday life.

One of the most striking arenas for thinking about this issue turned out to be my interviews with jali. Jali used interviews as performance spaces in which to tell not only of their professional talents but of the gender and caste considerations that gave them their status as jali. They prevailed upon me and my assistant to treat them as proper patrons should—with generosity and making opportunities. They made me self-conscious about my own performance as a researcher and, indeed, about the performative nature of describing cultural difference. This became (and continues to be) a central theme of my research.

Gambians pressed me to reflect on race as well as gender and caste as performances. They had their own ideas about African Americans, and they performed them. I became the audience for a number of performances by my Gambian friends in which they portrayed African Americans as depicted in the Hollywood movies they had seen repeatedly. In both memorized lines and scripted gestures, they could reenact scenes that portrayed African American men as tough gangsters who would kill for what they wanted. Because of my immersion in critical, reflexive anthropology, I had thought a great deal about Western stereotypes of Africans; I had thought much less about African stereotypes of Americans. Of course these images would come from the endless circulation of Hollywood action films. Just as African Americans' sense of Africa is formed within powerful media-generated images, so, too, in The Gambia, African Americans are represented in media styles. But what was particularly striking was how Gambian "performers" performed the common role allotted African Americans by using their bodies and voices to mimic violent gun-slinging thugs and criminals.[33] In another representation, they mimicked pop music icons Michael and Janet Jackson, singing their songs and copying their styles. Performance was the medium through which cultural difference was assimilated and understood.

These experiences, by calling my attention to the importance of performance in communicating about cultural difference, enabled me to formulate a new understanding of the themes that have characterized reflexive and critical anticolonial anthropology. In this regard, an important work that I see in dialogue with mine is Carolyn Martin Shaw's *Colonial Incriptions*.[34] She is attentive to issues of representation, but then she moves to trace the material effects of the interface between white African colonial presence and the making of Kenyan culture. This work is exceptional because in most discussions of colonialism's interface, representations of cultural difference have been seen mainly as textual and communicated in books.[35] Although texts have been important in creating stereotypes of difference, face-to-face interactions as well as formal ceremonies and scripted events are also key features of making difference. Attention to performance allows me to see how difference is negotiated and reformulated in context-specific enactments. It also makes it clear that representations need not be static and timeless.

Performance, then, is particularly relevant to my research because it is a central trope through which the continent of Africa is known in the rest of the world. Non-Africans imagine an Africa of performance. In turn, African performers, such as jali, build on this trope in presenting an "Africa" they want imagined through their performances. Everyday performances of difference augment and reformulate these understandings by making them part of personal repertoires. Thus, I came to appreciate that representations are always a performative issue. Today, performance critically informs my research not only in studying jali but also in studying the place of Africa in a global imagination.

FROM RESEARCH TO WRITING

When I returned to the United States to write about this research, I faced new challenges of navigating scholarly constituencies. One divide of particular concern for my research trajectory was the separation between African studies and African American studies. Historically these have been different worlds.[36] Until recently, African American students and scholars of African American studies have been actively discouraged from contributing to African studies. Researchers of European background have been considered more objective. Because of this history, many African American scholars have gone their own direction; indeed, they have emphasized the critique of objectivist standards of scholarship. Thus, somewhat different epistemological standards have come to characterize the two fields. African studies scholars have often imagined their challenge as impressing the European and North American historians and sociologists who still set disciplinary standards. They are particularly concerned, in this context, with "setting the record straight" using rigorous standards of scholarship. In this light, archival records and demographic data appear solid, while oral history must be used very carefully to avoid its distortions. In contrast, African American studies has stressed the knowledge that can be gained outside of dominant conventions of scholarship. African American scholars find memory, oral history, and ritual performance particularly interesting sources of alternative knowledge. It is difficult to navigate across these differences. My solution has not been to evaluate each of these approaches but rather to show how each one contributes to cosmopolitan discourses of culture and, thus, to the making of contemporary history.

A feminist approach has also figured prominently in my work; I have come to appreciate the influences of gender analysis in allowing me to critique dichotomous categories of male and female and also to raise critical questions about the ease with which we sometimes rely on "the evidence of experience."[37] But there is one critical place where these, perhaps at times, abstract notions of feminist theory are able to speak to the world about the predicament of women in the throes of the global economy—my final retrospection.

A memory: Mariama, a Gambian friend, arrived in the Bronx, New York, and lived with family members. After she had been here for a few months, we talked on the phone. She said, "It's so dangerous here in New York. People are running around with guns. I hardly ever go outside; I only go just to get food at the store. It's so dangerous. I often wish I was at home." When I spoke with her after several more months, Mariama told me of her working conditions in a factory. The doors were locked all day. The women were stuck inside without any fresh air and it was so hot in here. "But Paulla," she said, "what can we immigrants do? No one can say anything. We're all just here." This is an issue of contemporary concern: the making of a United States citizen! The conditions of being a recent part of the African Diaspora are often times obscured from view by the hegemonic presence of African American dreams of homeland. Feminism is both a theory and a practice. This memory reminds me that all of the issues I have discussed through this auto/ethnographic approach are more than academic issues; critical stakes were and are involved in our stories about global relations.

In bringing closure, I suggest that similar to the ways form and content are linked in my presentation, our lives as feminists, anthropologists, scientists, and social scientists are positioned in cross-cutting debates wherein public responsibility and intellectual pursuits critically interface. As Donna Haraway suggests in her essay "Situated Knowledges,"[38] acknowledging the conditions under which we produce our ideas only makes for a stronger sense of the research we conduct. In this respect, it has been important for me to show how my research draws critically on my background and training as a black feminist anthropologist. However, I am not simply satisfied with identifying "the power" in an unmediated way. Instead, my sense of gender, to paraphrase Joan Scott,[39] is to find gender a useful category of analysis important for examining power and difference. This notion helps disrupt the imagined homogeneity of women and men and communities of binary opposition. It allows us to notice power-laden cultural intersections at which

standards of identity and proper behavior are being actively negotiated. As an analytic category, gender points to multiple intersecting and overlapping structures of identity and inequality. In my
work, it allows me to see the *performance* of all kinds of difference,
not just of gender but also of caste, class, ethnicity, and the conti-
nental representations that define the set of distinctions known as
"Africa."

NOTES

I am indebted to the keen insights of my readers: Kathryn Chetkovich, Miyako Inoue,
Carolyn Martin Shaw, Wilmetta Toliver, and Anna Tsing. Much appreciation!

1. Zora Neale Hurston, *Dust Tracks on the Road* (New York: Arno, 1942).
2. James Clifford's notion that ethnographies are "partial truths" is fitting here, for one
   includes yet also excludes many things when writing ethnographies. James Clifford,
   "Introduction: Partial Truths," in *Writing Culture*, ed. George Marcus and James Clifford
   (Berkeley: University of California Press, 1986), 1–26.
3. Current interest in travel and displacement has contradictory effects. On the one hand,
   it can loosen up stable objects—places framed and situated in ethnographies; on the
   other hand, its presumed fluidity can leave questions about who has access and who
   can make claims around this imagined mobile community unattended. Theories have
   the same effect; they can seem to be "traveling," and yet they are also situated moments
   that need their location specified. See Janet Wolff, "On the Road Again," in *Resident
   Alien* (New York: Routledge, 1997), 115–134.
4. During Alex Haley's visit to The Gambia in the early seventies, he encountered a *jali*, a
   praise singer and oral historian, who provided a genealogy of the Kinte family. According to the jali, a distant relative of Haley's, Kunta Kinte, was reportedly captured, made
   a slave, and brought to the United States. Haley's account of the jali's narrative provided
   for many a moment of intimate (re)connection of African Americans to Africa. The
   village of Juffrey, where Kunta Kinte reportedly resided, has become the celebrated site
   in the quest for a homeland. For further discussion, see Paulla Ebron, *Performing Africa*
   (Princeton: Princeton University Press, 2001).
5. Alex Haley, *Roots* (New York: Doubleday, 1976). Also see *Roots: The Next Generation*, written by Alex Haley and produced by Stan Margulies and David Wolper in 1977 for Warner
   Brothers.
6. When one traces out the history of the African Diaspora, the more common set of references are made to those whose relatives departed from Africa long ago. Much more
   difficult to place in the history of Diaspora is the migration of Africans at the present
   moment. In may ways, we in the Diaspora feel we own this history of the continent, yet
   at the expense of intimate engagement with the present. A notable exception is the
   organization TransAfrica and its activities.
7. See, for example, Gayatri Spivak, *In Other Worlds* (New York: Routledge, 1987).
8. Notable among these are Sidonie Smith and Julia Watson, eds., *De/Colonizing the Subject:
   The Politics of Gender in Women's Autobiography* (Minneapolis: University of Minnesota
   Press, 1992); Carolyn Steedman, "Writing the Self: The End of the Scholarship Girl," in
   Cultural Methodologies, ed. Jim McGuigan (London: Sage, 1992), 106–125; Ann Gray,
   "Learning from Experience: Cultural Studies and Feminism," in *Cultural Methodologies*,
   87–105; Deborah Reed-Danahay, *Auto/ethnography* (New York: Berg, 1997); and Frances
   Marcia-Lees, Patricia Sharp, and Colleen Ballerino, "The Postmodern Turn in Anthropology," *Signs* 15, 1 (1989): 7–33.
9. See, for example, Renato Rosaldo, *Culture and Truth* (Boston: Beacon Press, 1989).
10. Essays about these concerns have been published in two notable anthologies: Talad
    Asad, ed., *Anthropology and the Colonial Encounter* (New York: Humanities, 1973); and
    Dell Hymes, ed., *Reinventing Anthropology* (New York: Vintage, 1972).
11. I view the distinction here as one focused on the circulation of political visions and

social moments in contrast to the globalism of today, which takes inspiration from the spread of corporate, primarily U.S. culture.

12. Benedict Anderson, *Imagined Communities* (London: Verso, 1991).

13. Two influential texts of the period were Roger Bastide, *African Civilizations in the New World*, trans. Peter Green (New York: Harper and Row, 1971); and Julius Nyerere, *Ujamaa: Essays on Socialism* (Dar es Salaam: Oxford, U.K., 1968).

14. Texts such as Amilcar Cabral, *Revolution in Guinea* (New York: Monthly Review, 1970), and the struggle in Mozambique against the U.S. company Gulf Oil were of key interest to those involved in political struggles on the African continent during this period.

15. See Paulo Freire, *Pedagogy of the Oppressed* (New York: Seabury Press, 1970).

16. One important account among many is that of Aimé Césaire, who recounts his time in France with a number of Third World and French intellectuals and philosophers, including Jean-Paul Sartre. See Aimé Césaire, *Une voix pour l'histoire* (San Francisco: California Newsreel, 1994). These students would later return to their countries to become heads of state after the colonial regime. One of the features mentioned by a tour guide in London was a plaque left at the site of a former restaurant in which Ho Chi Minh had worked as a chef, "until he changed careers."

17. Some of these works included Gloria Joseph and Jill Lewis, *Common Differences* (New York: Anchor/Doubleday, 1981); Audre Lorde, *Zami: A New Spelling of My Name* (Trumansburg, N.Y.: Crossing Press, 1983); Elly Bulkin, Minnie Bruce Pratt, and Barbara Smith, *Yours in Struggle* (Brooklyn, N.Y.: Long Haul Press, 1984); and Michelle Cliff, *Claiming an Identity They Taught Me to Despise* (Watertown, Mass.: Persphone Press, 1980).

18. Cherrie Moraga and Gloria Anzuldúa, *This Bridge Called My Back* (New York: Kitchen Table Press, 1983).

19. Gloria Hull, Patricia Bell Scott, and Barbara Smith, *All the Women Are White, All the Blacks Are Men, but Some of Us Are Brave* (Old Westbury, N.Y.: Feminist Press, 1987).

20. Anderson, *Imagined Communities*.

21. E. Frances White, "Africa on My Mind: Gender, Counter Discourse and African American Nationalism," *Journal of Women's History* 2, 1 (1990): 73–97. Two collections of essays on African women that were less critical of nationalism as a discourse but that addressed the place of black women in Africa and the Diaspora are Rosalyn Terborg-Penn, Sharon Harley, and Andrea Benton Rushing, eds., *Women in Africa and the Diaspora* (Washington, D.C.: Howard University Press, 1987); and Filomina Steady, ed., *Black Women Cross-Culturally* (Cambridge, Mass.: Schenkman Publications, 1981).

22. Linda Gordon, in a recent essay, frames these two moves as Difference I and Difference II, the former referring to differences between men and women and the latter to differences among women. See Gordon, "The Trouble with Difference," *Dissent* 46 (Spring 1999): 41–47.

23. Bonnie Thornton Dill, "Dialectics of Black Womanhood," *Signs* 4 (Summer 1979): 543–555.

24. Sandra Morgen, ed., *Gender and Anthropology* (Washington, D.C.: American Anthropological Association, 1989); Faye Ginsburg and Anna Tsing, eds., *Uncertain Terms* (Boston: Beacon Press, 1990). See also Ann Bookman and Sandra Morgen, eds., *Women and the Politics of Empowerment* (Philadephia: Temple University Press, 1990). For a parallel analysis of gender in history in non-Western contexts, see Margaret Strobel and Cheryl Johnson-Odum, eds., *Expanding the Boundaries of Women's History* (Bloomington, Ind.: Journal of Women's History, 1992).

25. Paulla Ebron and Anna Tsing, "In Dialogue: Reading across Minority Discourse," in *Women Writing Culture*, ed. Ruth Behar and Deborah Gordon (Berkeley: University of California Press, 1995), 390–411.

26. Gloria Anzaldúa, *Borderlands/La Frontera* (San Francisco: Spinsters/Aunt Lute Books, 1987). See also Hull, Scott, and Smith, *All the Women Are White, All the Blacks Are Men, but Some of Us Are Brave*.

27. By suggesting that I could occupy male status, I mean that I was able to draw upon the privilege of status and mobility that many men can take for granted; of course class status and age-ranking systems temper some men's abilities to move about freely. This "harp" is one of the two key instruments associated with the jali tradition. The second instrument is the xylophone-like *balaphon*.

28. Paulla Ebron, "Traffic in Men," in *Gendered Encounters*, ed. Maria Grosz-Ngate and Omari Kokole (New York: Routledge, 1997), 223–244.

29. Judith Butler, *Gender Trouble* (New York: Routledge, 1990).

30. Patricia Williams, *Alchemy of Race and Rights* (Cambridge: Harvard University Press, 1991).

31. Anthologies relevant here include Rayna R. Reiter, ed., *Towards an Anthropology of Women* (New York: Monthly Review, 1975); and Michelle Rosaldo and Louise Lamphere, eds., *Women, Culture, and Society*, (Stanford: Stanford University Press, 1974).

32. An early work on Gambian jali by musicologist Roderick Knight is one example. See Knight, "Mandinka Jaliya: Professional Music of The Gambia," Ph.D. dissertation, University of California, Los Angeles.

33. For a penetrating look at Hollywood's creation of stereotypic roles for African Americans, see Robert Townsend, *Hollywood Shuffle* (Los Angeles: Virgin Vision, 1987).

34. Carolyn Martin Shaw, *Colonial Inscriptions* (Minneapolis: University of Minnesota Press, 1995).

35. Edward Said, *Orientalism* (New York: Vintage, 1978), is a critical work in signaling the centrality of the Other in the Western imagination.

36. A thoughtful discussion of this history can be found in Deborah Amory, "African Studies as an American Institution," in "The Politics of Identity on Zanzibar," Ph.D. dissertation, Stanford University, 1994.

37. Joan Wallach Scott, "Evidence of Experience," *Critical Inquiry* 17 (Summer 1991): 773–797.

38. Donna Haraway, *Simians, Cyborgs, and Women* (New York: Routledge, 1991).

39. Joan Wallach Scott, "Use of Gender as a Category of Analysis," in *Gender and the Politics of History* (New York: Columbia University Press, 1988), 28–50.

9

CHERYL RODRIGUEZ

A HOMEGIRL GOES HOME
Black Feminism and the Lure
of Native Anthropology

How do the experiences of homegirl and Black feminist intellectual merge with the identity of native anthropologist? How do these identities influence the researcher's areas of interest, her methodologies, and her ethnographic representations? How does a Black feminist anthropologist define and negotiate the politics of home in her research endeavors? These are questions I answer by considering my own evolving relationship to feminism. In particular I examine the intersection of three important elements of native Black feminist anthropology: the historical and contemporary struggles of the Black feminist intellectual, the significance of naming for the Black feminist, and the politics of home. It is my position that an awareness of these underlying elements contributes to a richer field experience for the native ethnographer as she attempts to capture and define Black feminist anthropology. Drawing upon my own oral narrative research project about Black women's activism in Tampa, Florida, I demonstrate how a native Black feminist project is consciously constructed and designed, and I analyze the implications this approach has for teaching, community activism, and further research into local Black women's lives.

In her discussion of the boundaries and possibilities for women within patriarchal societies, feminist poet Adrienne Rich argues, "The most notable fact that culture imprints on women is the sense of our limits."[1] As Black feminist anthropologists, we represent resistance to the limitations of culture (including the culture of a colonized anthropology) that historically have been imposed on people of the Black community in general and Black women in particular. In our efforts to decolonize anthropology, we paint pictures of empowerment and strength where others have left bleak images of savagery and inferiority.

Yet, before we can laud the value of our work in identifying, resisting, and dismantling the limitations of culture, we must acknowledge that there are still critical questions to ponder. For example, what is a native Black feminist project? How do formal education, intellectualism, and feminism affect our interactions in the field with other women of the Black community? As researchers, how can we learn from and appreciate Black women's ways of knowing without assuming intellectual authority over their stories and without appearing to appropriate their cultural treasures for our own advancement? These are critical questions for the Black feminist anthropologist who is concerned not only about the integrity and truthfulness of her work but also about the impact of her feminist perspective on people of the Black community. Although a number of scholars have explored the dimensions of native anthropology for the Black anthropologist, few have pondered the specific issues of the self-identified feminist who turns her gaze on her home community. I argue that it is critical for Black feminist anthropologists to examine those issues we take with us to the field that are specifically related to personal history, self-identity, and our own perspectives about the purposes of modern anthropology.

Through fiction, Black feminist writer Alice Walker grapples with some of these issues. Often her work speaks from the perspective of the native and creates a picture of the conflicts that arise when the observer and the observed meet face to face in a place they both call home. In her short story "Everyday Use,"[2] Walker provides a metaphorical critique of the native anthropologist and her intrusive, invasive gaze. While the story's main character is not an anthropologist, she is a cultural worker and artist who—like many Black women intellectuals—is attempting to create and negotiate her identities within the contexts of two very divergent communities: the community of her birth and the community in which she has chosen to live as an adult.

In the story, a college-educated woman makes a brief visit home to her mother and sister in a rural Georgia community. The protective back roads, the unassuming simplicity, and the comfort of day-to-day predictability are all qualities that the visiting woman once criticized, resisted, and rejected early in her life. She now returns home, having made an academic connection with her African and African American roots. The woman has renamed herself (instead of Dee she is now Wangero Leewanika Kemanjo), and she explains to her mother, "I couldn't bear it any longer being named after the people who oppress me." (Her mother's response to this is, "You know well as me you was named after your aunt Dicie.")[3] Although she does not state this directly, the woman's main purpose for visiting is to collect family artifacts that she now views as culturally significant—precious and crudely artistic examples of the folk art tradition. Further, the woman is convinced that her mother and sister have no hope of appreciating the value of these artifacts, which have been a part of their everyday lives for generations. She lovingly admires the benches that her deceased father made because the family could not afford to buy chairs for the dinner table. Her hand closes over an old butter dish that belonged to her grandmother. She grabs a well-used handmade churn top and declares that she will use it in her apartment as a table centerpiece. However, when she asks for two family quilts, a conflict arises. Against the strength of her daughter's intellectual will, the mother insists that the quilts must remain where they are, possibly to be put to everyday use.

The first time I read this story, I understood the relevancy of its powerful symbolism to my work as a native anthropologist. However, Walker's work is valuable for other reasons as well. First, I believe that one of the ways in which we, as Black feminist anthropologists, have named and empowered ourselves is by embracing "subaltern intellectual production."[4] That is, we are comfortable with cultural workers whose methodologies, perspectives, ethnographic representations, and ways of knowing would not be acceptable to traditional anthropologists. Not only are we inspired by these subaltern voices, but we use them to transform the anthropological canon so that it reflects the richness and validity of Black feminist thought. As some scholars have argued, some of the most visible manifestations of Black feminism have been presented through the fiction of Walker and others.[5] When we as Black feminist anthropologists prominently feature these non-anthropological works in our writing, we challenge conventional epistemological underpinnings of the discipline while engaging in the critical process of self-definition. I also use Walker's fiction because she is indeed an interlocutor to anthropology. Faye V. Harrison argues that Walker's work resonates strongly with the scholarly discourse of several disciplines and particularly that of anthropology.[6] I agree with this analysis and would add that Walker's autoethnographic genius lies in her keen ability to observe, critique, and creatively interpret the intricate conflicts that define and legitimize Black women's culture in particular.

These creative and political uses of Walker's work notwithstanding, there remains a more apparent and immediate reason for introducing this chapter with the story "Everyday Use." The story resonates with three enduring themes that are often interwoven in Black feminist thought and theory: the historical and contemporary struggles of the Black feminist intellectual, the significance of naming, and the politics of home. For the Black feminist ethnographer who chooses to conduct her research in Black communities, these themes intersect and shape the unique contours and textures of Black feminist anthropology, sometimes serving as a framework for the ethnographic and epistemological issues addressed by the researcher.

In my research among Black women activists in Tampa, Florida, "the field" is my hometown as well as an ethnographic setting. Having been socialized in the ways of the Black community as well as those of the larger society, I enter and negotiate the field with multiple cultural perspectives. As a "homegirl," I have been socialized into the historic realities, cultural values, and linguistic norms of Black southern life. Thus, when conducting anthropological research among Black women, I perceive myself to be someone who has an intimate understanding of some of the most defining aspects of their lives. However, my education, my role as an anthropologist, and my own feminist activism have socialized me to "rename, recategorize, reclassify, and reconceptualize" many cultural phenomena associated with home. [7]

Similar to the character Dee in Walker's story, I often grapple with the painful conflicts that characterize the "ongoing crisis of being a black or brown intellectual."[8] This ongoing crisis is particularly poignant and treacherous for the Black feminist scholar who must balance the potentially colonizing impact of education with the fact that education is also a tool for empowerment. Like Dee, who assumes the appellation Wangero Leewanika Kemanjo, I have assumed names in my professional and political life that may appear just as foreign. While these names—"anthropologist" and "feminist"—may privilege me in some settings, they can also distance me from the people in my home community. Consequently, these three themes are elements that are psychically embedded in our work as native Black feminist anthropologists. They are a part of the cultural knapsack we take into the field.

My own evolving relationship to feminism derives from some of the mysterious and personal contents of my own cultural knapsack. While I remain an unequivocal Black feminist, I am also aware of the problems and conflicts this identity can raise even as I attempt to engage in liberatory and empowering research. Although scholars and activists credit the second wave of the women's movement with the astounding changes in women's social, economic, and political lives, feminism—as the ideological foundation of these changes—remains woefully misunderstood. Even at the dawn of a new century, feminism continues to face numerous challenges. For example, Black feminism—as both political stance and lived experience—continues to be misrepresented, distorted, or dismissed as though being both Black and feminist are two mutually exclusive and/or conflicting experiences.

Because of the misconceptions and confusion surrounding Black women's varying relationships to feminism, it is important for me to identify the sources of my own feminist consciousness. This dictates a discussion of the intersection of three important elements of native Black feminist anthropology mentioned previously: the historical and contemporary struggles of the Black feminist intellectual, the significance of naming for the Black feminist, and the politics of home. I argue that an awareness of these underlying themes contributes to a richer field experience for the native ethnographer as she attempts to capture and define Black feminist anthropology. Just as the definition of Black feminism continues to be elusive, so the definition of Black feminist anthropology will also remain nebulous if we fail to understand the critical components that form the core of our endogenous (or native) research.

Toward this end, I wish to describe an oral narrative research project involving Black women's activism in Tampa. This study, which was consciously constructed and designed as a native Black feminist project, has implications for teaching, community activism, and further research on local Black women's lives. My involvement in this project was not merely an intellectual exercise that I stumbled onto accidentally or by default. For me, the lure of anthropology at home springs from a very fundamental sense of respect and concern for my community. As I explain, my early observations and experiences with resistance and change in the Jim Crow South not only influenced my belief in the power of activism; these experiences also shaped my feminist sensibilities as well as my interest in contributing to an anthropology of truth and liberation.

BLACK FEMINISM: PERSONAL AND POLITICAL TRANSFORMATIONS

> So many black people who are threatened by feminism have argued that by being a black feminist (particularly if you are also a lesbian) you have left the race, are no longer a part of the black community, in short no longer have a home.
>
> —Barbara Smith,
> "Introduction," in *Home Girls: A Black Feminist Anthology*, 1983

Black women's intellectual and political struggles with the racism and classism of Euro-American feminism have occurred simultaneously with our struggles to address sexism, colorism, and homophobia within the Black community. As Stanlie James argues, our feminism is rooted and nourished in Black communities even as we challenge those same communities to address issues of internal oppression.[9] In retrospect, I realize that while growing up, I witnessed Black women enduring many forms of oppression within the Black community. Sexist beliefs and practices were as common as rain and often appeared to be the natural order of life. Yet those of us who were born in the 1950s grew up at the doorstep of a new era. Despite our subordinated positions as girls, as well as our seeming acceptance of social expectations of feminine clothing and behavior, many of us who came of age during the 1950s and 1960s were aware of sexual oppression before we could actually name it. That is, we had a sense of gender consciousness that came from the stories and admonishments of grandmothers and mothers who knew about the dual dangers and vulnerabilities of being both Black and female.

Lisa Hogeland makes an important distinction between gender consciousness and feminist consciousness.[10] She defines gender consciousness as women's self-awareness—our acknowledgment of the distinctive nature of our femaleness. Although gender consciousness is a precursor to feminist consciousness, the two terms are not synonymous. Feminist consciousness—which came later in my life—implies the politicization of gender consciousness through an awareness of patriarchal hierarchies, structures of domination, and systems of oppression.

I gained my gender consciousness from my grandmother, who

understood quite clearly how Black women were sexualized by men—through harassment and physical violation—in both public and private spheres. Working all her life as a domestic, my grandmother also taught me about the dignity and courage of Black women as they resisted—in very subtle ways—the dehumanizing treatment of their employers. I learned that Black women walked bravely through symbolic, ideological, and physical minefields that were as long and wide as life itself. Black grandmothers and mothers had the awesome task of teaching their daughters how to negotiate minefields daily. However, to grow up amid blatant racism and sexism is also to grow up in a culture of contradiction. Lessons on dignity, courage, and self-reliance were often taught within the context of achieving ladyhood. Yet ladyhood was only bestowed upon those girls who were compliant, obedient, and most of all, silent.

Thus, young Black women during the 1960s received mixed messages from our families and the community about our roles in society. On the one hand, we were encouraged to perform well in school and seek all the opportunities that were emerging for us as a result of the Civil Rights movement. On the other hand, the notion of Black women consciously seeking independent, self-determined lives was eschewed in many different ways. So, while I was encouraged to obtain a terminal or professional degree, I was also socialized (at home and at school) to accept without question the cultural restrictions of being female. It was only after I was safely married and immersed in motherhood that I began to question and challenge the social and cultural forces that were confining and limiting my life as a woman. Reflecting on the ways that my relationship to sexism evolved, I contend that my own Black feminist consciousness derives from some very complex, multidimensional, and contradictory experiences with oppression.

My feminist consciousness also derives from living with the wrenching realities of racism. I was a part of the generation of southern Black children whose nascent awareness of second-class citizenship matured even as we turned the stained and torn pages of our battered, secondhand textbooks in our segregated classrooms. Our separation from white children taught us that not only were white people the Other but that they were a superior and dangerous Other. At the same time, I learned that an enduring part of our lives as Black people was to confront the restrictions imposed by the dangerous Other. For example, one of my most vivid childhood memories is the image of my parents indignantly leaving a store—and vowing aloud never to shop there again—after a white store clerk suggested that I try on a dress in a dark, musty broom closet rather than in the dressing room used by the white customers.

I developed a sense of racial pride by observing, reading about, and absorbing the tumultuous changes occurring during the Civil Rights movement, and I became aware that people from all walks of life were resisting racism. Although it was the formally educated men whose leadership we all sought, I eventually learned that the work of intellectuals was intricately interwoven with that of grassroots activists. My father was a local civil rights leader whose seemingly innate activism was fueled by a passionate quest for knowledge. The words and wisdom of our revered male leaders were a significant part of my home and school education. For example, I recall reading the biographies and essays of such great men as Toussaint L'Ouverture, Marcus Garvey, W.E.B. Du Bois, and Martin Luther King. These men's ideas on equality and human rights stimulated my thinking about the importance of freedom, although like many young Black women, I was not clear on my specific role in the struggle for racial equality. Further, I was even more confused on what I would be doing once equality was attained.

Attempts to clarify and define Black women's roles in the struggle formed the foundation of the essays and fiction by Black women scholars and activists during the 1970s. In fact, Black feminist writings that emerged during the second wave of the feminist movement were extremely influential in shaping the feminist consciousness of contemporary Black feminist thinkers—including my own. My formal introduction to Black feminist ideas came through the literature that I discovered in the waning years of the Civil Rights movement. This was an electric time for Black women who had grown weary of attempting to find their voices in the patriarchal structure of most civil rights organizations. Black feminist writers asserted themselves and became visible in liberatory spaces that previously had been occupied and defined by Black men or white women. As Nancie Caraway argues, Black feminism "deconstructed the images, identities, presumptions, and methodology of hege-monic theory—not only androcentric world views but those of white feminism as well."[11] Yet even more courageously, Black femi-nist writers challenged the blatant sexism of the Black community, including that of Black male revolutionaries. These writings would become the single most important influence in my life as an intel-lectual, a community member, a social scientist, a teacher, and as a Black woman in a racialized, sexualized and, certainly class-driven America.

Classic political statements by the National Black Feminist Or-ganization and the Combahee River Collective and paradigmatic essays by scholars such as Barbara Smith, bell hooks, Audre Lorde, and E. Frances White continue to provide important analyses of the genesis of Black feminist theory and activism.[12] Although in-dependently diverse in their perspectives and analyses, these revo-lutionary works speak to the inherent value of Black women, the significance of identity politics in eradicating Black women's oppression, and the organic relationship of feminism to the Black experience. These writings also acknowledge a Black women's in-tellectual tradition rooted in Black women's awareness of the in-tersection of gender, race, and class. I remember the very first time I opened the pages of a remarkable book titled *All the Women Are White, All the Blacks Are Men, but Some of Us Are Brave* and realized that Black women's lives could be studied systematically.[13] This was the first time I had ever read the term *Black women's studies*, and indeed this was the first major text on this still-emerging discipline. Through essays, poetry, and fiction, Black feminists legitimized Black women's lives as contributors and revolutionaries. Their words illuminated the intersection of the insidiously oppressive forces we had lived with but had not named.

In the 1980s I transformed my intellectual and theoretical re-lationship with feminism into a relationship that was defined by public activism. I became involved in a chapter of the National Or-ganization for Women (NOW) in Chicago, Illinois. On the national, state, and local levels, NOW was predominantly white, more main-stream than radical, and painfully racist. However, in the absence of any other activist organization in suburban Chicago, NOW be-came the vehicle that ushered me into feminist and community politics. Through NOW I became involved in organizing reproductive rights marches, editing the chapter newsletter, building coalitions with other women's organizations, and bringing feminist education to local public schools. My leadership responsibilities increased, and eventually I became the chapter president. All of this was done while simultaneously challenging the local NOW membership to come to terms with their own individual and collective racism.

My experiences with NOW are interwoven with memories of growing up Black and female in the Jim Crow South during the civil rights era. These life events document my complex transition from gender consciousness to feminist consciousness. However, these events are also indicative of the experience of multiple consciousness. For example, in my activism with NOW in the early 1980s, I understood the immediacy and relevancy of the issues that we—as a community of women—were attempting to address. At the same time, as the only woman of color in the group, I was always keenly aware of the power and privilege bestowed upon these women simply by virtue of their whiteness. Moreover, although I understood that there were Black women who were claiming, redefining, and revolutionizing feminism, I also understood many Black women's absolute rejection of feminism.

As I shifted my interests and gradually transitioned into the academic world, this multiple consciousness would serve me well, particularly in the execution and analysis of projects that focused on Black women's lives. As Harrison contends, "anthropologists with multiple consciousness and vision have a strategic role to play in the struggle for a decolonized science of humankind. Anthropologists with dual or multiple vision may be uniquely able to convert their 'extra eyes' into useful research tools and effective political weapons."[14] The ethnographer who is also a Black woman and a feminist thinker brings not only a multiple vision but a distinct consciousness to native anthropology. This consciousness is influenced by our own lived experiences with struggles against race, gender, and class oppression. It is also influenced by our knowledge of the historic struggles of our Black feminist foremothers. Accompanying this distinctive consciousness, I contend, should be an awareness of the themes and elements that form the core of native Black feminist anthropology.

NATIVE ANTHROPOLOGY: CORE ELEMENTS OF OUR WORK

The villagers did not like her style of writing, her focus and the new name she called herself—feminist.

—Makeda Silvera,
Her Head a Village and Other Stories, 1994

Although some may question the efficacy, the objectivity, and even the methodological rigor of anthropology conducted in one's own society, the notion of anthropology at home is supported by a diverse and innovative body of research. As Donald Messerschmidt contends, "More than ever before we are staying home, where we study communal living, neighboring and cooperation, health and healing, old age and alienation."[15] Although it may not be considered an exotic or adventurous anthropology in the traditional sense, research conducted in our own environs challenges us to deconstruct notions of familiarity in that we are required to gaze deeper into the strangeness of the everyday realities we take for granted. We become students of our own communities and develop a more refined sense of who we are in relationship to the community. At the same time, anthropology at home can awaken us to the creativity, resiliency, and diversity of our communities.

Just as we prepare and reinvent ourselves for living and working abroad, we must also change ourselves in some very distinctive ways so that we can work in our own culture. In some cases we must recapture some aspects of our former selves to reconnect with our home communities. For example, Linda Nelson describes her initial feelings of alienation upon returning to Brooklyn—the community of her youth—to conduct a study of cultural themes in Black women's narratives: "I was annoyed by my anxiety since these were the very streets I had traveled alone, regularly, day and night, with little more preparation than a reminder to myself to 'just be cool.' In short, I had lost much of my street savvy."[16] As Nelson's revelation implies, fieldwork at home removes the façade we can comfortably assume when we are naïve strangers.

Anthropology at home has been called an anthropology of issues in that it implies an attempt to link the theory–practice dichotomy. As Messerschmidt argues, it is anthropology of action and planning.[17] In addition, I believe it is an anthropology that explores the interconnectedness between history, social change, and the future. Anthropology at home does not relegate the ethnographer to a minor role in the discipline, nor does it diminish the meaning of the anthropological experience. "In turning homeward, we are abandoning neither our methodological heritage nor our holistic perspective. Rather, we are building on them with confidence and innovation."[18]

Anthropology *at* home becomes the anthropology *of* home for the native anthropologist. When we claim insider status with our informants on the basis of factors such as ethnicity, kinship, social class, or gender, one assumption is that accessibility and rapport are minor issues. As Nelson muses, "On first consideration, anthropological research among one's own people promises much of the certainty and ease of a tender voyage home."[19] She goes on to explain the unwitting cultural blunders we commit and the varying degrees of acceptance from community informants that make this statement more idealistic than true. However, in general, native anthropology for the Black anthropologist promises a level of cooperation and a richness of spirit that is embedded in Black community traditions of racial uplift. Zora Neale Hurston alluded to this support when she wrote: "I hurried back to Eatonville because I knew that the town was full of material and that I could get it without hurt, harm or danger."[20] Similarly, John Gwaltney discussed the fact that Black informants' cooperation with the native anthropologist is often seen as "an act of racial solidarity and civic responsibility."[21] Assumptions of cooperation, racial solidarity, and even shared identity all relate to the anthropologist's general knowledge of the folks who compose her community of informants. Yet for us as Black feminists, what are some of the core elements that influence our approach to native anthropology? What do these core elements of native Black feminist anthropology tell us about ourselves as we engage in transforming the discipline and its relationship to the Black community?

One of the first issues we must understand is the historic and contemporary struggles of Black women intellectuals. This issue is a core element in our work as native anthropologists. When we engage in native anthropology, we often think of the corrective impact our research will have on the discipline. After all, we attempt to give voice to silence and to represent our communities in ways that are empowering. Moreover, in some respects, Black feminist anthropological analysis should be a vehicle for shedding new light on ongoing problems. Yet we must remember that our work as native anthropologists is intellectual work. In fact, I see native Black feminist anthropology as intellectual activism. We can examine the writings by and about our Black feminist foremothers in anthropology as well as the work of other Black women to find a very substantive tradition of intellectual activism. As Patricia Hill Collins argues, "Black women intellectuals have laid a vital analytical foundation for a distinctive standpoint on self, community, and society and, in doing so, created a Black women's intellectual tradition."[22]

Historically, however, Black women's contributions to social change have been distinguished from Black women's work as intellectuals. For example, Reginald Blaxton describes the American Negro Academy as America's first Black learned society. Founded in 1897, it was composed of major Black thinkers who sought to promote the life of the mind while simultaneously providing leadership in the Black community. Blaxton notes, however, that despite the existence of Ida B. Wells and other Black women who were intellectual activists, the American Negro Academy remained an all-male organization.[23] Thus, in our own communities, Black women intellectuals have had to struggle to have our ideas heard. Unfortunately, in many ways, this struggle to be recognized as intellectuals continues.

Contemporarily, the ongoing struggles of the Black feminist intellectual occur in several dimensions and locations of our professional lives. We struggle with the irony of composing careers within a discipline whose origins are grounded in racist ideology and whose discourse has influenced the development of a highly racialized society. Adrienne Andrews speaks to this particular dilemma as she attempts to understand her own conflicted relationship with anthropology: "I am the other. As a member of a group whose members are often perceived of as others (African Americans) I have been plagued with feelings of ambivalence surrounding my membership in the group of others known as anthropologists."[24] Just as we attempt to come to terms with our roles as anthropologists, we also must acknowledge the ways in which we are rendered invisible by white feminist scholarship. We come to anthropology as the colonized, as those who have historically been examined and displayed. Our lives as thinkers and creative spirits still remain a mystery to scholars—including white feminists. In the American feminist movement it is certainly true that "opposition movements retain residues of that which they oppose."[25] Consider Audre Lorde's questions in her open letter to Mary Daly:

> Have you read my work, and the work of other black women, for what it could give you? Or did you hunt through only to find words that would legitimize your chapter on African genital mutilation in the eyes of other Black women? And if so, then why not use our words to legitimize or illustrate the other places where we connect in our being and becoming?[26]

We also struggle with what Black feminist writer Gloria Wade-Gayles calls "the politics of validation."[27] Thus, like other Black intellectuals, we understand the distinctive and disparate burdens that accompany our decisions to work in white institutions or historically Black institutions. As Wade-Gayles laments, "We know the rule: only white institutions of higher learning have the power to validate us in white America."[28] The same is true for the departments we choose as our academic homes. We understand that there are distinctive rewards, implications, perceptions, and consequences in our choices to have academic homes in anthropology or Black studies or women's studies. As Black feminists, our anthropological work is as much about these intellectual struggles as it is about the words and ways of others.

Another core element of native Black feminist anthropology is the significance of naming. Bettina Aptheker contends, "Naming is a central motif in feminist thought. . . . Consider the connections between naming and identity, between naming and language, between naming and silence."[29] Gloria Hull and Barbara Smith, in a discussion of the critical need to study Black women's lives, argue, "Like any politically disenfranchised group, Black women could not exist consciously until we began to name ourselves."[30] Naming is a political strategy; it is a foundation, a force that connects divergent and contradictory experiences. Naming ourselves as feminists always situates us at a very critical ideological and political juncture, from which we resist demands (from others) to rank the oppressive forces that subjugate Black women. Despite Pearl Cleage's definition of feminism as "the belief that women are full human beings capable of participation and leadership in the full range of human activities,"[31] Black women's identification as feminists is often interpreted as a sign of our disconnection to Black communities. Black feminist intellectuals engage in some deeply emotional struggles with this perception. For example, through fiction, Makeda Silvera writes about the anguish of the Black feminist cultural worker who attempts to discuss her life (as a writer) from a feminist perspective. She struggles with the reality that writing and being among other feminist writers are indeed her work—things she is compelled to do. In her head, however, she hears the harsh criticisms of the home folk:

> "What about the danger of your writing being the definitive word for all Black women? What about the danger of writing in a liberal white bourgeois society and of selling out? Why don't you write about these things?" She screamed at them to shut up and give her a voice, but they ignored her and talked even louder. "Make it clear that you, as a Black woman writer, are privileged to be speaking on a panel like this."[32]

Despite a deep, reflexive sense of duty to ourselves and our people, we Black feminists navigate treacherous waters when we turn our gazes on the social conventions of our home communities. Collins raises two issues about Black feminism that have implications for our work as native anthropologists. First, she argues that Black feminism disrupts the historical and typically unquestioned code of Black racial solidarity.[33] Thus, the implication is that our presence in Black communities might be less controversial (or threatening) if our questions were about race rather than the intersection of race and gender. How much overt and institutionalized resistance do native Black feminist researchers encounter when their inquiry involves topics such as domestic violence, rape, absentee fathers, or child support issues in Black communities? This would be an interesting question to explore among Black feminist anthropologists.

Second, Collins makes the point that Black feminism conflicts with certain elements of Black religious traditions.[34] Thus, if our ethnographic interests led us to explore women's invisibility in leadership positions in the Black church, or if we wanted to examine the Black church's silence on issues such as AIDS or sexual harass-ment, or if we wanted to conduct interviews with Black lesbians, would we risk a form of alienation from our communities that could permeate our research? How can we speak about these issues in pro-fessional settings if people in Black communities view our work as disrespectful or misguided? As difficult as these questions may be, they are basic challenges that the native Black feminist anthropolo-gist must consider before making the journey home.

While we struggle with the complexities of expressing ourselves as intellectuals and naming ourselves as feminists, we must remain aware that our engagement in these particular struggles signifies a certain privileged status. Our realities as feminist scholars and re-searchers are distinctly different from the realities of large numbers of Black women who remain illiterate, undereducated, or perpetu-ally disempowered by poverty.[35] As Black feminists, we should be about the business of developing ethnographic projects that inter-weave our realities and struggles against patriarchy with those of all Black women. This includes giving voice to strengths and weak-ness, pain and troubles, the issues that affect Black women as women, and the issues that define Black women's relationships to Black men.[36] How we bridge the gap between the realities of the anthropologist and those of the informant is a critical aspect of the politics of home. I argue that the journey home for the Black femi-nist anthropologist should speak to intellectualism that embraces a range of experiences and worldviews—not simply those of the researcher. In revisiting Alice Walker's short story "Everyday Use," we find a critique of a Black woman whose intellectualism contrib-utes little to her home folk. Rather, her quest for enlightenment is self-serving, brutal, and oppressive: "She used to read to us with-out pity; forcing words, lies, other folks' habits, whole lives upon us two, sitting trapped and ignorant underneath her voice. She washed us in a river of make-believe, burned us with a lot of knowl-edge we didn't necessarily need to know."[37]

Bridging the gap between ourselves and our informants does not mean that we attempt to use our research to change all of the social conventions of the Black community that we deem oppressive to Black women. For me, bridging the gap means theorizing about issues of identity, self-definition, power, difference, and privilege in Black women's lives. Bridging the gap means employing what Moraga and Anzaldúa call "theory in the flesh." That is, theory in which all of our divergent realities—those shaped by color, class, sexuality, and varying levels of privilege—all merge in the creation of a "politic born out of necessity."[38] In my work among local Black women, theory in the flesh makes Black women's history, beliefs, and agency a catalyst for understanding myself as well as the women who share their stories.

In addition to an emphasis on activism, identity, resistance, and home, my native research projects focus on memory and connections. Similar to the thoughts of Gloria Wade-Gayles, I conduct research in the Black community to ensure that I do not forget: "It is my way of always being where I can see [my people] coming and going and to be reminded, therefore, of who I am and whose I am." Further, as Wade-Gayles contends, what we receive from our connections to the Black community is the gift of memory, "a gift so precious that without it no person is whole or, for that matter, happy."[39]

Native Black feminist anthropology involves negotiating the challenges of our lives as Black women who are also feminists and researchers. It involves reinventing ourselves not only as anthropologists but also as those who are capable of building bridges across contradictory realities. This is something that is rarely done.

LOCAL KNOWLEDGE AND HOME TRUTHS: EXPLORING BLACK WOMEN'S ACTIVISM

If she does not ravel and unravel his universe, she will then remain silent, looking at him looking at her.

—Trinh T. Minh-ha,
"The Language of Nativism: Anthropology as a Scientific
Conversation of Man with Man," in *Woman, Native, Other*, 1989

In 1994 I began a study of local Black women's grassroots activism. I consciously constructed this research as a native Black feminist ethnographic project, that is, a project that would explore the "multilayered texture of Black women's lives" from the perspective of a Black feminist researcher.[40] The most immediate goal of this project was to document Black women's contributions to social change in Tampa. The larger and far-reaching goal of this ongoing project is to determine how Black women can gain more political visibility and electoral power in Tampa.

Through recorded personal interviews, I sought to compare the stories, strategies, and insights of women who were activists during the years of Tampa's Civil Rights movement with the activist experiences of contemporary Black women. I also sought to explore the ways in which local Black women expressed their experiences with multiple forms of oppression. Further, I wanted to document the issues or situations that stimulated Black women's community activism during and after the civil rights years.

Local knowledge about Black women's historical and contemporary grassroots leadership in Tampa remains obscure, scattered, and sometimes difficult to uncover. There are several reasons for this. First, there is limited knowledge of African American community history in Tampa. Although African Americans established stable and enduring communities and traditions in Tampa, it has only been within the last ten to fifteen years that the systematic study of historic institutions, organizations, ceremonies, and practices has developed. There is also limited historical documentation of race relations in Tampa. In fact, few local citizens are aware of the activism that occurred in Tampa during the Civil Rights movement. Once again, scholarly efforts to document struggles against Jim Crow and other racist policies and practices are recent and few. Finally, the ethnohistorical literature on African American activism in Tampa focuses primarily on the work of educated African American men, particularly ministers, attorneys, and businessmen who were leaders of local, state, and national civil rights initiatives.

Clearly, this history is of the highest import, yet the exclusion of African American women makes this history an incomplete one. Another reason for the invisibility of Black women's activism in Tampa's community history is that with few exceptions, scholars have not interviewed local Black women about the roles they have played in social change. All of these factors contribute to a gaping chasm in local knowledge about Black women's visions and voices in this southern community. Through a number of research projects (as well as through teaching and community activism), I hope to fill this void.

To get at the history of Black women's activism in Tampa, I relied on the memory of local women activists. I conducted interviews with six women who have lived most of their adult lives in Tampa and who were involved in public forms of activism. Three of the women developed their activist consciousness during the civil rights era; however, only one informant from this group actually worked for a civil rights organization. The other two women were involved in community organizing, voter registration, and electoral politics. A second small group of women interviewed for this study consisted of three women who were (and continue to be) involved full time in grassroots activism in their respective communities. One of the women heads a task force on gay and lesbian rights issues; the other two are involved in community organizing and public housing issues.

I interviewed the activists in their homes or offices, most of which were located in historically Black neighborhoods. Prior to these meetings, I had not had extensive discussion with any of my informants; I knew of their activism through newspaper articles and, in some cases, mutual acquaintances. Although most of my childhood years in Tampa were spent in predominantly Black neighborhoods, some of my interviews took me to neighborhoods and places that I had never visited. I used my memories and childhood images of these neighborhoods to connect with my informants. For one interview session, I sat on the porch of a rickety old house in Seminole Heights. Formerly an all white neighborhood (and consequently not a community that I would have visited as a child), Seminole Heights is now a racially and economically integrated neighborhood.

The young woman who agreed to the interview felt it would be better if we sat outside and watched my car while we talked. A few days before our interview, her own car had been vandalized right in her front yard. As we sat and talked on the porch, teenage boys cruised by blasting rap music from their car stereos. My informant was initially uncomfortable with the interview process, but after we shared our mutual concerns and confusion about the problems of today's youth, she became more receptive to my presence. We spent an afternoon sitting on her porch swing, sharing our thoughts and learning from each other, the way that Black women have done for centuries.

To learn about the life and work of two other activists, I made several visits to the rental office of the Central Park Village public housing complex to interview a mother and daughter who have been living and working in public housing all of their lives. The office is a gathering place for the women's children, grandchildren, friends, and neighbors. As I made myself comfortable listening to stories, laughing, and joking with the women and their children, I thought about my childhood experiences at my grandmother's apartment in the "projects" across town. On another day, I drove to West Tampa to visit a woman who lived in a splendid old house that had intrigued me as a child. In fact, my friends and I would pass this house every day on our way to George Washington Carver Elementary School. On the day of the interview, I entered her house in awe—never having dreamed that I would one day be invited to see its grandeur.

On another occasion, one rainy Halloween evening, I found myself at a mall that had been long abandoned by the local middle-class citizenry. The mall's clientele were mostly low-income people of color. Perhaps this was why it was an appropriate place for the office of the Tampa NAACP. Amid the squeals of delighted trick-or-treaters, I interviewed a longtime activist who had taken charge of the embattled local chapter. My desire to learn about these women's lives required me to leave the familiarity of the predominantly white, suburban world that I have inhabited since early adulthood.

Because of Jim Crow laws, the white suburbs of Tampa were once as foreign to me as many urban Black communities are today. Now they have been my home for the past few years, one of the privileges gained when you become part of the established intellectual community. Now my research required me to establish a renewed relationship with the streets and sidewalks, the buildings and the billboards, the churches, schools, and offices that are all monuments to Black community life. In establishing a relationship with the field and in revisiting old memories and images, I am doing what Toni Morrison refers to as memory returning to the "archaeological site."[41] My memories help me to remain aware of my current roles as both an intellectual and a feminist. These memories also established a very effective connection between my informants and myself.

Elsewhere, I have analyzed and discussed some of the themes that emerged from these women's life histories and activist stories.[42] These themes include an acute and painful awareness of social oppression, a sense of spirituality that informs and guides their work, a sense of connectedness to the African American community, and attempts to develop effective working relationships with local and state political leaders. However, these themes do not include a discussion of the ways in which feminism or a feminist consciousness supports or serves their activism. Like many Black women activists, most of the women I interviewed spoke more about the barriers erected by racism than those created by sexism. Nevertheless, their powerful and truthful narratives reveal an understanding of Black women's roles in institutional change. As I have argued previously, "narratives of African American women activists represent the complex knowledge and strategies that compose a Black women's activist tradition."[43] Exploring and analyzing that tradition through this project is a very basic example of native Black feminist anthropology.

CONCLUSION

Through various research methodologies, Black feminist anthropologists have challenged the distorted images of Black womanhood that have been perpetuated through the social sciences. As we work to "retain our voices [and] to name and identify ourselves as independent women thinkers and actors inside the uniformity of institutions,"[44] we must also work to create an anthropology that acknowledges our struggles as intellectuals and feminists. These struggles are critical elements of our work as native Black feminist anthropologists. Our awareness of the unique nature of our research in Black communities will not only strengthen our connection to our home communities; this awareness will also redefine feminist politics and provide solutions to the problems that continue to oppress our people.

Determined to transform the anthropological canon so that Black women's stories will be told truthfully, I initiated a study involving interviews with women in my hometown. As I share these women's stories locally, my hope is that this research will raise awareness of the need for coalition building among Black women who work on diverse issues in Tampa. Without this kind of ethnographic work, the community has no systematic, written record of Black women's participation in social change and consequently gives the perception that we have no role models. Without the knowledge of these activist role models, young Black women may not feel empowered to become involved in local leadership. I also argue that aside from their contribution to the anthropological canon, studies such as this one are invaluable in the classroom, for

> when students are taught about Black women's roles in the creation of womanist scholarship, they must also be taught the role of nonacademic women in the ongoing development of Black women's studies [and anthropology]. In my classroom, the assumptions are that Black women—globally and locally—have worthy ideas to express and can offer insight and solutions to diverse, complex problems. These assumptions reinforce not only the notion of naming but also that of the inherent value of Black women's lives.[45]

This belief in the inherent value of Black women's lives—a guiding principle in Black feminist thought—is the essence of my anthropological endeavors. This, I strongly feel, is the nature of the home truths I have learned and the theory in flesh I seek to create. It is what draws me to work in my community, and it is the inspiration for my ever-evolving roles as both researcher and homegirl.

NOTES

The fieldwork described in this chapter was supported by a grant from the Division of Sponsored Research at the University of South Florida. I express my appreciation to the Black women activists of my local community, who continue to inspire and guide my native Black feminist projects.

1. Adrienne Rich, *Of Woman Born: Motherhood as Experience and Institution* (New York: Norton, 1976), 246.
2. Alice Walker, "Everyday Use," in *Black-Eyed Susans/Midnight Birds*, ed. Mary Helen Washington (New York: Anchor Books, 1990), 303–312.
3. Ibid., 308.
4. Faye V. Harrison, "Writing against the Grain: Cultural Politics of Difference in the Work

of Alice Walker," in *Women Writing Culture*, ed. Ruth Behar and Deborah Gordon (Berkeley: University of California Press, 1995), 242.

5. E. Frances White makes this point in her article on Black feminists as creators of theory. White contends that "Toni Morrison, Alice Walker, Toni Cade Bambara, and many others spoke to us and for us. Now a small but highly visible cadre of women have taken up their pens to construct the feminist theories that complement the ongoing literary renaissance." E. Frances White, "Listening to the Voices of Black Feminism," *Radical America* 18, 2–3 (1984): 7.

6. Harrison, "Writing against the Grain," 235.

7. Michele Foster, "Like Us but Not One of Us: Reflections on a Life History Study of African American Teachers," in *Unrelated Kin: Race and Gender in Women's Personal Narratives*, ed. Gwendolyn Etter-Lewis and Michele Foster (New York: Routledge, 1996), 216.

8. Harrison, "Writing against the Grain," 238.

9. Stanlie James, "Introduction," in *Theorizing Black Feminisms*, ed. Stanlie James and Abena Busia (New York: Routledge, 1993), 2.

10. Lisa Hogeland, "Fear of Feminism," *Ms. Magazine* 5, 3 (1994): 18–21.

11. Nancie Caraway, "Introduction," in *Segregated Sisterhood* (Knoxville: University of Tennessee Press, 1991), 5.

12. See Beverly Davis, "To Seize the Moment: A Retrospective of the National Black Feminist Organization," *Sage* 5, 2 (1988): 43–47; Combahee River Collective, "The Combahee River Collective Statement," in *Home Girls: A Black Feminist Anthology* (New York: Kitchen Table Women of Color Press, 1983), 272–282.

13. Gloria Hull, Patricia Bell Scott, and Barbara Smith, *All the Women Are White, All the Blacks Are Men, but Some of Us Are Brave: Black Women's Studies* (Old Westbury, N.Y.: Feminist Press, 1982).

14. Faye V. Harrison, "Ethnography as Politics," in *Decolonizing Anthropology: Moving Further toward an Anthropology for Liberation*, 2nd ed., ed. Faye V. Harrison (1991; reprint, Arlington, Va.: Association of Black Anthropologists and American Anthropological Association, 1997), 88–110.

15. Donald Messerschmidt, "Introduction," in *Anthropologists at Home in North America*, ed. D. Messerschmidt (New York: Cambridge University Press, 1981), 4.

16. Linda Nelson, "Hands in the Chit'lins: Notes on Native Anthropological Research among African American Women," in *Unrelated Kin: Race and Gender in Women's Personal Narratives*, ed. Gwendolyn Etter-Lewis and Michele Foster (New York: Routledge, 1996), 195.

17. Messerschmidt, "Introduction," 4–5.

18. Ibid., 5.

19. Nelson, "Hands in the Chit'lins," 183.

20. Zora Neale Hurston, *Mules and Men* (New York: Harper, 1990), 2.

21. John L. Gwaltney, "On Going Home Again—Some Reflections of a Native Anthropologist," *Phylon* 30 (1976): 236.

22. Patricia Hill Collins, *Black Feminist Thought* (New York: Routledge, 1991), 5.

23. Reginald Blaxton, "The American Negro Academy," *American Visions* 12, 1 (1997): 17–20.

24. Adrienne Andrews, "Balancing the Personal and Professional," in *Spirit, Space and Survival: African American Women in (White) Academe*, ed. Joy James and Ruth Farmer (New York: Routledge, 1993), 179.

25. Louise Newman, "Coming of Age, but Not in Samoa," in *White Women's Rights: The Racial Origins of Feminism in the United States* (New York: Oxford University Press, 1999), 159.

26. Audre Lorde, "An Open Letter to Mary Daly," in *Sister Outsider* (Trumansburg, N.Y.: Crossing Press, 1984), 69.

27. Gloria Wade-Gayles, "Going Home Again: The Dilemma of Today's Young Black Intellectuals," in *Rooted against the Wind* (Boston: Beacon Press, 1996), 135.

28. Ibid., 133.

29. Bettina Aptheker, *Tapestries of Life: Women's Work, Women's Consciousness, and the Meaning of Daily Experience* (Amherst: University of Massachusetts Press, 1989), 20.

30. Gloria Hull and Barbara Smith, "The Politics of Black Women's Studies," in *All the Women Are White, All the Blacks Are Men, but Some of Us Are Brave: Black Women's Studies*, xvii.

31. Pearl Cleage, *Deals with the Devil and Other Reasons to Riot* (New York: Ballantine Books, 1993), 28.
32. Makeda Silvera, "Her Head a Village," in *Her Head a Village and Other Stories* (Vancouver: Press Gang, 1994), 15.
33. Patricia Hill Collins, "What's in a Name? Womanism, Black Feminism and Beyond," *Black Scholar* 26, 1 (1996): 13.
34. Ibid., 14.
35. Collins challenges us to think about this issue: "One might ask how closely the thematic content of newly emerging black women's voices in the academy speak for and speak to the masses of African American women still denied literacy." Ibid., 15.
36. I believe that Black feminist anthropology should address issues of masculinity as well as issues that are relevant to the political, social, and economic survival of Black men. In this essay, however, I am concerned with the origins of a Black feminist consciousness and the ways in which this consciousness becomes a part of our anthropological methodologies.
37. Walker, "Everyday Use," 305.
38. Cherrie Moraga and Gloria Anzaldúa, *This Bridge Called My Back: Writings by Radical Women of Color* (Watertown, Mass.: Persephone Press, 1981), 23.
39. Wade-Gayles, "When Race Is Memory and Blackness Is Choice," in *Rooted against the Wind*, 191.
40. Combahee River Collective, "The Combahee River Collective Statement," 276.
41. Toni Morrison, "The Site of Memory," in *Inventing Truth: The Art and Craft of Memoir*, ed. William Zinsser (Boston: Houghton Mifflin, 1987), 103–124.
42. Cheryl Rodriguez, "Activist Stories: Culture and Continuity in Black Women's Narratives of Grassroots Community Work," *Frontiers: Journal of Women Studies* 19, 2 (1998): 94–112.
43. Ibid., 96.
44. Joy James and Ruth Farmer, "Introduction," in *Spirit, Space and Survival*, 1.
45. Rodriguez, "Activist Stories," 108–109.

Notes on Contributors

A. LYNN BOLLES, Ph.D. (1981) and M.A. (1978), Rutgers University, is a professor of women's studies and affiliate faculty in anthropology, Afro-American studies, and comparative literature at the University of Maryland, College Park. Her research focuses on the African Diaspora, particularly in the Caribbean. Among her works are *We Paid Our Dues: Women Trade Union Leaders in the Caribbean* (1996); *Sister Jamaica: Women, Work and Households in Kingston, Jamaica* (1996); *In the Shadow of the Sun* (with C. D. Deere et al., 1990); and *My Mother Who Fathered Me and Others: Gender and Kinship in the English-Speaking Caribbean* (1988). At present, Bolles is finishing a project on race, class, and women tourist workers in Negril, Jamaica, and a textbook on Pan-Caribbean women's experiences. She is also the president of the Association of Feminist Anthropology and a former president of the Caribbean Studies Association.

JOHNNETTA B. COLE, Ph.D. (1967), Northwestern University, in 1987 became the first African American woman to serve as president of Spelman College, historically a college for Black women. After a decade of service at Spelman, she joined the faculty at Emory University as Presidential Distinguished Professor of Anthropology,

Women's Studies, and African American Studies. Two of Cole's books, *Anthropology for the Nineties* and *All American Women: Lines That Divide, Ties That Bind*, are used in college classrooms. Her articles appear in scholarly journals, and she publishes for general audiences. She is a fellow of the American Anthropological Association and the American Academy of Arts and Sciences and a member of the Association of Black Anthropologists. Johnnetta B. Cole has received more than forty honorary degrees.

Paulla A. Ebron, Ph.D. (1993), University of Massachusetts, Amherst, is an assistant professor of cultural and social anthropology at Stanford University. She has conducted research in The Gambia and South Carolina. Her interests focus on Africa and the African Diaspora and questions of representation and performance. She is the author of *Performing Africa* (2001); other works include "Regional Difference in African American Culture," *American Anthropologist* (1999); and "Tourists as Pilgrims: Commercial Fashioning of Trans-Atlantic Publics," *American Ethnologist* 24, 4 (1999): 910–932.

Angela M. Gilliam, Ph.D. (1981), Union Graduate School, is a member of the faculty at Evergreen State College, Olympia, Washington. She has conducted research in Mexico, Brazil, and Papua New Guinea and organized the first and second international film festivals in independent Papua New Guinea in 1979 and 1980. She represented the International Women's Anthropology Conference at the United Nations when that nongovernmental organization petitioned the Trusteeship Council and the Fourth Committee around issues of decolonization in the Pacific. In 1994–1995, she was a Senior Fulbright Scholar in the graduate program in anthropology at the University of Brasilia. She continues to publish around themes germane to the intersection of race, gender, and class in Brazil and is also currently working on a memoir. Among her works are "Women's Equality and National Liberation," in *Third World Women and the Politics of Feminism* (1991); *Confronting the Margaret Mead Legacy: Scholarship, Empire, and the South Pacific* (with L. Foerstel, 1992); *Social Construction of the Past: Representation as Power* (with G. C. Bond, 1994); "Militarism and Accumulation as Cargo

Cult," in *Decolonizing Anthropology* (2nd ed., 1997); and "Global-ização, identidade e os ataques à igualdade nos Estados Unidos: Es-boço de uma perspectiva para o Brasil," in *Revista Critica de Ciências Sociasis: Número Especial: Identidades* (1997).

IRMA McCLAURIN, Ph.D. (1993), M.A. (1987), and M.F.A. (1976), University of Massachusetts, Amherst, is an associate pro-fessor of anthropology and an affiliate of the Center for Latin American Studies, the Center for African Studies, and the Center for Research on Gender and Women Studies at the University of Florida, Gainesville. Her research focuses on women's narratives, gender inequality, gender and migration, and domestic violence in the African Diaspora. She has conducted research in Belize, Suriname, and The Netherlands. She is author of *Women of Belize: Gender and Change in Central America* (1996); her other works in-clude "Salvaging Lives in the African Diaspora: Anthropology, Eth-nography, and Women's Narratives," *Souls* 1, 3 (1999); "Gender and the Environment" (with Heather McIlvaine-Newsad), *Anthropology News* 450, 7 (1999); and "Incongruities: Dissonance and Contra-diction in the Life of a Black Middle-Class Woman," in *Uncertain Terms: Negotiating Gender in American Culture* (1990). Her current research is on cross-cultural approaches to domestic violence and an intellectual biography of Zora Neale Hurston as an anthropolo-gist. She is the author of three books of poetry, and her poetry has appeared in more than sixteen magazines and anthologies. She is a former member of the editorial board of *Feminist Studies* and is currently editor of *Transforming Anthropology* as well as a member of the executive boards of the Association of Black Anthropologists and the Association of Feminist Anthropology.

CHERYL MWARIA, Ph.D. (1985) and M.A. (1974), Columbia University, is an associate professor of anthropology and the di-rector of Africana studies at Hofstra University. Her research con-centrates on medical anthropology and Africa, and she has conducted research on medical issues and women in Kenya, Cuba, and the United States. Among her more recent works are *African Visions: Literary Images, Political Change and Social Struggle in Con-temporary Africa* (with Silvia Federici and Joseph McLaren, 2000);

"The Immorality of Collective Punishment: A Closer Look at the Impact of the U.S. Embargo on the Health of Cubans," *Souls* 1, 2 (1999); and "Physician-Assisted Suicide: An Anthropological Perspective," *Fordham Urban Law Journal* 24, 4 (1997). She has served on the executive boards of the American Ethnological Society and the Society for the Study of Anthropology of North America.

CHERYL RODRIGUEZ, Ph.D. (1992), University of South Florida, is an associate professor of anthropology and Africana studies at the University of South Florida. A major focus of her research is the exploration of Black feminist or womanist theory and its relevance to the social, political, and economic lives of African Diasporan women. Her current research examines the manifestations of womanist perspectives in Black women's community activism. She also teaches and conducts activist community research, which involves the engagement of local people in historical and cultural community awareness. Her publications include "Recapturing Lost Images: Narratives of a Black Business Enclave," *Practicing Anthropology* 20, 1 (1998); and "African-American Anthropology and the Pedagogy of Activist Community Research, *Anthropology and Education Quarterly* 27, 3 (1996). Rodriguez is the president of the Association of Black Anthropologists for 2000–2001.

CAROLYN MARTIN SHAW, Ph.D. (1975), Michigan State University, is a professor of anthropology at the University of California, Santa Cruz, where she has served as the chair of the anthropology department and the provost of Kresge College, one of the campus's residential colleges. She is the author of *Colonial Inscriptions: Race, Sex, and Class in Kenya* (1995) and has served on the editorial boards of *Feminist Studies, Gay and Lesbian Quarterly*, and *Cultural Anthropology*. She is a former program chair for the Association of Black Anthropologists (1996–1997) and is a past member of the executive board of the Association of Feminist Anthropology.

KIMBERLY EISON SIMMONS, Ph.D. (2001), Michigan State University, is the resident director of the Council Study Center for Spanish Language and Caribbean Studies in Santiago de los Caballeros, Dominican Republic, through the Council on International Education Exchange. She is also a research associate with the Center for Latin American and Caribbean Studies at Michigan State University. She served as a researcher-in-residence with the African Studies Diaspora Research Project at Michigan State University from 1994 to 2000, and is now an affiliate. Her dissertation is titled "Reconfiguring Dominicanness: Competing Discourses Surrounding Race, Nation, and Identity in the Dominican Republic."

KARLA SLOCUM, Ph.D. (1996), University of Florida, M.A. (1992), SUNY Binghamton University, is an assistant professor of anthropology and African and Afro-American studies at the University of North Carolina–Chapel Hill. She is completing a monograph on social movements and alternative discourses to globalization among banana growers in St. Lucia.

Index